P9-DUT-250

GOD MATTERS

GOD MATTERS

Conversations in Theology

Graeme Garrett

A Michael Glazier Book
THE LITURGICAL PRESS
Collegeville, Minnesota

The author and publisher would like to thank the following for permission to reproduce material used in this book: Peters Fraser & Dunlop for the sketch by Alan Bennett, "Take a Pew," from *The Complete Beyond the Fringe* (London: Methuen, 1987) 103–104, used in chapter 3, and material quoted from Alan Bennett's play "Bed Among the Lentils," from *Talking Heads* (London: BBC Books, 1988) 29–41 used in Part III; Penguin Australia for the Leunig sketch "We're Church of England aren't we?" from *The Travelling Leunig* (Melbourne: Penguin, 1990) 31, and Michael Leunig/*The Age* for the other two sketches taken from Karl Rahner & Michael Leunig, eds., *A Common Philosophy*, introduced and arranged by John Honner (Melbourne: Aurora Books, 1992) 27 and 83, which appear in chapter 2; *Scottish Journal of Theology* for an earlier version of chapter 3, originally published as "My Brother Esau is an Hairy Man: An Encounter Between the Comedian and the Preacher," Vol. 33, No. 3, 239–56; Alan Cadwallader for an earlier version of chapter 4, originally published as "Theology and the Uses of Childhood," in Alan Cadwallader, ed., *Episcopacy: Views from the Antipodes* (Adelaide: Anglican Board of Christian Education, 1994) 257–74; *St Mark's Review* for an earlier version of chapter 5, "Yahweh Doesn't Show His Face in Reproductions," No. 148 (Summer 1992) 2–9; *Pacifica* for an earlier version of chapter 10, originally published as "Rule 4? Gender Difference and the Nature of Doctrine," Vol. 10, No. 2, 173–86.

A Michael Glazier Book published by The Liturgical Press

Cover design by Ann Blattner. Watercolor by Ethel Boyle.

© 1999 by The Order of St. Benedict, Inc., Collegeville, Minnesota. All rights reserved. No part of this book may be reproduced in any form or by any means, electronic or mechanical, including photocopying, recording, taping, or any retrieval system, without the written permission of The Liturgical Press, Collegeville, Minnesota 56321. Printed in the United States of America.

1   2   3   4   5   6   7   8

Library of Congress Cataloging-in-Publication Data

Garrett, Graeme, 1941–
    God matters : conversations in theology / Graeme Garrett.
        p.   cm.
    Includes bibliographical references.
    ISBN 0-8146-5944-6 (alk. paper)
    1. Theology, Doctrinal.   I. Title.
  BT80.G365   1999
  230—dc21   99-18656
                                                                CIP

To Pam, Catherine and Jane

Table of Contents

Acknowledgments

Many gifts, intellectual and personal, have shaped my perceptions. Most important have been conversations with friends. My special thanks are due to Peter Llewellyn, Heather Thomson, Winifred Wing Han Lamb, Rosamund Dalziell, John Parkes, Jane Foulcher, Wayne Hooper, and Fran Gray. Thorwald Lorenzen and John Langmore generously read the manuscript in full. Their gracious and perceptive criticisms were invaluable. Paul Collins' broad and disturbing eco/theological vision has unsettled (though he may think not enough) my tendency to become absorbed in matters christological to the neglect of God's Earth, as he calls it. Graham Little also read the book in preparation. To friendship with him across more than three decades I owe more than I can say. Linda Maloney guided the editorial process from start to finish with wonderful good humor and wisdom. Finally, my thanks go to students and colleagues at St. Mark's, particularly John Painter, without whose patient encouragement this project would not have seen the light of day.

Introduction:
Mountains, Jungles, and
Theological Ad Hocery

To have lived in the Church across the latter half of the twentieth century is to have lived in a state of almost permanent theological crisis. At any rate that is how it feels to me. Of course it could be argued that this is nothing more than the experience of life itself. To be in crisis is to feel one's existence under judgment (Greek=*krisis*). This is a continuous process. Accepted ways of thought, feeling, and action are always being thrown into question before the bar of self or society or God, or some other tribunal, real or imagined. Tomorrow's theology will never be the same as yesterday's theology. Today's theology is always in the awkward position of trying to negotiate the straits between the two. This inevitably calls for judgment about what to change and what to preserve. Thus crisis is a permanent state, another name for history. *Ecclesia semper reformanda*. The Church is always in reformation mode.

On the other hand, if everything is a crisis nothing is. A genuine crisis, as distinct from the routine changes of life, is an *abnormal* state, a situation in which the expected run of things is suddenly and thoroughly disrupted. Certain periods *are* more critical than others. Far-reaching judgments are made in them. Large changes in the balance between old ways and new are negotiated. Recently it has become fashionable, following Thomas Kuhn, to refer to such wholesale changes as "paradigm shifts." The changes in question are not merely about this or that detail. Rather the fundamental way of looking at the world, the "entire constellation of beliefs, values, techniques and so on, shared by the members of a given community," is under challenge.[1] It is easier to name and understand such a

---

[1] Thomas S. Kuhn, *The Structure of Scientific Revolutions* (Chicago: University of Chicago Press, 1970) 178. Cf. Hans Küng, *Paradigm Change in Theology: A Symposium for the Future* (Edinburgh: T & T Clark, 1989) 7. Argument goes on as to which

shift once it is past. In the midst of the crisis everything is unclear. That is what it means to be in crisis. Many sensitive observers believe we are now in a moment of such major transformation. A paradigm shift is brewing. The Church and its theology are facing deep uncertainty, under challenge from within and without, and groping for the way forward. Old certainties are gone. But the shape of the new has yet to emerge.

One indication that this might indeed be the case is that a sense of crisis is not confined to the experience of Christians or the task of theology. It seems to be part of a wider cultural and historical phenomenon, at least in the Western tradition. The elusive and ugly word 'postmodernism' has become an accepted way of describing the condition. It crops up in discussions of art, literature, philosophy, politics, and even science. Of course, as the medical skeptic said to the patient, "just because the doctor has a name for your complaint doesn't meant she knows what it is!" The term postmodernism still seems a kind of shot in the dark. The postmodern is whatever comes after the modern. And as Stephen Toulmin remarks, "statements like 'The modern age has come to an end' are easier to resonate to than to understand."[2] There is a sense that something is up, that a period is coming to an end. But it is easier to see what is no longer the case than what is emerging to take its place.

Where the quest for certainty was a hallmark of the modern, a deep sense of uncertainty marks the postmodern. Where absolute truth was a modern ideal, pluralism of interpretation is the postmodern reality. Where clarity was modern, ambiguity is postmodern. In the famous phrase of Lyotard, postmodernity means the loss of "meta-narratives."[3] The hope for a single, all-inclusive, coherent vision of the world has lost plausibility for many people. Reality seems to be in pieces, truth irreducibly relative, the unity of experience fragmented. These are imprecise descriptions and highly controversial, but they would fit the description of a paradigm shift. Even if they are only partially applicable to our times they signal a climate in which theology has some serious reconstruction

---

changes and what periods deserve to be so described, but the major junctions in the unfolding story of Christian life and thought are tolerably clear—the Gentile Mission (Paul), the classic Hellenistic creeds (Chalcedon), the Medieval Synthesis (Aquinas), the Reformation (Luther), Liberalism (Schleiermacher) and, in our own century, the so-called "crisis theology" associated with the name of Karl Barth.

[2] Stephen Toulmin, *Cosmopolis: The Hidden Agenda of Modernity* (Chicago: University of Chicago Press, 1992) 5. This is one of the most illuminating discussions of the meaning of "modernity" I know. It provides a helpful background at least for trying to understand what is being *displaced* in a move to a post-modern world.

[3] See especially J. F. Lyotard, *The Postmodern Condition: A Report on Knowledge*, translated by G. Bennington and B. Massumi (Manchester: Manchester University Press, 1984).

to do—and perhaps some humble pie to eat. Like Renaissance humanism, its intellectual ancestor, postmodernism calls at the very least for "a decent feeling for the finitude of human power."[4] Whatever the headaches a postmodern ethos may be causing, such a feeling for the finitude of human power seems no bad thing for theology. A renewed sensitivity is in order to the prophetic observation that in matters theological "as the heavens are higher than the earth, so are my ways higher than your ways and my thoughts than your thoughts," says the Lord (Isa 55:9).

Mountains and Jungles

How might theology proceed? If it is right to assume that postmodernism is a broad cultural phenomenon it should be possible to draw some useful comparisons between the transformations taking place in theology and those occurring in other areas of cultural expression, in the hope that such comparisons might throw light on the forces shaping theology in the contemporary world and suggest ways in which it might fruitfully respond. Any number of conversation partners could be chosen—literature, art, social theory, philosophy, and so on.[5] But for my purposes the history of recent science, especially physics, provides a useful starting point.

In his Gifford lectures of 1985 the Princeton physicist Freeman Dyson wrote: "God did not only create mountains, he also created jungles."[6] Dyson was making a point about two types of science, two types of physics in fact. He called one the "unifying" and the other the "diversifying" type. Einstein and Maxwell are dominating examples of the first, the unifying type. Their concern is with "mountains." Throughout his life Einstein sought for a broad, rational, unified theory of the physical world and its components. His most famous shot at it was the theory of relativity. Maxwell plotted the dynamics of electromagnetism in a brief series of elegant, far-reaching equations. Both thinkers drew together vast ranges of experimental data in their theories. Their aim was to bring more and more

---

[4] Toulmin, *Cosmopolis* 70.

[5] For an interesting attempt to set the "theology of crisis" in context with the movements in art, literature, and science in the early twentieth century see Karl-Josef Kuschel, *Born Before All Time? The Dispute over Christ's Origin*, translated by John Bowden (London: S.C.M. Press, 1992) 67–83; for theology in dialogue with social theory see the monumental study by John Milbank, *Theology and Social Theory: Beyond Secular Reason* (Cambridge, Mass.: Basil Blackwell, 1990). And in his recent Stanton Lectures, "Transcending Humanity: Versions of Finitude," Fergus Kerr carried on a fascinating theological conversation with seven contemporary philosophers. (The Divinity School, University of Cambridge, Lent Term 1995.)

[6] Freeman Dyson, *Infinite in all Directions* (New York: Harper & Row, 1988) 6.

of the observed phenomena within the scope of a few fundamental principles: in short, to discern the unity of things, how they hang together.

On the other hand, Rutherford and Eddington stand for Dyson's diversifying science. The diversifiers are in love with complexity, with the myriad details of the world. They live in the "jungle." What fascinates them is the uniqueness of particular entities, the hard and messy "givenness" of things. They don't care so much how things hang together as what they are really *like*. Dyson tells the story of an occasion at dinner when Eddington, the astrophysicist, speculated that perhaps the theoreticians were right and that electrons, those tiny negatively charged bits of the atom, were really just useful mathematical notions that might not have any concrete existence. To which Rutherford snorted, "Not exist, not exist,—why I can see the little beggars there in front of me as plainly as I can see that spoon."[7]

Dyson sums up the history of physics over the past 100 years as follows:

> It turned out that God's creation was richer than either Maxwell or Einstein had imagined. There was a time in the 1920s and 1930s when it seemed that the landscape of physics was almost fully mapped. The world of physics looked simple. There were the mountains explored by Maxwell and Einstein and Rutherford and Bohr, the theories of relativity and the quantum, great landmarks standing clear and cold and clean in the sunlight, and between them only a few unimportant valleys still to be surveyed. Now we know better. After we began seriously to explore the valleys in the 1950s, we found in them flora and fauna as strange and unexpected as anything to be seen in the valleys of the Amazon. Instead of three species of elementary particle which were known in the 1920s, we now have sixty-one. Instead of three states of matter, solid, liquid and gas, we have six or more. Instead of a few succinct equations to summarize the universe of physics, we have a luxuriant growth of mathematical structures, as diverse as the phenomena they attempt to describe.[8]

Dyson respects the work of the unifiers but clearly prefers the style of the diversifiers. The world is infinitely rich. It is unlikely, perhaps even *hubris*, to suppose we can bring it under the control of a few humanly devised equations however brilliant. "Seek simplicity and distrust it" is his motto.

Now it seems to me that this analysis of the situation in physics has interesting analogues in theology, in two ways. First, the basic, if rough, distinction between styles seems to apply. The history of theology exhibits a remarkably parallel tension. The unifiers are the systematicians, the dogmaticians, the creed writers. They try to map the territory of theological reality comprehensively, logically, and inclusively. They are after the

---

[7] Ibid. 43.
[8] Ibid. 7.

mountain peaks. "I believe in God the Father Almighty . . . and in Jesus Christ his only Son, our Lord . . . and in the Holy Spirit, the Lord, the Giver of life"—three paragraphs for a theory of God, the world, and everything. It is elegant. It is powerful. And it is of fundamental importance to the Church, and perhaps to the world. The unifiers have a rightfully honored place in the theological tradition. In the New Testament the primary example is St. John, whose gospel is an elegant artistic unity presenting the Christ-figure in a series of interlocking images that have a cumulative effect on the reader—the way, the truth, the life, the light, the water, the bread, the wine, the door, and so on. From there the line continues through Origen, Aquinas (possibly the greatest of the type), Calvin, Schleiermacher, up to Rahner, Tillich, Pannenberg, and Elizabeth Johnson. And this is to mention merely some of the big names.

The advantages of the unifying approach to theology are many. I will note two only. First: wholeness. Systematic construction, say in trinitarian form, helps us to see the object of theology in its fullness in which, as Tillich argues, "many parts and elements are united by determining principles and dynamic interrelations." To put it another way, the systematic approach reduces the temptation to theological distortion through unjustified concentration on a part of the picture at the expense of the whole. Heresies from docetism to unitarianism have suffered from this tunnel vision, seeing the trees but missing the wood. The second great virtue of the unifiers is consistency. Talking sense in theology, as in other studies, means not contradicting yourself too often or too spectacularly. This is extremely hard in theology, as anyone who has tried it knows. The discipline of systematic thinking forces a certain responsibility on us. In trying out a new statement or new thought in theology—and here I am again quoting Tillich—"the necessity of surveying previous statements in order to see whether or not they are mutually compatible drastically reduces inconsistencies."[9] In other words, it helps save us from talking too much nonsense.

The diversifiers find all this a bit tedious, abstract, speculative, and reductionist. Where's the teeming jungle of real life in it? Søren Kierkegaard, a doyen of the diversifiers, was tireless in his mockery of the pretensions of the unifiers. He wrote whole books with titles like *Philosophical Fragments* and *Concluding Unscientific Postscript*. A lot of what he had to say appears in short journal entries in the famous diaries. "The philosopher contemplates Christianity for the sake of interpreting it with his speculative thought," he writes.

[9] For the citations given see Paul Tillich, *Systematic Theology* 3 (London: James Nisbet & Co. Ltd., 1964) 3–4.

> But suppose this whole proceeding were a chimera, a sheer impossibility; suppose that Christianity is subjectivity, an inner transformation, an actualization of inwardness, and that only two kinds of people can know anything about it: those who with an infinite passionate interest in an eternal happiness base this their happiness upon their believing relationship to Christianity, and those who with an opposite passion, but in passion, reject it—the happy and the unhappy lovers.[10]

Subjectivity, inwardness, infinite passion: these are Kierkegaard's equivalents of Rutherford's electrons, the "little beggars" right there in front of him. In the New Testament the ancestor is Paul. Paul was no systematician, but a missionary, the apostle to the Gentiles. His job was to take the gospel across cultural boundaries. So he had to cope with the concrete, messy, irreducible plurality of human experience, language, and custom. It is hard to mount a unified case when today you're debating with Jewish traditionalists, tomorrow it is the group at the Hellenized synagogue, and next week Greek skeptics who haven't the faintest idea of the tradition of the Torah. Paul doesn't have time for the nicely structured treatise, the elegant and extended formulation of a coherent vision. He writes on the run. Excessive spiritualism is the problem at Corinth, theological legalism in Galatia, the question of the economy of salvation in Rome. He develops his pneumatology, his theology of the cross, his doctrine of justification in response to the concrete situations, languages, and cultural backgrounds of the people he speaks with. It's a jungle out there. The little beggars are everywhere. You have to deal with them as they are, not as you would like them to be. Paul goes so far as to make the unabashed claim that he shifts the grounds of his argument to suit the demands of the occasion: "I have become all things to all people, that I might by all means save some" (1 Cor 9:22; but see also vv. 19-23). If ever there was one, this is a claim calculated to drive at least some unifiers to distraction.[11] The diversifiers also have a long and respected pedigree: Tertullian, Augustine (a mixture), Luther, Julian of Norwich, Kierkegaard, Barth (the early period), Reinhold Niebuhr, Gustavo Gutierrez, Rosemary Radford Ruether are a few of the names that come to mind.

The advantages of the diversifying style in theology are exactly the reverse of those of the unifiers. Comprehensiveness is an illusion. It almost always suffers from the problem of ideology. By ideology I mean the claim to be in possession of a more or less universal understanding of

---

[10] Søren Kierkegaard, *Concluding Unscientific Postscript*, translated by David F. Swenson (Princeton: Princeton University Press, 1968) 51.

[11] Cf. Walter Kaufmann, "On examination, it turns out that what theists agree on is a formulation, not a state of affairs; and this formulation, to cite the admirably candid words of St. Paul about himself, means 'all things to all men.'" *The Faith of a Heretic* (New York: Doubleday Anchor, 1961) 120.

human existence, of how to live and act as human beings in the world. Unfortunately such claims, when examined, usually turn out in fact to function as a justification of the particular interests of a given group or individual by presenting those interests as the requirements of universal truth and the practice of disinterested justice.[12] It is the mote and beam all over again. The unifier thinks he can see clearly. But his vision is more a projection of the plank in his own eye than a clear perception of the mote in the eye of the other. It is better to stick to a conversation with particular people on particular issues and not pretend you can speak for all people on every matter under the sun. "[T]heologians have to proceed in a piece-meal fashion, confronting one problem or question at a time. . . . This seems a better procedure than the endeavor to reduce all questions in theology to a basic systematic position which can then be applied ready-made to any and all problems that come along."[13] Liberation and feminist theologians have much of importance to say on this point.

Diversifiers are also suspicious of too much consistency. Since when were things human, especially things religious, consistent? Paul's writing is full of inconsistency. "I do not understand my own actions. For I do not do what I want, I do the very thing I hate" (Rom 7:15). "My strength is made perfect in weakness" (2 Cor 12:9). It is hard to avoid this kind of oxymoron if you take seriously a *theo*-logy of the cross, that is, the essence of God revealed in the death of a criminal. Tertullian spoke of absurdity, Kierkegaard of paradox, Barth of dialectic. In the more abstract words of Eberhard Jüngel, the truth of faith needs "to be sought in some other place than the non-conflictual functioning of . . . principles within a system devoid of contradictions."[14] Living, and especially living in the presence of God as revealed in Jesus the Christ, is not always neat or logical. Theology must mirror ontology. That is, it must take note of what is actually there in lived experience and the given history of revelation, not pretend that life and revelation must mirror whatever the theologian thinks of as logical. To put it bluntly, you have to feel your way along the jungle trail and face whatever leaps out at you. You can't know what that will be in advance. What worked at the last turning of the track may not be useful at the next. Doing theology is more like cutting a path in a swamp than thinking mathematics in a chair.

The second similarity between Dyson's view of the history of modern physics and how theology seems to work concerns the balance of

---

[12] I am indebted here to the discussion of ideology in theology by Schubert M. Ogden, *The Point of Christology* (London: S.C.M. Press, 1982) 94–96.

[13] Hans W. Frei, *Theology and Narrative: Selected Essays*, edited by George Hunsinger and William C. Placher (New York: Oxford University Press, 1993) 58–59.

[14] Eberhard Jüngel, *Theological Essays II*, edited by J. B. Webster, translated by Arnold Neufeldt-Fast and J. B. Webster (Edinburgh: T & T Clark, 1995) 34.

power between the two styles. The unifiers, the big-picture people in physics, according to Dyson, held sway in the first part of the twentieth century, but since the 1950s the diversifiers have started to come into their own. The tidy and universal world of Einstein and Maxwell has given way to the weird, unpredictable world of contemporary particle physics with its black holes, superstring, quarks, mesons and gluons; its fractals, strange attractors and chaos; its curved space and time that runs backwards. Not that the great unifying theories have become obsolete or uninteresting; it is just that they are less dominating now. Their limits have been exposed by the stubborn unpredictability and stunning profusion of the world out there. The *logos* may be in the *cosmos*, as the prologue of the Gospel of John asserts. But it seems to be a *logos* of depth and tangled mystery considerably beyond our capacity to comprehend. And if Gödel's theorem is correct this unreachability is built in in principle, not simply in practice. It is not that we just haven't got it "taped" at this point. It is that every time we do "tape" something—whether it is Mandelbrot's sets or Dyson's butterflies—we discover the tape won't stick. There is endless color and complexity in the little piece we've got our tape around, and every question answered generates two more beyond itself. Reality, it seems, is "infinite in all directions."

Theology has followed a somewhat parallel course. Between the 1920s and the 1960s it was dominated by the unifiers. Brunner, Tillich, Rahner, Barth all presented vast and integrated systematic statements of the Christian faith. They were (and are) marvelous constructions, full of insight and order that are still of great value. But in the later part of the century, the postmodern bit in which we now live, such systems have gone off the boil. People don't write like that any more, or not as confidently. And many people don't read like that any more. It all seems a bit abstract and overconfident. Dietrich Bonhoeffer, that mercurial theological genius of the diversifying type, was one of the earliest to detect a change in the mood of things. In his prison cell in 1944 he wrote of Tillich's effort at a broad apologetic theology: "he . . . sought to understand the world better than it understood itself; but it felt that it was completely misunderstood . . . the world unseated him and went on by itself." And of Barth of the *Church Dogmatics* he coined the famous phrase that his theology had become a "positivism of revelation," that is, a theology that does not take the actual human context of its utterance seriously enough. It thinks it speaks the Word of God universally. But it doesn't.[15]

After that wave upon wave of unease broke on the theological shores. Bultmann's demythologizing project emerged with its effort to rethink

---

[15] Dietrich Bonhoeffer, *Letters and Papers from Prison* (London: S.C.M. Press, 1971 [1st ed. 1953]) 327–28.

theology in a technological age. Thomas Altizer and his colleagues, with the "Death of God" experiment, began wondering how theology might proceed in the face of a declining sense of the transcendent. Then came Gustavo Gutierrez and his radical critique of the ideology of power. Classical theology was shown to be often on the master side of the master/slave symbiosis. New theology began to adapt to the jungle of the poor and oppressed. East not West, South not North became the prominent geo-theological compass points. Then came Mary Daly and the feminists. Classical theology was under fire as a western, patriarchal, phallocentric, misogynist mentality. New theology began blazing trails "beyond God the Father," regardless of where they might lead, and scornful of systema-tizers who tried to point out the "dangers" of this new woman-driven road-cutting machinery. Then came Thomas Berry and the ecologists. Classical theology was accused and convicted of anthropocentrism, an ideological preoccupation with human interests, as if God had been twid-dling her thumbs through fifteen billion years of cosmic history awaiting the appearance of *Homo (un)sapiens*. New theology plunged into the chaos of cosmic process in search of the elusive light of revelation. The old paths of Scripture and christology began to look strangely circum-scribed, circular at best, dead-end at worst. The cumulative weight of this onslaught has led to a more modest, even tentative stand on the part of theologians. Local theologies and particular issues appear more manage-able and interesting. We live in a pluralist world. God seems to have made it that way. Therefore we need to work and think within a pluralist diver-sity rather than a universalist unity.

Theological Ad Hocery

What might theology look like in such a pluralist situation? Obvi-ously it would be silly and self-defeating to try to give a comprehensive answer: silly because the issue is too big, self-defeating because pluralism, if it means anything, means *not* being open to unified comprehension. Postmodernism is all about *difference*. There is no longer one center. There are many. Theology simply has to get used to what David Tracy calls "the unsettling reality of our polycentric present."[16]

The essays that follow could be described as an exercise in "ad hoc apologetics" or to be more exact, "ad hoc theological conversations." The essays are *theological* in the sense that they try to express as clearly as possible what it means to affirm this world as created and redeemed by

[16] David Tracy, *On Naming the Present: Reflections on God, Hermeneutics, and Church* (Maryknoll, N.Y.: Orbis, 1994) 4. For a lucid discussion of various theologi-cal options in relation to postmodernism see Peter C. Hodgson, *Winds of the Spirit: A Constructive Christian Theology* (London: S.C.M. Press, 1994), especially ch. 5.

God, as God is revealed in the biblical narrative culminating in the story of Jesus Christ. The essays are *conversational* in the sense that they adopt a dialogical style by seeking an exchange of ideas between partners who share some common interests, but may differ quite strongly on important matters of outlook, attitude, and belief. The essays are *ad hoc* (lit. "to this") in the sense of being fitted for a particular purpose or end. An ad hoc solution is one designed to meet a specific problem or immediate challenge. It makes no necessary claim to completeness or universality and is not easily transferable to other contexts or circumstances.

The idea of "ad hocery" in theology derives from an important essay published in 1986 by William Werpehowski entitled "Ad Hoc Apologetics."[17] The phrase reflects the style. Classical apologetics in its more robust form tried to demonstrate that Christian faith is the truth of life to which all human beings, if they are clear-headed and honest, must adhere. You are simple or irrational if you don't. In its softer versions it sought to show only that it is not irrational for human beings to pursue a Christian identity. But by and large, soft or hard, apologetics had wide-ranging ambitions.

Again Tillich is a good example of the classic, or unifying, style in apologetics. One part of the task of Christian theology, according to Tillich—but not only to him of course—is to communicate the gospel to others who do not as yet share its grace and claims. Part of such communication, as the liberationists insist, is living a particular kind of life, a life of love and justice, not to put too fine a point on it. The gospel is action as well as reflection. Tillich wouldn't argue. But let me stick to the reflection side of the equation for the moment. True communication of the gospel means making it possible for people to decide for or against it. To do this they must understand it. But if they are to understand it we, who try to communicate it, must find some common ground with the hearers, otherwise the message will simply be misunderstood. So the argument runs. But what is that common ground? Tillich's answer is well known. "*They* [the hearers along with us the speakers] *all participate in human existence.*" And he continues: "This is a very *universal* answer."[18] Shared human existence is the common ground for communication of faith. Tillich then proceeded to analyze this common existence in a variety of ways. In particular he was concerned with the human experience of anxiety, and in three types: the anxiety of death, the anxiety of guilt, and the anxiety of meaninglessness. These are human universals in Tillich's opinion. We suffer them just because we are human. They manifest our

---

[17] William Werpehowski, "Ad Hoc Apologetics," *Journal of Religion* 66:3 (July 1986) 282–301.

[18] Paul Tillich, *Theology of Culture* (New York: Oxford University Press, 1959) 202. Italics in the original text except for the word "universal."

humanity. The gospel addresses these human anxieties in terms of the message of the grace of God in Christ as life, justification, and truth. The theological answers match the human questions.

What's wrong with that? The diversifiers, beginning with Bonhoeffer, have a chorus of responses. The first complaint is this. Tillich assumes a uniformity of human nature that is just not the case. Get some distance on Tillich's work and it starts to look as if his universal humanity is, in fact, the *angst*-ridden humanity of affluent male European intellectuals who lived through the social traumas of the early parts of this century and found their souls' expression in the dark artistry of the existentialists. In short, it is Tillich writ large. But that is hardly humanity *per se*. The jungle's a good deal thicker than that. What can be said of Tillich's theology is that it did speak to a certain group of people at a certain time who shared certain specific but historically relative characteristics. In that context it was brilliantly done. But it is context specific. And it won't travel well in the South or East, to say nothing of the brave new world of Mary Daly's "Gyn/ecology."[19]

This is part of what Werpehowski means by "ad hoc" in his apologetics. There is still a strong commitment of theology to *public* discourse. After all, God understood in the Christian tradition either really is the source and hope of the world or is nothing. And either all human (and other) beings are really "creatures of God" or none are. Therefore, as Eberhard Jüngel argues, "talk about God either concerns everyone or no one." Theology "definitely cannot be pursued as a hobby."[20] But in a postmodern world Christian "talk about God" takes place in a public arena marked by many different kinds of talk, including many different kinds of talk about God. Challenges are thrown up from a variety of contexts that presuppose different beliefs, attitudes, and practices, in short different traditions. It is hard to imagine that a single, unified approach could deal with all the issues presented to theology by, say, medical technology, economic rationalism, Islamic fundamentalism, feminist philosophy, or deep ecology, to mention just a few. "The Christian apologist thus seeks to establish common ground with the non-Christian as creature [of God] with reference to a *particular context of action or a particular contested question*."[21] If theological conversation is to make sense it needs to

---

[19] Mary Daly, *Gyn/ecology: the metaethics of radical feminism* (Boston: Beacon, 1978).

[20] Eberhard Jüngel, *Theological Essays II*, 1. This is not to deny the importance of the theological task of critical reexamination of the basic dogmas of the faith for the sake of the faithful. Faith needs to seek understanding for itself within its own tradition. But I am concerned with the articulation of faith within a wider cultural context.

[21] Werpehowski, "Ad Hoc Apologetics," 287 (italics added). To be fair to Tillich it should be noted that he was aware of limitations. "None of us is asked to speak to

resist the temptation to universalize its observations. Any such attempt runs the danger of misconceiving the nature of the human experience it purports to describe and relate to. Human beings are shaped, that is, made human, in particular traditions, languages, and cultures. That *is* their humanity, not some ultimately unimportant veneer laid over a deeper, universal structure. It is particularity that must be taken seriously in theological conversation. Hence "it cannot but be an ad hoc affair."[22]

A second complaint against the older apologetics is that it too readily adopted a position of superiority, implicitly if not explicitly dealing with outlooks and traditions other than its own as if they were somehow incomplete and in need of Christian supplementation or correction. Tillich's famous "method of correlation" expressed it nicely. "Theology formulates the questions implied in human existence, and theology formulates the answers implied in divine self-manifestation under the guidance of the questions implied in human existence."[23] Human existence raises the questions; theology, on the basis of revelation, gives the answers. Moreover, "it is as if we [i.e., theologians] held up a mirror in which they [i.e., nonbelievers] see themselves."[24] It would be unfair to take such quotations out of context and baldly convict Tillich of adopting an arrogant attitude of Christian supremacy toward all other views. The theological task is always a risk, he argued, and can only be undertaken in humility and with a willingness to learn from others.[25] Still, this theology does give the impression that it understands the "others" better than they understand themselves. In a postmodern world that attitude is unlikely to cut much ice. "The time is past," writes Jeffrey Stout, "when theology can reign as queen of the sciences, putting each other voice in its place and articulating, with a conviction approaching certainty, the presuppositions all share." Christianity "as a voice in conversation . . . must take its place among the other voices, as often *to be corrected* as to correct."[26]

For this reason I prefer to speak of *conversation* rather than apologetics.[27] Despite the best intentions in the world, the word apologetics

---

everybody in all places and in all periods. Communication is a matter of participation" (*Theology of Culture* 204).

[22] Werpehowski, "Ad Hoc Apologetics," 287.

[23] Tillich, *Systematic Theology* 1:69.

[24] Tillich, *Theology of Culture* 204.

[25] For example: "Medicine has helped us to rediscover the meaning of grace in our theology." Ibid. 211.

[26] Jeffrey Stout, *Ethics After Babel* (Boston: Beacon, 1988) 164–65 (italics added).

[27] I gratefully acknowledge my indebtedness in what follows to the discussion of conversation found in William C. Placher, *Unapologetic Theology: A Christian Voice in a Pluralistic Conversation* (Louisville: Westminster/John Knox, 1989) ch. 7, *passim*. See also Keith Ward, *Religion and Revelation: A Theology of Revelation in the World's Religions* (Oxford: Clarendon Press, 1994) Part I, especially 31–34.

has connotations of "demonstrating the correctness" of a Christian position over against alternatives. There is nothing wrong with such an endeavor, of course, and it will no doubt always be a part of the theological task. But apologetics—Tillich calls it "answering theology"[28]—inevitably seems to be in the position of delivering answers to others rather than fielding questions from them. By contrast, a conversation is a commitment to a common exchange in which the differing interests, convictions, and opinions of both (or many) sides are acknowledged and respected, and which is open-ended in the sense that the outcome is not predetermined in some way. "Truly speaking," said Emerson, "it is not instruction, but *provocation*, that I can receive from another soul."[29] Such conversational provocation can take place in contexts of conflict and disagreement where the aim is to decide an issue of contention, or of simple curiosity and a shared search for deeper clarity over some puzzle of thought or action. Or the motivation might be sheer conviviality and the delight in sharing experiences and swapping jokes. As with most conversations the resolutions achieved in such exchanges, precisely because they concern particular issues and are between participants with particular backgrounds, commitments, and values, are likely to be provisional, subject to reconsideration, and rarely equally convincing to all observers. It's the jungle, not the mountain.

To be successful such theological conversations need to satisfy at least two criteria. On the one hand they try to clarify and support Christian identity. They take seriously the gospel witness to God's action in the crucified and risen Christ. In this sense they are "faith speaking." Christians live in particular contexts too. We need to understand and live those contexts in the light of the revelation of God. Conversation with others is an attempt to clarify, explain and—yes, at times—to commend the implications of this revelation. Often it is precisely the fact that the other does *not* share the faith perspective that provokes, as Emerson argued, new insight and deeper understanding of faith.

At the same time the particular context or disputed issue must make sense to the non-Christian likewise placed in a particular context. If it is to be helpful, or even interesting, the talk must sustain and nurture the independent identity of the conversation partner in the area of action and understanding under discussion. If in the course of the exchange particular features of the Christian faith seem illuminating to the other and precipitate change in a direction sympathetic to faith, well and good. But the

[28] Tillich, *Systematic Theology* 1:6.

[29] Ralph Waldo Emerson, from "An Address Delivered before the Senior Class in Divinity, Cambridge, Sunday Evening, 15 July, 1838," quoted by Stanley Cavell, *The Claim of Reason: Wittgenstein, Skepticism, Morality, and Tragedy* (New York: Oxford University Press, 1979) title page (italics added).

change may also go the other way. Theology may find itself under pressure to adapt or modify its position. "Discussion bears fruit when a common language is found. Then the participants part from one another as changed beings. The individual perspectives with which they entered upon the discussion have been transformed, and so they are transformed themselves."[30] The street is definitely two-way.

Many things can be achieved through talk. Mutual respect and mutual clarification are genuine and interesting possibilities. At some point, however, the conversation partners are likely to be run up against fundamental convictions that are presupposed in all their discussion but are simply incommensurable. I believe that ultimately this world is grounded on divine love as manifest in the life of Jesus Christ. You can make no sense of that. The world seems to you at best indifferent to human aspiration, at worst hostile. We may fruitfully argue about how to work for compassion and justice in human society and we might find much to say and do in common, but at this fundamental level it seems to be either/or. You believe that religious awareness is a projection of unconscious fears and hopes. I think it is a form through which fellowship with a divine "other" is mediated. We may talk successfully about the fascinating mix of psychological and sociological factors in religious (and other) experience, but at this basic level we face irreducible difference.

A hard-nosed postmodernism simply lets it rest at that. In the jungle of particular outlooks and traditions we just have to accept the breakdown of anything like the classic notion of truth as one, coherent, and universal. In Nietzsche's famous phrase, "facts are precisely what there is not, only interpretations."[31] Whether such a radical relativism can be sustained is a moot point—one of the things to talk about, no doubt! Postmodernism seems to be right to this extent, however, that there is no Archimedean position from which to adjudicate the question. And yet a hankering for something of the mountains seems to remain. We each argue our case as best we can *as if* convinced that our position makes better sense of the world as a whole—and this includes those convinced that it makes no sense at all to speak of "the world as whole." There are no easy victories. But perhaps we may hope for some progress toward a deeper grasp of the implications involved, and the difficulties inherent, in the various life-stances we adopt.

The hope from which these conversations set out, at least, is that a Christian perspective—while it agrees that all search for truth, its own in-

---

[30] Hans-Georg Gadamer, *Reason in the Age of Science*, translated by Frederick G. Lawrence (Cambridge, Mass.: M.I.T. Press, 1981) 110–11, quoted in Placher, *Unapologetic Theology* 112.

[31] Friedrich Nietzsche, *The Will to Power*, translated by Walter Kaufmann and R. J. Hollingdale (New York: Vintage, 1968) 481.

cluded, is tradition-shaped, and that none of us choose or express our fundamental beliefs with impartial or universal rationality—does not imply that Christian truth is purely *Christian* truth and not (ultimately) truth for everyone.[32] Presumably a Freudian, Marxist, feminist, or even radical relativist believes that some of what he or she sees and says is of as much importance to others as to himself or herself. Why else bother with conversation? At any rate faith in one God seems to demand some such hope. It believes "that the world created and redeemed by God and Jesus Christ as depicted in Scripture is our one and only world."[33] On this ground theology, at least the theology in these pages, believes conversation with the "provocative other" is possible and fruitful.

Because the style is ad hoc, the chapters that follow, though having many lines of connection, can be read separately. Part I, "Humor and Theology," revolves around the search for a theology that laughs, or at least one that can see and make the joke. Theology has traditionally taken dialogue with philosophy, history, psychology, sociology, and science very seriously. But while comedians seem more than happy to take on theology—religious jokes abound—theologians have been remarkably shy to take on the comedians. This is a pity. Religious comedy can be a source of delight and amusement, part of the grace of life. It can also be a critical conversation partner, challenging and encouraging the faithful to examine the nature of their commitments. We all get the point when Woody Allen has one of his film characters say, "my aunt rejected the Bible because it had an unbelievable central character," even if we are not quite sure how to respond to it!

Religious humor "speaks" to a wide range of people. Many more people see the drift of a Michael Leunig cartoon on the meaning of Christmas than are interested in a sermon on the same topic. Theology ought to take note of this. What are the comedians saying about God? And what can we learn from it? The partners in the conversation here are contemporary comedians. Like the public at large, comedians take widely differing attitudes toward religion from the highly critical (Alan Bennett) to the warmly supportive (Michael Leunig), with a good deal of ambivalence between (Woody Allen, Garrison Keillor and others). Chapter 2 is an attempt to analyze four different types of religious humor—blasphemy, mockery, irony, and euphemy—and the kind of contribution each

[32] Cf. the words of Keith Ward: "The Christian claim is that God is redemptive love, that the human goal is personal union with God, and that the way to the goal is one of participating in the Divine love itself. This is final in that these truths are irreformable. No doubt they allow and invite many developments of understanding . . . . But they are irrevocably true, and any view which denies them must be regarded as ultimately false" *(Religion and Revelation* 279).

[33] Werpehowski, "Ad Hoc Apologetics," 300–301.

might make to theological thought. Chapter 3 is an extended discussion of one of my favorite religious jokes, Alan Bennett's wonderful spoof on preaching: "My brother Esau is an hairy man, but I am a smooth man!"

Part II, "Experience and God," deals with various aspects of belief in God in a world not convinced of its plausibility. Theological language, particularly the language that arises out of childhood experience and speaks of God as "Father," has become highly controversial in our time. Sustained, though very different, critiques have been offered of it by Freud on the one hand and feminists on the other. The ensuing controversy is the focus of Chapter 4. In Chapter 5 an attempt is made to look for "moments of grace" in ordinary (as distinct from religious) experience. Can we find "signals of transcendence" or "rumors of angels" (as Peter Berger calls them) in the details of common human life, especially human life under threat or facing suffering? The neurologist Oliver Sacks and the psychiatrist Silvano Arieti are the major conversation partners here. In the third chapter of this section (Chapter 6) the conversation turns to more technical theological issues. Christian identity has been associated with telling the story of Jesus, at least since the time of the writing of the gospels. But what does that story commit us to in a postmodern situation? What does it imply about God and God's dealings with the world? Critiques made by the philosophers Friedrich Nietzsche and Jean Paul Richter raise the questions here and a sprinkling of theologians—Niebuhr, Barth, Moltmann, and Macquarrie among them—help in making a response.

Part III, "Existence and Christ," moves into matters of christology, or more precisely, soteriology. The controlling question of this section is: What does it mean to speak of "salvation" in Jesus as the Christ? Is such a claim merely dogmatic hogwash? If not, what does it mean in concrete experience? Where is such grace found in the Church? As in the other sections, a variety of conversation partners appear. Alan Bennett is central once again, this time in his role as playwright rather than comedian. The four chapters of the section arise in discussion of Bennett's television play, "Bed Among the Lentils." The play was originally produced by the BBC as one in a series called *Talking Heads*, and was shown several times on public television in the early 1990s. It tells the story of a vicar's wife called Susan who has lived in and served the Church all her life, but seems to have experienced very little of what could be called "saving grace" for her trouble. How does she see Christ? What does theology have to say in response to her strong disillusionment with churchy talk of redemption? Chapter 7— "Mrs. Vicar"—introduces Susan and her story. The following chapters then pick up different aspects of her life in the Church and especially the view of Christ that has been mediated to her through this involvement.

Part I

Theology and Humor

2

The Most Significant Event
Our Faith Has to Offer?

Uneasy Conversations between the Comedian and the Believer

The American theologian William H. Willimon tells a story that taps into every preacher's nightmares. "I was preaching in a large auditorium in the West," he writes.

> Jet lag had taken its toll—at least that's the best excuse I can find. The person who introduced me told the crowd of students that I was a great preacher, much in demand, interesting, controversial and expensive. The pressure was on.
>
> I launched into my sermon, a simple piece unworthy of such an extravagant introduction. "When the sermon is weak, say it louder," somebody once told me. So I was loud, emotional, passionate.
>
> "And what is the most significant event our faith has to offer?" I asked. "The erection," I bellowed.
>
> Someone in the front row screamed.
>
> "I mean the *resurrection*!" I said the correct word at least 12 more times. It didn't seem to do any good. Church was out.
>
> "I'm sure I shall remember your sermon for the rest of my life," a young woman told me after the service. I could hear her laughing as she walked out of the building and down the street.

"A slip of the tongue in the middle of a sermon," Willimon comments wryly, "is called Freudian by some, evidence of the humility-producing power of the Holy Spirit by others."[1] But whatever its source, one thing is sure—laughter and religion live in an uneasy relationship with each other. Along with politics and sex, religion is one of the inexhaustible mines that comedians quarry for material. The paydirt they throw up is often distinctly uncomfortable for the faithful. In this instance Willimon, unwittingly and

---

[1] William H. Willimon, "Sermon Slips," *The Christian Ministry* (Nov.–Dec. 1988) 39.

unwillingly, became his own comic commentator, a parody of himself as preacher. The result was much delight for his youthful audience and much embarrassment for himself. This mixture of humiliation and delight in laughter is intriguing and has fascinated philosophers since Plato's time.

On the one hand Willimon is "put down" by the laughter. His sermon is in ruins and his self-esteem badly dented. He looks a fool. He is supposed to be talking of high spiritual matters. But his mind, apparently, is fixated in another place. And the doctrine he preaches is likewise mocked. Faith talks of new life through resurrection, but after the slip we feel we know where the source of new life *really* resides! So humor can be cruel. "As laughter emerges with man from the midst of antiquity it seems to hold a dagger in its hand."[2] Standing helpless in the pulpit, Willimon could resonate with such a classic and aggressive evaluation of the function of laughter in human life.

On the other hand, the retelling of the story is delightful. There is real pleasure in it. Willimon comes across as someone who doesn't take himself too seriously, as preachers often do or are thought to do. He doesn't mind acknowledging his bumbling fallibility. That lets us loosen up and puts us on side. If this sort of thing happens to the best of them perhaps we can all "play up" a bit in church. There is relief in the levity. Religious existence is often too serious. Theology is frequently practiced as if it were no laughing matter. We don't find it difficult to understand why Nietzsche squirmed beneath what he felt to be a deadening quality of the devout life. "One has to be very coarse," he said, "in order not to feel the presence of Christians and Christian values as an oppression beneath which genuine festive feelings go to the devil." The joke is a way of softening this depressing estimation of belief. Laughter can help liberate faith. Willimon is even prepared to interpret the laughter as "the power of the Holy Spirit"! If this seems implausible, at least we might read the young woman's delighted exit from the church as a "signal of transcendence," an echo of the divine delight in the rich, confusing mixture of a world in the process of being made.[3]

---

[2] Quoted by Arthur Koestler, *The Act of Creation* (New York: Macmillan, 1964) 52. The original is taken from J. C. Gregory, *The Nature of Laughter* (London: Kegan Paul, 1924).

[3] I have been unable to locate the source of the Nietzsche reference. On Peter Berger's understanding of laughter as a "signal of transcendence" see, *A Rumor Of Angels: Modern Society and the Rediscovery of the Supernatural* (New York: Penguin, 1973) 69–75; also *The Precarious Vision* (New York: Doubleday, 1961) 212. For a recent and fascinating discussion of theology and humor see Karl-Josef Kuschel, *Laughter: A Theological Reflection,* translated by John Bowden (London: S.C.M. Press, 1994). The section on a "theology of tears" (pp. 45–47) is an illuminating analysis of the weight given in Christian tradition to tears over laughter in our dealings with God.

What follows is a look at some of the uses of laughter in and at religion. I want to explore the way comedians deal with religious matters and what theologians might learn from them. The range of material is endless. In this essay I can only sketch a simple typology that might help us think about it, making no claim to completeness.

The typology moves between two extremes. At one extreme is blasphemy. This is the point where the negative face of humor, its aggressive quality, is set unremittingly against religion. Here the humorist is anti-theologian with a vengeance. The laughter of blasphemy, at least as far as the believer is concerned, sounds like the shrieking guffaws of hell. At the other extremity we have, for want of a more elegant term, "euphemy."[4] If blasphemy speaks hurt and curse, euphemy utters grace and beauty. Its etymological meaning is "speaking well." A euphemism is a phrase that "puts it nicely." At this extreme the comedian almost *becomes* the theologian. The humor is intended to bless and affirm. The laughter is of heaven.

Between these extremes lies a whole spectrum of possible relations between humor and belief. We will examine two: mockery and irony. By "mockery" I mean the type of humor that makes fun of something, "sends it up," so to speak. It may be cutting. But it wounds to heal or at least amuse. Its touch is light, drawing attention to the distortions and foibles of belief without the overtones of contempt that consign religion as a whole to the dustbin of stupidity or corruption as with blasphemy. "Irony," on the other hand, is the form of humor that thrives on situations of *self*-contradiction. An ironic situation is one in which I tie myself up in knots of my own making. Religious humor that works with irony generates laughter by drawing attention to circumstances where religious life contradicts its own intentions. In short, it fails according to its *own*—not someone else's—lights.

It is neither possible nor necessary to draw firm and fast lines between the types. Often the same jokes can be read in more than one mode at the same time. But we can summarize the differences roughly as follows. The humorist as blasphemer says to the believer, "Look, your belief is disgusting and contemptible." The mocker says, "Can't you see, your position is ridiculous." The ironist raises an eyebrow, "It looks to me," she says, "as if you've tripped yourself up with your own fancy footwork." The euphemist is on side. "Look at the possibilities," his humor says. And, with a glance back at the others, "Aren't they laughable when you look at them from this (believing) angle?"

---

[4] I borrowed the word from David Lawton's excellent study, *Blasphemy* (New York and Sydney: Harvester/Wheatsheaf, 1993) 14.

Blasphemy: "How far can you go?"

The horizon of blasphemy extends beyond the field of humor, of course. One can blaspheme without being funny or trying to be funny. The outburst made by Job's wife, born of frustration and pity, that he "curse God, and die" (Job 2:9), could be seen as an invitation to blaspheme, but certainly without making a joke of it. Nevertheless, since Plato's day laughter has been suspected of deeply irreverent intentions— a risky game to play in the temple of God. As with pornography, what constitutes blasphemy in law or in the minds of individuals varies with time and place. One group's gentle mockery is another's open sacrilege. The case of Salman Rushdie has made that terrifyingly clear in our time. This is not the place to try to sort out the details of such boundary disputes. David Lawton has done an excellent job for any who are interested.[5] I want simply to emphasize the traditional connection that has been made between blasphemy and humor.

The moral sensitivities of people in seventeenth- and eighteenth-century England were no doubt a good deal more exercised by questions of blasphemy than we in our times. The words of Henry Hooten, writing in 1709, nicely capture both the gravity and the nature of the problem at the time. Speaking of the "blasphemies of his age," Hooten writes:

> To this Head may be reduced the ill practice of such as set their Mouths against Heaven, by prophanely making Holy Writ the subject of their Mirth, and Drollery, ridiculing Vertue and Religion, and (in as much as in them lies) laughing all Piety, out of Countenance, without which, Cicero tells us, No Faith could be secured, no Society amongst Men could be preserved, nor that most excellent Vertue of Justice itself subsists (*sic*); And therefore, to speak loosely, and wantonly about holy Things, or Persons; to make any thing nearly relating to God and Religion, the Matter of Sport and Mockery; or to turn the Sentences and Phrases of Holy Scripture into Jest, and Ridicule, is (notwithstanding the commonness thereof) a very great Sin.[6]

If blasphemy were so defined today, and the penalty for it were the cutting out of the tongue as it was in Hooten's time, one could think of a small army of contemporary comedians who would now be without the power of speech. The statement takes for granted an essential connection between blasphemy and laughter. Sport, mockery, mirth, jest, ridicule, drollery, in short a wide range of what might be called shades of comic meaning, are one and all condemned in reference to religion. The common complaint is that they take holy things—Scripture, religion, faith, God—and debunk them. In the final analysis that is tantamount to defying *God*, setting "their

---

[5] See n. 4. In what follows I am drawing heavily on Lawton's work.
[6] Quoted by Lawton, *Blasphemy* 15.

Mouth against Heaven." It is a short step from here to the famous Leviti-can definition of the blasphemer as the one "who curses God" and so "shall be put to death" (Lev 24:15-16). In such a climate one would select one's religious jokes with care.

The fact that in the West these days this position seems bizarre may be one indicator of the decline in even a generalized sense of the sacred in common consciousness. It was obvious that most newspaper commentators could only interpret the Islamic death threat against Rushdie as a sort of grotesque barbarity. Without a genuine sense of the sacred, the concept of blasphemy—the abuse of the sacred—loses emotional impact. "Is nothing sacred?" has become a lightweight rhetorical question. We find it hard work to be *that* offensive or *that* offended, at least in religious matters! On the other hand, so-called "political correctness" in our time often stridently demands the sort of propriety of speech in gender, racial, and political matters that provides something of a secular equivalent to the theological offense associated with blasphemy in earlier days.

Even with a much reduced sense of the outrage that blasphemous humor once provoked, we can still feel something of its potency. Take the limerick: There was a young lady called Alice / Who pissed in a Catholic chalice / But the Bishop agreed / She peed out of need / And not out of Protestant malice.

Most of us probably feel that these words are not utterly dreadful. The second half of the rhyme softens what might otherwise be felt as a pretty nasty theological and denominational affront. The outrage is lurking there, but its raw impact is blunted by the explanation that the action arose from biological desperation, not malicious intent. The "sin" is the outcome of bodily necessity rather than spiritual wickedness. Thus the humor has its own in-built brake, as it were, which cuts the momentum of what seems to be a headlong rush toward the religiously abhorrent. If we laugh at it we might do so just a little out of relief at this let off.

But the reprieve is not absolute. Even in dire physical need it is hard to think of circumstances where *such* a solution would be the best or even the only one available. The weight of the humor falls on the awful exchange of fluids in the eucharistic cup. This is an age-old, almost stock-in-trade device of derisive attacks on religious belief. The blasphemy trial against Sir Charles Sedley reported by Samuel Pepys in his *Diary* entry for 1 July 1663 makes this patently clear. Pepys describes how in a drunken state, on a balcony of an Oxford house, Sedley stripped himself naked and performed a mock religious service:

> . . . acting all the postures of lust and buggery that could be imagined, and abusing of scripture and, as it were, from thence preaching a Mountebanke sermon from that pulpit, saying that there he hath to sell such a pounder

as should make all the c***s in town run after him—a thousand people standing underneath to see and hear him.

And that being done, he took a glass of wine and washed his prick in it and then drank it off; and then took another and drank the King's health. . . .[7]

To call this comic incongruity seems woefully inadequate. Like the black mass, this action is a brutal inversion of religious sense and sensibility. The wine of the eucharist is for many believers the blood of Christ. It is the sacred drink that, taken into the body, gives life and nourishment to the soul and holds death and corruption at bay. "The medicine of immortality," the early Church called it. Urine is the excrement of the body and represents waste, corruption, putrefaction and, *in the wrong place*, all that is poisonous to life. Yet this is the exchange envisaged by the limerick and Charles Sedley's behavior. Excrement for nourishment. Exit for entrance. Death for life. In a sacramental context it comes as near to calling the good evil, the pure filthy and the sublime disgusting as is conceivable. Humor that occupies this territory is blatantly anti-theological. It wounds to kill.

Even so theology may have things to learn from what is undoubtedly a painful encounter. For one thing, blasphemous humor is a blunt reminder that faith is called to live in the midst of a world that may well be deeply opposed to its values. "I am sending you out like lambs in the midst of wolves," said Jesus (Luke 10:3). The gospel itself is offensive. It is an offense to what is offensive to God. A theology judged not worth affronting might well be salt that has lost its savor.

A less comforting reading also presents itself. Blasphemous humor puts the question: *Who* really is offended? The passion story of the gospels includes the accusation of blasphemy made by the religious authorities (and that of sedition by the political authorities) against *Jesus*. The vision of God embodied in his language and life was interpreted as an attack on theological orthodoxy by the representatives of that orthodoxy. With levitical zeal they had him done to death as an offense against God. In other words, the one who in Christian history came to be revered as God incarnate was, in the first instance, regarded as a theological obscenity. Which is the blasphemy? Which is the reversal of theological truth?

The passion story ought to give theologians pause to examine their motives. It doesn't take any great acumen to see that accusations of blasphemy are frequently made by, and designed to serve the interests of, those who have power, politically or religiously. The pious complain that blasphemers have "set their Mouths against Heaven." But it is often a

---

[7] Quoted by Lawton, *Blasphemy* 24. The original is found in *The Diary of Samuel Pepys* (1663), edited by Robert Latham and William Matthews (Berkeley and Los Angeles: University of California Press, 1970–) 4:209–210.

human rather than a divine realm that is at stake. Both priest and king have something to fear in Sedley's antics. It is not only the eucharistic cup but also the loyal toast he attacks. It is worth noting that while atheist tyrants may not resort to terms of blasphemy, the cry of "treason" or "sedition" can perform a parallel linguistic function. Secular tyrants have as little patience with comedians as do religious fanatics, and for the same reason. Comedians loosen the guy ropes of control. They insist that Church and State are human, all too human, and not the vice regents of heaven on earth, whatever their claims.

There is such a thing as blasphemous humor—the joke that "murders" God and "mutilates" holy things. But some caution is needed in making judgments. What functions as blasphemy in one context may operate to uncover theological fraud in another—that is, the kind of theology that uses the name of God to justify ungodly enterprises. It is difficult at times to distinguish between the comic gesture that says in effect "nothing is sacred because there is no God" and the one that says "this sacred *claim* is overblown, and whatever it pretends, *it* is not God." But the distinction matters. Both gestures may be painful for the believer. The first is the pain of theological offense, the poisoned chalice offered; the second of theological truth, the idolatrous sacrament named.

Mockery: "You don't expect me to believe that!"

To mock is "to poke fun at." The phrase is illuminating. To poke means to prod with a pointed instrument, to probe, to needle, to jab. The aim of the action may be various: to get attention, to awaken, to tickle, to hurt. If we poke a fire the intention is to rearrange the material in the hope of creating a better blaze, to get something going. To have fun "poked" at you, then, implies that the joke is roughly pushed at you like a sharp stick. The intention is to get under your skin. This comic approach won't easily be brushed aside. The impact on its object, in our case the believer/theologian, may be to startle, disturb, prod into action, or crush. But in contrast to blasphemy the action of this humor is more like the application of a scalpel than the thrust of a sword.

The sharpness of this humor depends on the exposure of (real or imagined) foolishness, fraud, arrogance and, especially in our time, impotence in religious life. That is why the bumbling clergyman is such a favorite of comedians. Rowan Atkinson as the priest in charge of one of the weddings in the film *Four Weddings and a Funeral* is a textbook example. He's a beached whale. He stammers, fluffs his lines, moves awkwardly in his anachronistic robes, and finally pronounces a blessing on his flustered congregation with the words, "In the name of the Father, the Son and the Holy Goat"!

The long slide of the Church from a position of social dominance to one of marginal influence is an obvious feature of our social landscape. The Church often lays claim to an authority it does not command, or presumes to offer moral leadership when its own house is a shambles. Atkinson as priest symbolizes all these things. He is foolish, ignorant, presumptuous, and acting in bad faith. Above all he is impotent. He can't do it. The sharpest jabs are aimed at theology itself, the God-talk. The supposed expert can't get it right. Moreover, the language about God seems as close to contemporary mumbo-jumbo as ghost is to goat. In the end what difference does the substitution make anyway? This God died the death of a thousand qualifications ages ago. The priest, God's tongue-tied representative, is a ludicrous demonstration of the "real absence" of the deity in today's world. William Willimon's hapless experience of preaching, though less devastating, is a similar case in point.

The rivalry that exists between different religious traditions or persuasions is a field ripe for mocking exploitation. The laughter of the denominational put down is irresistible: "you think my religion is odd, look at yours!"

> A rabbi and a Catholic priest were traveling opposite each other on a train. After a while the priest asks the rabbi, "Tell me, rabbi, as a man of the cloth in your faith, you're not supposed to eat pork, are you?"
>
> "That's correct."
>
> "Tell me then, man to man, have you ever tried it?"
>
> "When I was a young man," the rabbi answered, "I must confess that I did try it. Tell me, father, as a man of the cloth in your faith, you're not supposed to have sexual relations with women, are you?"
>
> "No, that's right."
>
> "Would you tell me, man to man, have you ever tried that?"
>
> "To be honest with you," said the Catholic leader, "when I was a young man I did try it."
>
> "Hm . . .," reflected the rabbi. "Better than pork, isn't it?"

A nice collusion is at first set up by the emotional drift of the story. The two religious leaders are alone in the train. A mood of intimacy develops. Shared secrets are possible. "Let's be honest, man to man, we both bend the rules a bit, it's only human!" So it looks as if the story is about what holds diverse religions together and gives them some common ground. Whatever faith we profess, human foibles and fallibilities are common to us all. We're in this thing together. Don't believe it! Common humanity is not enough to stifle religious antagonism.

Commitment to faith of any kind demands sacrifice. It is an important aspect of serious obedience to God. But what kind of religion arbitrarily bans the eating of pork? What conceivable purpose, divine or human, can be served by such an extraordinary prohibition? What view of God lies behind such an irrational demand? And what sort of blind religious obedience goes along with it? Such are the unspoken implications of the priest's inquiries. Paul Newman and Robert Redford's *Sting* has nothing on the rabbi's comeback. If we're swapping estimations of irrational religious demands and the gods who require them of their followers, what is a pork-free diet compared to celibacy?! Christian superiority is neatly debunked. Who really is "on top" here?

Another area of contemporary religious controversy comes under comic scrutiny in this variation on the child's "let's-see-what-we've-got-down-here" scene.

Oh, so that explains why I can't be ordained!

Debates on women's ordination have been heated and complex. The cartoon cuts through the tangled sophistication of it all and confronts us with the fundamentals. When all is said and done, boy and girl stand side by side. Can anyone seriously believe that biology is destiny in this *theological* sense? Is a glance down the diaper really going to settle the question of divine vocation for half the human race?

The famous feminist quip, "When God made man she was only joking," takes the matter a stage further. Aggression sits close to the surface. The joke is a two-pronged attack designed to unseat not merely this or that example of sexism, but patriarchy *per se* from its place. First comes the anthropology. An abrupt reversal of the Aristotelian/Thomist tradition that depicts woman as a deformed man, "defective and misbegotten,"[8] structures the humor. Any attempt to reduce woman to the design specifications of man is laughable, the joke asserts. If the truth be known, the vaunted human prototype, the male according to the Genesis account, is nothing but the creator's cartoon, a rough (and disposable?) sketch for the real portrait to follow. The unspoken implication is clear: the true *imago dei*—the authentic image of God—is woman.

Then comes the theology. The divine "she" breaks rudely into the flow of a sentence that two thousand years of theological and liturgical use has honed for the inevitable anticipation of "he." The gender reversal strikes like a blow, dislodging the masculine pronoun for God and destabilizing the whole issue of sex and God. It highlights the fact that the use of gender-specific language in describing God has deep implications for understanding both divinity and humanity. The distortions that follow its uncritical application are thrown up at us by the humor. Men feel the poke of a feminist critique of theology.

Religion, like politics, will always take a caning from the comedian. And as with any spanking there will always be argument as to whether or not it is deserved. Sometimes it isn't. Joke makers, like the rest of us, have mixed motives lying behind their actions. Clear-eyed spotting and naming of discrepancy, fraud, and coverup represent only one of these, albeit an essential one for the art. But comedians also want success and fame and money. Their route to these glittering prizes is laughter. "Anything for a laugh" edges toward an economic truism in the trade. As Michael Leunig notes: "Let us be clear on one thing—a joke is not *necessarily* a truth."[9] Anger, envy, and resentment in comedian and audience alike make a fertile culture for the growth of the laughing virus. Though we may not like to be reminded of a grace and judgment that transcend our control we know Atkinson doesn't represent all priests, nor is his benediction the last word on a doctrine of God in the modern world.

Nonetheless humorists as mockers are important critics of the faith. Theologians do well to be in dialogue with them as seriously as with the philosophers and sociologists, perhaps more so if communication with ordinary people and not only intellectuals is part of the theological agenda. A religious joke that generates a laugh is touching something in the human appreciation of the sacred. It invites thought. And it might, like the iron in the fire, just disturb things long enough to get a blaze going again.

---

[8] Cf. Thomas Aquinas, *Summa Theologica* (New York: Benziger, 1947) I. Pars Prima, q. 92, reply to objection 1, p. 466.

[9] Michael Leunig, "Laughter and life: seeing the extraordinary in the ordinary," *St Mark's Review* (Summer 1995) 6.

Irony: "God's Loyal Opposition"

"Irony," says Kierkegaard, "perceives that the individual has given himself away."[10] Self-entanglement is the nub of it. We trip *ourselves* up on obstacles of our own making. The religious humor of the third type plays on this possibility. It is not wholly different from mockery. The categories blur, as we said. Mockery tends to attack religion by declaring it out of step with some prevailing music regarded (by the comic) as guiding the dance of contemporary values and aspirations. Religion can't or won't play the game. So we have portrayed spiritual impotence in the face of secular power (the bumbling clergyman), or the consulting of old maps on terrain that is new (sexist language). And so on.

Ironic humor, by contrast, makes its point by drawing attention to discrepancies between intention and performance in religious life. Woody Allen's quip: "I'm not an atheist. I'm God's loyal Opposition!" encapsulates the genius of ironic religious comedy. In politics the Opposition attacks the Government, but not arbitrarily or with any weapon at hand. It attacks in the name of loyalty to the same task that (supposedly) motivates the Government: the well-being of the society. The most telling barbs of the Opposition are those that expose the Government for failing to live up to its own expectations. The same is true of religious irony. It sends up belief from the point of view of its (i.e., religion's) own "better self."

The ironic approach can take two major forms. The first is the comedy associated with falling short of religious ideals, the second with getting them mixed up. In the comedy of the "short-fall" the ironist contrasts experienced reality with professed aspiration. Sunday's unedifying homily is set in the light of a theology of the Word of God. Alan Bennett's famous sermon joke on the text, "My brother Esau is an hairy man, but I am a smooth man," is a great example of the genre.[11] William Willimon is an instance in real life. The comedy of the "mixup" plays on tensions inherent in religious belief. It uncovers contradictions and incoherencies that seem to be implicit, but often go unnoticed, in the life of faith.

> "Why was God depressed yesterday?"
> "He failed to make a stone so heavy he couldn't lift it."
> "Why is he depressed today?"
> "He succeeded in making a stone so heavy he couldn't lift it."

The point? Omnipotence is a self-contradictory idea.

Because irony works with rather than against the grain of religion it has a special contribution to make to theological work. It holds a mirror

---

[10] Søren Kierkegaard, *On Authority and Revelation*, translated by Walter Lowrie (New York: Harper & Row, 1966) 125.

[11] This comic sermon will be discussed in detail in the following chapter.

up to the believer that invites *self*-reflection and *self*-examination more directly than other forms of humor. Thus irony can be a stimulus to constructive theological development, a pointer toward ways of being truer to ourselves as believers.

My earliest religious emotions were shaped in the community of the Plymouth Brethren. So it is no wonder I find the story about the orientation tour of heaven has a delicious resonance.

> A bunch of new arrivals is being shown around the celestial city. At the conclusion of the tour the angel in charge asks them if they have any questions about what they have seen.
>
> "Yes," says one. "That high wall we passed a few minutes ago. What's behind it?"
>
> "Oh," replies the angel, "that's where the Brethren live. They think they're the only ones up here. And we wouldn't want to disappoint them!"

This joke works ironically. And conveniently it illustrates the humor of both the shortfall and the mixup. Read in terms of shortfall the joke looks like this: Heaven is the destiny God intends for creation. But, as the spiritual puts it, "Everybody talkin' 'bout heaven ain't a-goin' there." Life is serious. It is possible to miss one's eternal destiny. That is the final sting of evil. Who then will make it?—a time-honored and controversial theological question. Exclusive religious sects may be convinced that salvation is a gift of God. But it is a straight gate and a narrow way that leads to eternal life. And *they* are ones who tread it. Others, who see things differently, must therefore be on the path to destruction. In the story it turns out that this sectarian expectation is realized—and yet paradoxically not realized—eschatologically. The exclusivists make it to heaven, as they anticipated. But they are (blissfully?) unaware that paradise is bigger than they think. The irony is that in excluding others they have really excluded themselves. They are not punished in some vindictive way for their failings. They just can't cope with heaven's generosity and need to be sheltered from it so as not to be disappointed.

Anybody with a minimal theological understanding can get the point. But the more the hearer knows of the theology of reconciliation the sharper the point becomes. If heaven is the destiny God intends for creation, and if God in Christ accepted the cross as the price for saving the world from losing this destiny, is it likely that this divine intention will be of such marginal effect that, of all the teeming billions of creatures, paid-up members of the Brethren sect alone will stand before God at the last? None of this is said directly. What is said is that, in the final analysis, exclusives exclude themselves. The joke works as a theological critique of religious bigotry made in the name of a more generous doctrine of reconciliation. Brethren eschatology is a "fall short" theological position.

But there is more in this irony than a jibe in favor of a theology of universal redemption against those who sell it short. We can as easily reverse the comic grammar and read the joke as an *attack* on the doctrine of reconciliation using religious exclusiveness as the charge. Then the logic of the ironic "mixup" comes to the fore. The theology of final reconciliation of human beings with God and each other (i.e., in heaven) is often understood to imply a state of undifferentiated unity in which all serious differences are leveled out. Enmity between groups and individuals is overcome. Each is reconciled to all and all to each. The high-priestly prayer of Jesus, "that they [i.e., his followers] may be one, as we are one . . ." (John 17:22) seems to point in this direction. But is this really conceivable?

Michael Leunig's cartoon of the countercultural couple filling in the census form is not set in heaven. But it raises the question.

"We're Church of England aren't we?"

The Brethren (sectarian) view of religious faith places the stress on the ultimately serious character of human existence. It is possible to squander our opportunities and eventually lose our eternal destiny. Therefore the choices we make in history really matter. It is vital to know the true way, God's way, and to follow it with heart, soul, mind and strength.

At the other end of the scale stands the Leunig "Church of England." Here tolerance reigns. Love, generosity, inclusiveness are regarded as the marks of the life of faith. But where does that lead? If you were unkind you might say in the end (eschatologically?) it means anything goes. It doesn't matter much who you are or what you believe, Leunig seems to be saying. If you don't actually read yourself out of the Anglican Church, you're in! If you can't think of anything else to say in a tight spot, say you're C. of E. Who's to know? And who's to care? It doesn't commit you to anything. This view of religious life seems so bland as to have no cutting edge, so accommodating as to have no identifiable message to bring to the social debate, so open-ended as to have no recognizable vision either to offend or to recommend. The gates of hell won't do much trembling in face of this onslaught! And will heaven care?

The Leunig cartoon and the Brethren joke when read together seem to clash two theological principles, both of which appear essential to a Christian understanding of history and eschatology. The first is reconciliation conceived as unity. Final reconciliation surely means earthly hostilities are overcome. Otherwise eternity is simply the hatreds of history recycled. Heaven must be broad enough to accommodate all sorts (Leunig). The second principle is bliss understood as the fulfillment of individual character. Heaven means the state of completion in which, by the grace of God, we reach the full stature of our human potential. But the realization of human potential is not a trivial matter. Deep and demanding moral and spiritual choices confront us in history and unless we are prepared to commit ourselves to the right choices, virtue and justice will be trampled upon. Choice matters, eternally (Brethren seriousness).

But this creates a dilemma. If the Brethren stay behind the wall they can be happy (i.e., fulfilled). What they stood for so earnestly in historical life seems finally vindicated and they are at one. But their bliss is purchased at the price of delusion. They are in fact *not* the only ones in heaven. All sorts of C. of E. eccentrics are there too! On the other hand, if the wall comes down they cannot be really happy. For then they will discover that their deepest faith and earnest moral endeavor are misplaced. The "enemies" they believed headed for hell are in heaven. And they are as alien as they ever were on earth. So what was the point of all that struggle and sacrifice? In other words, it seems the Brethren in heaven can be fulfilled but not part of the whole, or part of the whole but not fulfilled. It is a case of *either* happiness *or* unity, but not both. Or, looked at the other way, tolerance can cope with unity, but it loses religious and moral seriousness.

The theological question is this: Is it possible to conceive a state of being in which the differences that characterize this world are transcended in the sense that they no longer generate hatred, strife, and war—the marks of a "fallen world"—and yet they are not so obliterated that the basic identities of those who have been historically shaped by those differences are simply annulled? Can there be a common destiny for

Muslim and Jew, Anglican and Brethren, in mutual relationship, without holy war or holocaust, and yet *also* without sacrifice of the serious spiritual substance and moral endeavor that make each what he or she is?

This is a vital question. Isaiah Berlin rejected all "teleological views" of human existence because of it.[12] For Berlin the three religions mentioned—Islam, Judaism, and Christianity—each assume that human beings, and indeed the universe as a whole, have a basic God-determined purpose. The ultimate meaning of life is found in moving toward that predestined goal, symbolized by the idea of "heaven." The difficulty, as Berlin sees it, is that all teleologies—including anti-theological movements like Marxism—depend upon the notion of an ultimate *unity*, a "one world" view of destiny. And therein lie the seeds of tyranny, the determination to force everyone into the value system of the favored faith on the grounds that all other modes of being are corruptions of the one true purpose of human life.

An eschatological extrapolation of this doctrine lands the believer in incoherence, according to Berlin. A heavenly unity is supposed to bring harmony to the historical dissonances between Jewish, Muslim, Christian, and any number of other value systems. But by their very natures these value systems are contradictory. Harmony between them is not simply difficult to devise in practice. It is literally inconceivable. Heaven, in the sense described, is not an as-yet-unrealized possibility. It is a nonsense. The only way to avoid delusion in eschatology (and tyranny in history) is to understand human purposes as ends freely chosen and pursued by human beings themselves, not as predetermined by God, or Nature, or the Dialectic of History, or whatever other principle of unity may be espoused. The crucial thing for a free society to know and defend is that the ends pursued by people and cultures may not necessarily be compatible. Some values will never be harmonized: Brethren commitment and C. of E. tolerance, Christian humility and Homeric fortitude, for example. Difference must be affirmed and defended. On these grounds, among others, Berlin dismisses Christian views.

In the final analysis this is the substance of the two jokes and the question they put to theology in the name of theology. The wall surrounding the heavenly enclave of Brethren souls, and the "anything goes" of the C. of E. census form, are comic symbols of ultimate puzzles about unity and difference that a doctrine of reconciliation faces, and of the mess we get ourselves into trying to solve them. Berlin may be wrong in arguing that reconciliation is an idea that cannot be thought through to the end and so is a state that cannot rationally be hoped for. But our jokes are

---

[12] Isaiah Berlin, "Introduction," in James Tully, ed., *Philosophy in an Age of Pluralism: The Philosophy of Charles Taylor in Question* (Cambridge: Cambridge University Press, 1994) 1–3; also Henry Hardy, ed., *The Crooked Timber of Humanity* (London: Fontana Press, 1991) chs. 1 and 2.

at least half on his side. Christian theology must try to show how Berlin's point can be acknowledged without his conclusion being drawn. Real "otherness" in human values must be accommodated in any workable eschatology. Without this, reconciliation is either impossible (the wall will never be breached) or it implies a collapse of distinctions that make history serious and interesting (the wall is torn down and its sheltered inhabitants forcibly "integrated" with the rest). Heaven becomes either a repetition or a negation of earth and in neither case its fulfilment.

Euphemy: "The Last Laugh?"

"He who laughs last laughs longest," the saying goes. This implies a battle of wits, a tangle of give and take. But it also poses the inevitable question: *Who* has the last laugh? Our fourth comic type is concerned with both issues, the battle and the victory. Although it has received far less attention from mainstream interpretations of humor—the laughter of "bad mouthing" has tended to dominate discussions—what I am calling euphemy, or the laughter of "well saying," is of great significance to theology. Here the religious humorist is directly, or almost directly, "on side."

At least one strand in classic atonement theory (Rufinus; Gregory of Nyssa) interprets the cross of Christ as a sort of ultimate practical joke played by God on the devil. The lure is the life of the Son of God. The prize is the souls of the damned. The devil takes the bait. But having swallowed it he finds to his horror that he can't "keep it down." Tricked once and for all, he loses both hostages and ransom in the great "punch line" of the resurrection. Heaven and earth ring with the joyful (laughing?) praise of angels and mortals alike. It may not be the most subtle of atonement theologies but it does make a point. Resurrection is an undoing of an undoing, a battle and a victory. If true it is euphemy indeed. The words of Julian of Norwich—"All will be well. And all manner of things will be well"—turn out to be an exegesis of the last and longest laugh of all.

There are dangers here, of course. The laughter *of* believers (rather than *at* believers) may try to claim the victory rather too easily. There is a "my-cup-is-full-and-running-over" brand of piety that manages to ignore the horrors of the world around and belie its own advertising with an empty head and timid heart. It smells of "cheap grace."[13] Comedians are quick to pounce on it. The fixed pious smile and nervous "I'm-everybody's-best-friend" giggle of the comedian-as-parson (Rowan Atkinson again or Alan Bennett's Vicar Geoffrey[14]) is the caricature presentation. Genuine euphemy will have none of it.

[13] Bonhoeffer's famous term.
[14] In his play, "Bed Among the Lentils." See Alan Bennett, *Talking Heads* (London: BBC Books, 1988) 29–41. This play is discussed in detail in chs. 8–11 below.

As with irony, euphemistic comedy comes in two forms. The first is what might be called "boomerang humor," or the comedy of "the double negative." If faith can be lampooned, so can unfaith. Boomerang humor mocks the mockers of the sacred and in that sense comes to God's defense. Woody Allen says somewhere, referring to some cogent defense of belief in God, "Stop it. I don't like having my doubts undermined like that!"

While history runs, of course, the jury is still out on the question of ultimate victory, the *real* last laugh. Theology's case for the defense rests finally on *faith* in God as creator and redeemer. It is a claim as strong and as weak as the witness to the resurrection is strong and weak. But *given* that faith, there is a laughter of belief, a joyful celebration in anticipation of a kingdom where alienation is overcome in reconciliation and difference is respected in integrity. This is euphemy proper—the humor of grace and beauty. For the Christian, religious celebration is most intensely expressed at the Eucharist. Perhaps this is why the battle is often most fiercely joined with blasphemy on eucharistic themes. It is a question of the last laugh. The pity of it is that real laughter is so seldom a part of the proceedings. Along with all other memories rightly evoked at the table of the Lord, we would do well to remember Nietzsche's great ironic joke. "If they want me to believe in their redeemer, they'd have to look a bit more redeemed!"

From a theological point of view Michael Leunig is one of the best exponents of both the comedy of the double negative and the joyful celebration. It is clear from his work that a dominating intention is to build up rather than break down, to affirm rather than deny. I have in mind especially the drawings, but the same thing holds true of his books of prayers. In his development as a cartoonist Leunig reports a growing disillusionment with the aggressive face of laughter. Speaking of his early career in political cartooning he says: "I was cruel many times. There can be real cruelty in just drawing someone with exaggerated face or features, even if it is done in the spirit of fun. It made me realise the world is fragile."[15] Two important lessons emerged from this disaffection. First Leunig came to appreciate the difference between laughter and truth. Just because something is funny doesn't mean it is true or fair.[16] Second, he became suspicious of comic motivation, especially in professional humorists. A smoldering anger seems to lie not far from the surface of much public humor. "This anger is spurted out on politicians and public figures. . . . It is usually done in the name of serious concern. 'I'm the conscience of the community and I must keep them honest.' Maybe. But often it is also a matter of satisfying a great rage."[17]

---

[15] Leunig, "Laughter and life," 4.
[16] See n. 9 above.
[17] Leunig, "Laughter and life," 6.

Leunig turned away from traditional cartooning that concentrates on the external world of politics and important events in order to "draw that other world, which is basically the personal world."[18] It was to be a world of the ordinary rather than the grand, the world of every man and every woman with their weals and woes, their ducks and teapots and fairy tales. The method he developed was introspective, but the results were anything but individualistic. The fact is, Leunig argues, "the most intensely personal is also most universal."[19] In looking for a way to give expression to the underlying forces and conflicts at work in society, but which are often hidden and ignored, Leunig became increasingly aware of the destructive aspects of modern western societies: of fragmentation and a loss of human community, of pollution and an attitude of irreverence to the natural world, of technological reason that banishes mystery, magic, and a sense of infinitude from human consciousness, of bureaucracy that seems unaware of any value beyond economic efficiency. He decided to look for ways to counteract the trends.

> I want to know what is worth *affirming*. . . . I'm not a post-modernist who says, "Just let it rip and see what happens. The way it turns out is the way it is." I think we have to make choices about what we want and stick by them . . . instead of every day re-inventing values according to whatever the latest market research indicates. . . . What it comes to is that I am a conservationist. I am trying to conserve cultural and spiritual things to the extent that I can.[20]

It is this *affirming* attitude that is the hallmark of Leunig's humor. His cartoons are like adult "fairy gardens"[21] into which the viewer/reader is invited in order to explore unexpected ways of being and relating. In the final analysis this work of conservation follows the two major routes noted earlier: the laughter of the double negative and the laughter of joyful celebration. Of an enormous range of possible examples I will choose just one of each.

The Double Negative—In Defense of the "Sacred Cow"

Leunig is certainly familiar with the humor of deconstruction. "I once thought what a funny fellow I was to go around knocking down 'sacred cows.' . . . My generation was like that. We went around smashing and breaking things."[22] Nor does he reject this approach out of hand. Such humor can be critical and cleansing. The problem is where to draw a line.

[18] Ibid., 3.
[19] Ibid., 10.
[20] Ibid., 9, 10.
[21] Ibid., 7.
[22] Ibid., 9.

I thought I could destroy this or that sacred cow, because there would always be other sacred cows somewhere else. . . . But now I find there are few sacred cows left. I'd love to see a sacred cow! I'd like to go and worship the damned thing . . . well, you don't call a sacred cow "a damned thing!"[23]

Leunig's disillusionment with disillusionment is depicted in this drawing.[24]

The picture might well be labeled "the hermeneutics of suspicion." In the last two hundred years the application of this hermeneutics has seen theology reduced to anthropology, anthropology to psychology, psychology to economics, economics to biology, biology to chemistry, chemistry to physics, physics to . . . questions of the "Big Bang" and all that. Much has no doubt been illuminated along the way. But the limitations of the skeptical stance that claims to "see through" every value, every action, every art form, every sacrament is neatly debunked in the picture of the man with X-ray eyes. In seeing through everything he sees nothing at all, not even his own motivations—that is, "the back of his own head."

In this negation of the negative there lie hints of something more. The Leunig moon appears twice in the cartoon, small and distant but present still, as if silently waiting for a glance upwards, beyond the closed cycle of earth-bound critical thinking. In the little book in which he pairs the writings of Karl Rahner with the pictures of Michael Leunig, John Honner has

[23] Ibid.

[24] The cartoon is taken from John Honner, ed., *Michael Leunig & Karl Rahner: A Common Philosophy* (Melbourne: Aurora Books, 1992) 27.

emphasized this positive consequence of the logic of the double negative: "In the fact that we affirm the possibility of a merely *finite* horizon of questioning, this possibility is already surpassed, and we show ourselves to be beings within an *infinite* horizon."[25] There's more to the world than meets the skeptical eye. But you have to know where to look, and how.

The Laughter of Celebration—Cartoon Christmas

"The cartoonist is very good at recognising corruption, but not very good at recognising a saint."[26] Is it possible to present holy things in comic form, positively, and not simply as the debunking of the debunkers? Examples of Leunig's attempt at an affirmative answer to this question could be taken from pictures that deal with subjects as diverse as the activities of guardian angels and the archaeology of manners. But I want to take a specifically theological theme: the nativity of Christ.[27]

This is a cartoonist's picture of Christmas. But is it a "real cartoon"?[28] Or is it some other more serious kind of depiction? A drawing

[25] Honner, *Michael Leunig & Karl Rahner* 26. The Rahner quote comes from his *Foundations of Christian Faith* (New York: Darton, Longman & Todd, 1978) 31–32.

[26] Leunig, "Laughter and life," 9.

[27] Honner, *Michael Leunig & Karl Rahner* 83.

[28] I am using the word to refer to the typical modern newspaper cartoon, not the technical artistic reference to a preliminary sketch for a later more detailed work.

can be said to be a cartoon, I would argue, if it satisfies at least the following criteria. (1) It intends to convey a "message" usually, but not necessarily, of a controversial kind. (2) It looks for immediate impact, so the message is presented in the most economical way possible. A cartoon is like a pictorial parable. Extraneous detail is cut to the minimum in order to focus on the key ideas. (3) This means that figures in the picture are deliberately stylized, a few lines only suggesting the form, and caricatured, in that features are distorted to convey a particular interpretation of character or mood. (4) Finally, the genre is comic. An unfunny cartoon is a failure.

The nativity scene above fits the type. There is no mistaking the theme. This is obviously Christmas, with Mary, Joseph, and holy child in a simple shelter, stars above, animals around (point 2). The figures of both humans and animals are sketched in typical cartoon fashion (point 3). Joseph and Mary are the Leunig everyman and everywoman, here in Eastern garb. They are slightly hunched, with prominent nose—"full of unsnuffled tears"[29]—and an expectant eye. The animals are humanoid. They share the same stance, same posture, same eye as everyman. Nature is mirror and *alter ego* of the human. The message, too, is there, kerygmatic and controversial (point 1). The picture confronts us with difference, a significant difference from what we know to be the cliché of Christmas. At first glance it *looks* like a standard Christmas card scene, and is meant to. But then we notice something odd. The animals are misplaced. Not only are the usual cows and sheep replaced by dogs, ducks, and cats (or is it rats?). But these animals have moved from their normal positions as stupefied spectators on the edge of a *human*/divine drama to center-stage front. Most disturbing of all, they gaze not at the human child, but at a haloed infant each of its *own* species!

Given a different artistic context it would be possible to imagine this as a clever restatement of the projectionist theory of religious experience. We make gods in the image of our own beings. Were that the case the cartoon would belong with the humor of mockery or irony. But in this instance affirmation, worship, delight—certainly not illusion—is the manifest intention. Everything is bathed in the light of heaven. The positive yet *different* thrust of the picture is to affirm the incarnation as *cosmic* occurrence. A purely anthropocentric reading of the Christ event is inadequate. The human incarnation is modestly placed to one side. It is not denied or mocked. It is merely put in a new place. That place is alongside and perhaps, for the time being, a little behind the place of other beings. The implication is that God's love for the world is not exhausted by its saving participation in human affairs. God relates as

[29] Leunig, "Laughter and life," 4.

companion to every level of being. Leunig may or may not be aware of the current theological critiques being made of classic christology by thinkers concerned with ecological sustainability, but his cartoon depiction of incarnation within the horizon of nature as well as history is right to the point.[30]

The fourth criterion of a cartoon is humor. Is the picture funny? I think it is. But if it is, it is gentle humor, merry and without malice. There is nothing of the raw edge of nativity humor found in the shout from the stable, "It's a girl!" where all the emotional hostilities of theological sexism rumble in the laughter generated—unless, that is, we are to assume that from the perspective of animals the joke on humans would appear just as deliciously vengeful! Leaving aside such inter-species speculation, the power of the humor seems to lie in its disclosure of the comic discrepancy between less and more. Your Christ is too *small*, the cartoon argues. Theologies that assume that the incarnation touches only the human realm have not yet understood the truly universal scope of the gift. With dogs and ducks and cats, and by extension all creation, "lift up your hearts," the mystery of God is greater than you dreamed of. If God is infinite, the discovery of God will presumably be an endless encounter with surprise, the delightful revelation of the laughable limitations of our apprehension of divine glory at this and at every point. The laughter of eternity will be the comedy of memory transcended without end.

The Comic Catenary

We can draw these reflections together in the following diagram, which I will call "the comic catenary." As we recall from school mathematics, a catenary is the shape assumed by a rope or chain when suspended between two points and left to hang under its own weight, or with a uniform distribution of other weight along its line, such as in the case of a suspension bridge. The "road" that bears the "traffic" between theology and humor moves back and forth across the line **F** to **G** which is suspended, so to speak, from the catenary above. This line represents specific examples of religious humor, i.e., particular jokes. I have noted along it the jokes referred to. The catenary represents the form or class of humor that underlies the particular examples and, in that sense, "supports" them. Like all attempts at classification, this model has its limits. Types of religious humor can be identified, but they are rarely pure. Most jokes have blurred edges and might well be placed at more than one point along the catenary.

---

[30] For one of many possible titles on this subject see Thomas Berry, *The Dream of the Earth* (San Francisco: The Sierra Club, 1988).

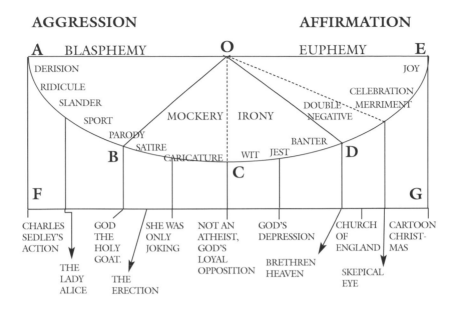

The two ends of the catenary represent the extremes of relationship between theology (or religion) and humor: blasphemy at one end, **A**, euphemy at the other, **E**. The dotted line from the center **O** to the midpoint of the catenary **C** marks the transition boundary from humor that is aggressive toward religion (left side) to humor that is affirming (right side). The impact of the humor on the left is theological critique, that on the right theological construction. On the aggressive side of the scale the segment **AOB** covers humor that wounds with the intent to kill. It is out to destroy or seriously discredit religious faith and no one can mistake its aim. The comedy of ridicule, derision, slander and, of course, blasphemy belong here. In the neighboring segment **BOC** we find the kind of humor that is still critical, but more gently so. This is the territory of mocking laughter. It may be cutting. But it is not deadly. Religious caricature, parody, satire, or facetiousness belong in this section.

On the right-hand side is the humor of affirmation. Segment **COD** represents the shading of humor across from the critical to the constructive. Comedy in this, the ironic section of the catenary may question religious expressions or dispositions, but it does so in a way that offers support and even positive encouragement to its subjects. Humor of this kind takes religion to task on its (i.e., religion's) *own* terms. It speaks to faith in the power of faith's own affirmations. Religious wit, jest, banter and the like belong under this heading.

As we move toward the euphemy end of the spectrum, segment **DOE**, it gets harder to find words to describe the kind of comedy represented. (This is a point that is not lost on those who wish to stress the aggressive interpretation of humor.) Can humor really build up as well as break down? If it can—and I hope we have shown it can—then we can speak of laughter as celebration, merriment, delight, and ultimately joy.

Thus the relationship of laughter to religion, of the comedian to the theologian, is complex and dynamic. Theology is right to be somewhat cautious of laughter. It has had long experience both as victim and as perpetrator of the joke that "sends up" and "puts down." On the other hand, a theology that takes itself too seriously, that cannot see the joke and will not laugh at itself, is a theology that has become too timid or too arrogant. It deserves what the humorist has to give in the way of a critical caning. That theology has often been reluctant to explore the positive contribution humor can make to its enterprise seems an unnecessary self-limitation. Religious laughter as "loyal opposition," as irony, as merriment, as euphemy, represents a rich resource on which theology might draw. Laughter may be a pip in the apple of Eden, as Baudelaire remarked.[31] But it is also one of the more piquant sauces in the banquet of heaven. It would be irony indeed if in trying to avoid choking on the one theology missed altogether the delightful taste of the other.

The next chapter can be read as a sample of the menu on offer.

---

[31] See Michele Hannoosh, *Baudelaire and Caricature: From the Comic to an Art of Modernity* (University Park, Pa.: Pennsylvania State University Press, 1992) 10.

3

Portrait of the Preacher as a Fool

The Foolishness of Preaching

In a famous passage Paul comes close to calling the work of preaching a job for fools. "God decided, through the foolishness of our proclamation, to save those who believe" (1 Cor 1:21). Whatever this foolishness is, Paul regards God as having a hand in it and therefore sees its consequences as beneficial, indeed saving. But that does not alter the fact that the phrase "the foolishness of preaching" (the King James rendition) seems to many people a deliciously apt description of the task. It is worth noting that in the text this judgment is not made by observers from outside. We would hardly be surprised if people who felt religious faith was pointless were to conclude that its expression in preaching is absurd. But Paul is speaking of "those who believe"—at the very least of those on the way to belief.

Foolishness can mean many things. Paul contrasts preaching with the accepted wisdom of his age, with *what* the philosopher knows and *how* the debater argues (1 Cor 1:19-20). On both counts the preacher seems to come off second best. Beside the philosopher the message of the preacher looks naïve, lacking rational content and universal principle. Against the debater the preacher's arguments appear unconvincing, more assertion than demonstration. By these lights the preaching of the gospel is judged foolish. It is at variance with what counts as clear thinking, sound argument, and good taste. And presumably this is when preaching is at its best! Nor have things improved much with the passage of time. Paul Scherer tells of a Roman Catholic observer who quipped that if ever Protestantism should be found dead of an assassin's attack, the dagger in its back would be the Protestant sermon.[1] By this assessment preaching is a kind of suicide, potentially fatal to the very life it is supposed to nurture.

---

[1] Paul Scherer, *The Word God Sent* (London: Hodder & Stoughton, 1966) 3.

I want to distinguish two types of foolishness. Let us call them *wayward* foolishness and *intrinsic* foolishness respectively. Both, I will argue, are important in a critical evaluation of preaching.

By *wayward* foolishness I mean the sort of behavior that leaps into a particular task but fails to take seriously the prerequisites for its successful completion. We say fools rush in where angels fear to tread. A foolish person doesn't see (or care) that what he or she is doing is likely to go badly given a sober estimate of the nature of the undertaking and the abilities of the one undertaking it. It's a fool who goes to a job interview without carefully studying the job specifications. And whatever the inducements, the backyard boxer who gets into the ring with Mike Tyson is a fool. It is not that these enterprises are somehow flawed. Job interviews and boxing matches, whatever we think of them, have a manifest coherence. Certain knowledge and skills are needed for any successful participation. A fool is careless about these requirements. He thinks he knows what it is all about, but in fact does not. A fool in the wayward sense is the incompetent.

By *intrinsic* foolishness I mean the kind of action that by its nature is somehow self-contradictory. The enterprise is inherently at odds with its own intentions and is bound to come to grief regardless of the capacities of those who may be involved. The gambler who always puts her money on the horse with the longest odds is intrinsically foolish. There is an almost inevitable contradiction in the procedure. She wants to make money. But the game she plays virtually guarantees her money will be lost. Smoking may be another such foolishness. The end—a desire to project an image of virility and sophistication—is at war with the means. A fool in the intrinsic sense is sawing away at the branch she is sitting on.

I will come back to this distinction and its application to the preacher in a moment. But first a step into comedy. In Shakespearian drama the "fool" is the clown or jester. The fool plays up and clowns around. But the jocularity has a serious intent. His antics point deftly to the contradictions, deceptions, and stupidities that inhere in the actions and qualities of the characters in the drama. Comedians are our modern equivalents. We argued in the previous chapter that a successful comedian is one who holds the mirror up to the human condition. He or she points out the incongruities and inconsistencies, the frauds and self-deceptions—in short, the foolishness—we are all prone to. The "fool" as comedian is dedicated to "outing" foolishness wherever it may be lurking in human affairs.

If the preacher is sometimes a fool it shouldn't be surprising if the "fool" (comedian) is sometimes the preacher. It takes one to know one, the saying goes. Any number of contemporary comics have turned their attention to the modern clergyman and clergywoman with spectacular results. Impersonations by Peter Cook, John Cleese, Rowan Atkinson, and

Dave Allan come readily to mind. In this chapter I want to examine my favorite sermon joke, a "fool's" view of the foolishness of preaching if ever there was one. The sketch is Alan Bennett's "Take a Pew," which first came to light as part of the famous Cambridge review, *Beyond the Fringe*. The humor is a potent mixture of mockery—a challenge to the very essence of preaching, and irony—an acute observation of common pulpit incompetence. Bennett simply takes a "text" and preaches a "sermon" on it. Of course a good deal of the humor resides not so much in *what* is said as in the *way* it is said. As we hope would be the case with the genuine article, so here. Reading the script of the comic "sermon" doesn't have quite the impact of hearing it delivered. But for all that, it isn't too hard to image the following words uttered with a pompous, parsonical tone: the worst kind of pulpit rhetoric.

Take a Pew

The 29th verse of the 14th chapter of the book of Genesis: "But my brother Esau is an hairy man, but I am a smooth man"—my brother Esau is an hairy man, but I am a smooth man. Perhaps I can paraphrase this, say the same thing in a different way, by quoting you some words from that grand old prophet, Nehemiah—Nehemiah 7:16.

> *And he said unto me, what seest thou*
> *And I said unto him, lo!*
> *I see the children of Bebai*
> *Numbering six hundred and seventy-three*
> *And I see the children of Asgad*
> *Numbering one thousand, four hundred and seventy four.*
> (more quickly) *I see the children of Bebai*
> *Numbering six hundred and seventy-three*
> *And I see the children of Asgad*
> *Numbering one thousand, four hundred and seventy four.*

There come times in the lives of each and every one of us when we turn aside from our fellows and seek the solitude and tranquillity of our own firesides. When we put up our feet and put on our slippers, and sit and stare into the fire; and I wonder at such times whether your thoughts turn, as mine do, to those words I've just read to you now. They are very unique and very special words, words that express as so very few words do that sense of lack that lies at the very heart of modern existence. That "I-don't-quite-know-what-it-is-but-I'm-not-getting-everything-out-of-life-that-I-should-be-getting" sort of feeling. But they are more than this, these words, much much more. They are in a very real sense a challenge to each and every one of us here tonight. What is that challenge?

As I was on my way here tonight, I arrived at the station, and by an oversight I happened to go out by the way one is supposed to come in; and as I was going out an employee of the railway company hailed me. "Hey, Jack," he shouted, *"where do you think you're going?" That at any rate was the gist of what he said. But, you know, I was grateful to him; because, you see, he put me in mind of the kind of question I felt I ought to be asking you, here, tonight: Where do you think **you're** going?*

Very many years ago, when I was about as old as some of you are now, I went mountain climbing in Scotland with a very dear friend of mine. And there was this mountain, you see, and we decided to climb it. And so, very early one morning, we arose and began to climb. All day we climbed. Up and up and up; higher and higher and higher. Until the valley lay very small below us, and the mists of the evening began to come down, and the sun to set. And when we reached the summit we sat down to watch this magnificent sight of the sun going down behind the mountain. And as he watched, my friend very suddenly and violently vomited.

Some of us think life's a bit like that, don't we? But it isn't. Life, you know, is rather like opening a tin of sardines. We are all of us looking for the key. And, I wonder, how many of you here tonight have wasted years of your lives looking behind the kitchen dressers of this life for that key. I know I have. Others think they've found the key, don't they? They roll back the lid of the sardine tin of life, they reveal the sardines, the riches of life, therein, and they get them out, they enjoy them. But, you know, there's always a little bit in the corner you can't get out. I wonder—I wonder, is there a little bit in the corner of your life? I know there is in mine!

So, now, I draw to a close. I want you, when you go out into the world, in times of trouble, and sorrow, and hopelessness, and despair, amid the hurly-burly of modern life, if ever you're tempted to say, "Stuff this for a lark;" I want you, at such times, to cast your minds back to the words of my first text to you tonight: "But my brother Esau is an hairy man, but I am a smooth man."[2]

Any number of attitudes might be taken toward this sketch, especially if we happen to be preachers. We could reject it out of hand as an impudent and impious attack upon a noble profession and thus unworthy of serious consideration. Certainly it is less than a wholehearted endorsement of our calling! Alternatively, we might enjoy it as a lighthearted romp, fun while it lasts and even cathartic. There is some comfort, as William Willimon found out, in being able to laugh about our own floundering efforts at preaching and so not take ourselves too seriously.[3] Then, of course, we could always take refuge in the assumption that if it applies, it applies to someone else. But we might also take Bennett as a genuine conversation partner, someone to listen to carefully. His comedy then un-

[2] "Take a Pew" is a sketch from the Revue "Beyond the Fringe," written and performed by Alan Bennett. *The Complete BEYOND THE FRINGE*, by Alan Bennett, Peter Cook, Jonathan Miller, and Dudley Moore, edited by Roger Wilmut (London: Methuen Paperback, 1987) 103–104.

[3] See above, p. 19.

covers something of the truth about preaching and preachers—a truth that invites thought.

The sketch is a caricature, a verbal cartoon. We know well enough how visual caricature works.[4] Political cartooning is the most obvious example of the art. The caricaturist takes the features of the subject, usually the face, and draws it so that while it is unmistakably the person intended (John Howard, Margaret Thatcher, Bill Clinton or whoever), some features are overdrawn to the point of gross distortion. The exaggeration, however, has an interpretive, often critical, purpose. The Thatcher cartoon hairdo, nose, and mouth signify a pugnacious, intrusive, aggressive style. The pictorial exaggeration stays near enough to the real features of the person to be recognizable, but is also sufficiently different to make the critical judgment of the artist crystal clear.

This is what Bennett is doing *verbally* to preachers and their art. He takes a "sermon" and "preaches" it. We recognize it immediately, as we recognize the Clinton or Thatcher face. He begins and ends with a biblical text. And what a text! He "exegetes" it with a variety of familiar homiletical techniques—repetition, a biblical quotation, a few vivid illustrations, a sense of being "with it" by appeal to the "lack that lies at the very heart of modern existence." Then he concludes with the customary personal challenge and exhortation. Unmistakably it is the sermonic form. Like a cartoonist who spatially distorts the features of his subject to draw attention to what he considers idiosyncrasies of character, Bennett focuses on certain features of the homiletical art that he regards as typical of the preacher's profession, and by a process of verbal exaggeration and simplification he enlarges these features to the point where their deficiencies become glaringly obvious. Thus the spoof functions as a sort of magnifying glass through which to scrutinize the person and work of the preacher. It yields a distorted picture. But it is distortion with a purpose. Abuses that in the normal course of events might go unnoticed through the dullness of familiarity or the timidity of conventional piety are made uncomfortably clear. The result is a pretty scathing assessment of preaching. This is humor well on the aggressive side of the comic catenary.[5] It plays hard on what it sees as a discrepancy between the intention of proclaiming the gospel and what is actually delivered: The foolishness of preaching portrayed.

The Wayward Fool

To return now to the initial distinction between kinds of foolishness: Alan Bennett certainly highlights a good deal of *wayward* foolishness

---

[4] See above, pp. 39–40.
[5] See above, p. 41.

about preaching. Wayward foolishness we defined as engaging in a task without caring enough about the rules and requirements for its competent performance. In this case it means shoddy preaching. Bennett catalogues a whole string of such wayward homiletical follies. As preachers we may blush in self-recognition at points. Without attempting to be exhaustive, let me outline some of his more obvious commentary.

(*i*) *Voice*. A preacher's instrument of communication is the voice. How it is used is fundamental to the success or failure of the task. Since the comic sketch is here in written form only, the points I want to make have to be taken largely on trust. But for those who know the original it is obvious that the comedian has worked hard to perfect what we might call the "parson's pitch"—a sing-song, wimpish, holier-than-thou presentation that by its tone and timbre screams the worst about the rhetoric of the pulpit. It is a caricature. But the critique stands. We have heard preachers do this sort of thing. The problem is inauthenticity. It sounds like a put-up job, a mask for the occasion. The preacher seems to be trying to make the message more plausible than it is by using a special aural code. But it winds up being artificial. We feel tempted to ask, "What's he trying to hide? Why doesn't he be himself?"

Bennett is particularly sharp on the matter of authority. The voice he adopts is a conventional expression of British class differentiation. It is an Oxbridge accent hammed up—lispy and upper-crust-ish. He talks down to the congregation as to those who are culpably ignorant and in need of instruction from on high. But the emperor has no clothes. This wayward foolishness of preaching might be summed up as the contradiction between form and content. The gospel is in essence good news to the poor. It is addressed with special compassion to those who labor and are heavy laden. To be proclaimed well it needs a form suited to this substance. In Bennett's version there is no generosity of tone, no solidarity in attitude, no humility in demeanor. Authority in this sermon is the fake sway of a person who talks loudly without knowing from experience the meaning of his subject.

(*ii*) *Language inflation*. Words are the preacher's currency. Through the medium of words he or she exchanges the riches of faith with the hearers. But there is an economics of words. If face value and real value are not necessarily the same thing in monetary, neither are they in semantic terms. Bennett's critique is clear. Talk is cheap. His preacher's words flow effortlessly. But despite the urgent reassurance that these words are "very unique and very special words, words that express as so very few words do" the deep matters of human existence—they don't really amount to a hill of beans. There is no serious preparation for the task. The man is still looking for something to say as he arrives at the station on the way to the church. Free association—"Is there a little bit in the corner of your life?" and immediate impression—"he put me in mind of the kind of question I felt I ought to be asking you, here, tonight"—provide such links as there are between one idea and the next. There is a liberal use of illustrations, of course. Stories of personal experience (the mountain climb) and complex allegory (the sardine tin) make up the bulk of the text. They are wonderfully vivid. Any preacher might envy the color and economy of their telling. But in this instance they act like skis under the feet of a novice who has strayed onto the steep slope. Once entered upon they gather a momentum of their own and take their hapless owner on an appalling ride to disaster.

Cheap grace is to ethical endeavor what cheap words are to homiletic responsibility. If there is a genuine short cut to proclamation I have yet to find it. As a child I remember a standard parental justification for refusing to fund some newly desired object: "you won't know the value of money until you've worked for it." Malcolm Fraser put it more bluntly with the famous remark: "There is no such thing as a free lunch." In our context the equivalents might be: you don't know the cost of preaching until you have had to do it yourself; and there is no such thing as an easy sentence. In my experience both things are true. Biblical texts have to be interpreted, ideas pursued until they yield their meanings, images crafted so they genuinely represent what is intended, stories explored to discover where the weight of their feeling lies, connections and contrasts, warrants and authorities placed and secured where their strength is most needed. And all this has to be coordinated under the controlling perspective of a coherent aim. Finally it has to be expressed one word at a time. As H. L. Mencken said in a different context, the challenge is always the same: "which words and in what order?"

(iii) Dereliction of Duty. The task of the preacher is to interpret the biblical witness to the present situation. This is the heart of the matter. Dutifully, therefore, Bennett takes a text. But the point he wishes to drive home is wickedly barbed. For the text—"My brother Esau is an hairy man but I am a smooth man"—is ludicrous and, lifted out of context, borders on the idiotic. The words in this instance are quoted correctly, but the reference is mischievously wrong. It doesn't come from the "29th verse of the 14th chapter of the book of Genesis," but from Genesis 27:11. The other quotation—"from that grand old prophet, Nehemiah"—by contrast, is correctly referenced, but this time the words quoted are wildly scrambled. The real text mentions Bebai and Asgad alright, but the number of descendants reported in the sermon are a complete fabrication (673 instead of 628, and 1474 instead of 2322) and the rest is simply made up. Thus without a word being said directly, Bennett quietly sets up the Bible as a meaningless, impenetrable text, hardly worth taking seriously. Both quotations are intended to highlight the hermeneutical gap that yawns

between the biblical message and contemporary experience of the world. The task and the problem of preaching are thus starkly set. The message of the Bible, embedded in a literature that comes from another age and couched in archaic terms, is supposed to be of crucial relevance to life as it is lived here and now. According to the Church, this is the Word of God. The preacher's job is to make it relevant or at least plausible. But this preacher falls woefully short of the mark. He has his texts, but not once does he refer to, much less explicate, them in the course of his sermon. They remain there at the end, as they were in the beginning, distant and powerless, alien realities from the strange land of the past. The wayward foolishness of the preacher is to undertake the hermeneutical task but be devoid of the skill to carry it through.

(iv) Shallowness of Spirit. Part of the preacher's job is to speak helpfully to the deep troubles of human existence—its mystery, its struggle with good and evil, its suffering. But the unrelenting demands of the job can lead to the temptation of easy answers. Bennett-the-preacher has only make-believe solutions for real problems. He trivializes the mystery (the comparison of life with a sardine can), sentimentalizes the struggle for meaning (slippers on, feet up, staring blankly into the fire), and cheapens the pain ("stuff this for a lark"). He plays at being profound with reference to "the lack that lies at the very heart of modern existence," but can't quite say what the challenge is that supposedly confronts us in this lack, and ends up with the shout of a railway clerk furnishing the central direction of his discourse.

I don't think anyone expects the preacher to have all the answers or even to know always what are the real questions that face and perplex people. But one who presumes to speak publicly on matters of life and death ought at least to know something about where the limitations of analysis lie and where the approximation of solutions fails. In an enterprise dominated by the demand to speak it is equally important for the preacher to know when and where to be silent. Not to feel a deep awe before the mystery of life and death is not to respect life and death as they deserve. We live more deeply that we can say.[6] Preaching becomes a parody of itself if the preacher doesn't know this.

(v) Grandstanding. The preacher in the pulpit is supposed to be an ambassador for God, a medium through which God's Word is spoken. But we are stuck with the reality, given classic expression by Phillips Brooks, that preaching is "truth through personality"[7]—*my* personality if I am the preacher. It is pointless pretending that the self in the pulpit is

---

[6] It was Alfred North Whitehead, I think, who said, "We live more deeply than we can think."

[7] See Phillips Brooks, *Lectures on Preaching* (Manchester: James Robinson, 1899) 5ff.

not also a self on show, and aware of the fact. There is a buzz in preaching that is akin to the power interests of the political orator and the applause interests of the stage actor. It is hard not to get tangled up in a confusion of means and ends. Policy's the thing. But woe betide the junior minister who doesn't know who's making it. The play's the thing. But watch out if the understudy shines too brightly on the star's night off. The gospel's the thing. But remember who's preaching it.

As with politics and acting, so with preaching, this essential connection of personality and function is no bad thing *per se*. What would the Gettysburg address be without Lincoln behind it? And how different would the character of Lear be without the aged Olivier's performance. Eberhard Jüngel puts a finger on it. "Each theologian [read also preacher] is personally grasped by the truth to which he or she must respond in thought, word and . . . deed. In this respect theology always also bears the individual characteristics of a life story. It is in part theological biography."[8] But this does not alter the truth that preaching is fundamentally talk of God. If *my talk* of God gets in the way of my talk *of God* a line has been crossed that spells the corruption of proclamation. It is this line that Bennett marks. In this comic pulpit the medium has become the message. The preacher's finger points steadily selfwards. God is scarcely mentioned.

Thus far we have considered the comedian's depiction of the wayward foolishness of preaching. To do the job well the preacher should in form, content, style, and language mediate the Word of God to the contemporary world in a way that is both faithful to the Word and relevant to the world. Moreover, the work must be intensely personal and reflect the theological and spiritual biography of the preacher. And yet it is Christ, not personality, who is to come to expression in proclamation. It's a tough assignment on all counts. Often we are not up to it in mind, or spirit, or discipline. We make wayward fools of ourselves in one way or another. And in the course of it we sometimes make the truth we are supposed to serve look foolish as well.

The Intrinsic Fool

But it is not only the question of wayward foolishness—the various ways in which the preacher can stumble in the task of proclaiming the gospel—that is at stake. The deeper issue is whether the gospel, *however* well it is preached, has anything of real value to contribute to the postmodern world. There can be only one outcome of the contest if David goes up against Goliath with a defective slingshot. What Alan Bennett is asking

---

[8] Eberhard Jüngel, *Theological Essays II*, edited by J. B. Webster, translated by Arnold Neufeldt-Fast and J. B. Webster (Edinburgh: T & T Clark, 1995) 3.

is not only whether David knows how to use the sling (i.e., is he competent?) but whether the stones in his hand carry enough weight for the job (i.e., is it possible?). I argued earlier that an enterprise deserves to be called intrinsically foolish when there is something inherently self-contradictory about it, when some antithesis exists in the heart of the action itself. Is preaching foolishness in this sense? Are we fools as preachers not just because we do a difficult task poorly, but because the task itself is inherently impossible? This is a question of theology, not practical competence.

The comic sermon works at this deeper level as well. It holds the mirror up to life, religious life in this case. Life obviously does have particular humorous discrepancies built into it. We run into them everywhere. They become the material of our jokes. But such humorous incidents are possible because human life itself is at bottom a potential joke. Our humanity is built from its foundations on essential tensions or polarities. I will call this, for want of a better term, the anthropological paradox. The two greatest theorists of humor in the modern period have both recognized the paradox although offering differing interpretations of it. Freud argued that the basic incongruity in human existence is the clash between the unconscious and conscious realms of the mind. From the dynamic interaction between these two realms the logic and emotion of much, if not all, humor derives.[9] His theory can certainly account for a wide range of jokes. A lot of funny things do arise out of the discrepancy between what a person says they are on about and what unconsciously, at another level of their being, they are really doing. William Willimon was the victim of a spectacular clash between the desires of the libido (unconscious) and the demands of the mind to speak spiritual truth (conscious). Id checkmates superego, and in public![10]

The French philosopher Henri Bergson argued that humor arises from the nature of our human embodiment, the "mechanical encrusted on the living," as he put it.[11] The tension between the feeling, thinking, deciding person—my inner self with all that entails for spiritual sensitivity and freedom, the tension between that and the material shell in which it is housed—the panting, devouring, excreting body, relentlessly determined by insensate laws of chemistry and physics, is the tap root of

---

[9] Sigmund Freud, *Jokes and their Relation to the Unconscious*, The Standard Edition of the Complete Psychological Works of Sigmund Freud VIII, translated by J. Strachey et al. (London: Hogarth Press, 1971; original publication 1905).

[10] See above, p. 19.

[11] Henri Bergson, *Laughter: an essay on the meaning of the comic*, translated by Cloudesley Brereton and Fred Rothwell (New York: Macmillan, 1911) 29, 37. Peter Berger uses a variation on the same theme with his view that humor reflects what he calls the "imprisonment of the human spirit in the world." See *A Rumor of Angels: Modern Society and the Rediscovery of the Supernatural* (New York: Penguin, 1973) 70.

humor according to Bergson. It generates the inexhaustible contradictions and mysteries that seed the marvelously varied crop of laughter in human life. This is perhaps a broader definition than Freud's. It accounts for a huge diversity of types of humor. Charlie Chaplin can be seen as a brilliant exponent of Bergsonian humor. His endless variations on the theme of the swaggering big-shot who fails to notice the banana peel on the ground and sails to a resounding cropper is the paradigm. Mindless gravity debunks high-flown pomp and circumstance. The anthropological paradox strikes again and again.[12]

All this bluntly stated theory may not seem very convincing. But look at how it operates in the sermon joke. Bennett certainly plays on the paradox throughout the sketch. The railway station, for example: Here is the preacher arriving on his way to proclaim the Word of God, a lofty enterprise of the human spirit. But the mechanical is encrusted on the living, and the unconscious takes over the functions of the conscious mind. The preacher behaves like a robot with a defective program. He claims to be a messenger of God but can't tell the difference between entrance and exit. He goes out "by the way one is supposed to come in." And an "employee of the railway company," no intellectual or spiritual giant we are led to presume, lets fly with a message that, even in its censored form— "Where do you think you're going?"—vibrates with an energy and life altogether lacking in the case of the homily itself. "Just how elevated is this character?" the comedian asks, without putting it into words, of course.

The most powerful exploitation of the anthropological paradox, however, comes in the wonderful mountain-climbing story. Here the comedian really baits the trap for us. The literary form of the story is deliberately designed to emphasize the grandeur of the human spirit. "All day we climbed," the preacher intones. The obvious intention is to paint a picture of an adventurer pitting courage, skill, and endurance against the brute challenge of the mountain. "Until the valley lay very small below us." Here is the conqueror whose spirit has won out over the mountain. He is at the summit. And then: "We sat down to watch this magnificent sight of the sun going down . . . ." This is the nicest touch of all. When we remember that the story is told in the context of a "sermon," the connotations are irresistible. Here is the human being as participator-in-divine-beauty who communes with the God "whose dwelling place is in the light of setting suns" (Wordsworth). Thus the grandeur of the human spirit is underlined with three luminous strokes, each bolder than its predecessor—Adventurer, Conqueror, Contemplator of Divine Beauty. But at the very moment of

---

[12] The same duality of being between the high and the low, the spiritual and the physical, is the source not only of comedy but also of tragedy. Were it a dear friend who took the spill and was injured in the fall it would not be funny, but sad for the onlooker.

climax the mountaineer is sick. A violent clash of majesty and degradation is precipitated in our minds. The adventurer and world-conqueror is disclosed as a victim of harsh bodily malfunctions like the meanest member of the animal species. The creature that gives itself airs as a partner in a divine dialogue is as much a prisoner of blind mechanical laws as the stones beneath his feet. The split between the spirit and the world, the mechanical and the living, could hardly be set out more sharply.

The same paradox forms the bedrock of the comic sketch as a whole, not just individual parts of it. After all, the sketch is a single joke about preaching and preachers. It is at this level that the real theological critique of preaching begins to emerge. In a *religious* context, symbolized by the figure of the preacher, the paradoxical elements of our life in the world come into sharpest focus. On the one hand the incommensurability between the Being of God and human being seems absolute. This is Kierkegaard's "infinite qualitative distinction." God is transcendent, spiritual, infinite, eternal. We, by contrast, are immanent, material, finite, and mortal. The Creator stands over against the creature. Humanity is divinely bound. This human limitation before God seemed crushing and outrageous to Nietzsche. In the name of human dignity he repudiated it in disgust. God must die for humanity to live.

On the other hand faith claims a relationship with God, a melting of the prison walls between the transcendent and the immanent, the infinite and the finite. The human spirit breaks out of its imprisonment in the world and soars to heaven. It is taken into fellowship with God, or even, as the mystics claim, into oneness with God. According to the New Testament this is true liberty: "So if the Son makes you free, you will be free indeed" (John 8:36). Humanity is divinely free.

The radical paradox that pertains to existence in the world as a life-in-relation-to-God is the spring of all *religious* humor. Bennett exploits it beautifully in his portrait of the preacher. Here is a person of Promethean spiritual aspirations beside which the exploits of the mountaineer look modest indeed. What is a climb to the mountain peak compared with a climb to heaven? The preacher takes it upon him- or herself to mount the pulpit, open the Bible, and speak in the name of God; indeed, to speak the Word of God itself. The comedian isn't convinced. And the fundamental thrust of his sketch is not simply to challenge what the preacher *does*, that is, the technique of pulpit oratory with its various forms of wayward foolishnesses. Rather it is to question what the preacher *is*—a religious believer, a person in a representative relationship with God. Is it credible that God's being and God's grace actually break into the horizons of our human world in such a way as this? The preacher claims to hold the key to unlock the heavenly mystery. But, says the comedian, about the most mysterious key in this collection is to a sardine tin. And "there's always a little bit in the corner you can't get out!" The preacher claims rightly to discern the Word of God. But authority here seems to rise no higher from the earth than discernment between a beard and a clean shave. So "stuff this for a lark!" "Take a good look," says the comedian. "This is no angel, or even saint. It's a rather ordinary man flapping paper wings."

The foolishness of preaching is not merely wayward. It is intrinsic. The task is an impossibility. How can human beings possibly claim to speak the Word of God? And particularly to speak it on the basis of the biblical text, which seems so alien, anachronistic, mythological, and patriarchal? (or whatever terms are in fashion these days). This is no new observation, of course, nor is it confined to the insights of the clown. We are reminded of the forceful words of Karl Barth. "*As ministers we ought to speak of God. We are human, however, and so cannot speak of God. We ought therefore to recognise both our obligation and our inability and by that very recognition give God the glory.* This is our perplexity. The rest of our task fades into insignificance in comparison."[13] Humorist and theologian come to the same conclusion by very different routes, the former "from below" via an anthropological path, the latter "from above" via a theological path. But both see clearly the incongruity between the humble and the exalted, the human and the divine, that is at the heart of religious existence in general and the preaching task in particular.

Divine Foolishness

The problem of the intrinsic foolishness of preaching goes deeper still. In one of his essays Stanley Cavell notes:

> Nothing an outsider can say about religion has the rooted violence of things the religious have themselves had it at heart to say: no brilliant attack by an outsider against (say) obscurantism will seem to go far enough to a brilliant insider faced with the real obscurity of God; and attacks against religious institutions in the name of reason [or humor!] will not go far enough in a man who is attacking them in the name of faith.[14]

If Paul may be thought of as a "brilliant insider," then in this instance it is certainly true that he presses the matter much harder than Bennett. For Paul the problem of preaching is not the immediately obvious one that God is in heaven and we humans on earth, so that the presumption of speaking for God is patently obvious and comically rich. More is involved

---

[13] Karl Barth, *The Word of God and the Word of Man*, translated by Douglas Horton (New York: Harper & Row, 1957) 186. (Italics in the original.)

[14] Stanley Cavell, *Must We Mean what We Say?: A Book of Essays* (New York: Charles Scribner's Sons, 1969) 174.

in "the real obscurity of God" than that. For the word we preach is not just any word about God. It is the word of the *cross*. "For since, in the wisdom of God, the world did not know God through wisdom, God decided, through the foolishness of our proclamation, to save those who believe. For Jews demand signs and Greeks desire wisdom, but we proclaim *Christ crucified*, a stumbling block to Jews and foolishness to Gentiles" (1 Cor 1:21-22, italics added). To claim to speak for God may sound foolish enough. But to speak for God by speaking of the cross is outrageous. How can God be identified with the suffering death of the condemned criminal Jesus of Nazareth? That makes the hermeneutical problem of "my brother Esau" look simple in comparison. Hegel puts this paradox in blunt terms:

> God has died, God is dead—this is the most appalling thought, that everything eternal and true is not, and that negation itself is bound up in God; bound up with this is the supreme pain, the feeling of the utter absence of deliverance, the surrender of all that is higher.[15]

This is the real foolishness of preaching. God undertakes all that belongs to the human lot: not merely our finitude, our obduracy, and our materiality, but also our fallibility, our failing, and our perishability. God enters the extremity of human alienation. God enters what can only be called— and here paradox seems to reach its limit in contradiction—godforsakenness. If the story of the gospel is true, then the reality of God that comes to word in the life of Jesus Christ is stranger even than the reality of God that comes to word in Jesus' own story of the prodigal son. In the gospel story God does not merely wait at home for the prodigal to return. God tracks us to the far country where we have wasted our substance. In the final analysis God in Christ becomes the prodigal himself—condemned, outcast, thrown to the dogs. This is the God who comes to word in what we proclaim.

Is it any wonder it looks foolish? To make sense of it would be impossible, but for one thing. "God's foolishness is wiser than human wisdom, and God's weakness is stronger than human strength" (1 Cor 1:25). If we are not to blunt the sharpest thrust of the story of the cross we are forced to speak in terms of the "death of God." The death of God is a necessary yet freely chosen self-giving of God through which the nihilating power of death is destroyed and the divine grace of life unleashed. God's life enters our death and overcomes it from within. The death of God is an appalling thought, as Hegel says. It appears to be the absence of any deliverance and the surrender of all that is higher. But he

---

[15] Quoted in Hans Küng, *The Incarnation of God: An Introduction to Hegel's Theological Thought as Prolegomena to a Future Christology*, translated by J. R. Stephenson (Edinburgh: T & T Clark, 1987) 1.

goes on, "the course of events does not grind to a halt here; rather a reversal now comes about, to wit, God maintains himself in this process. The latter is but the death of death. God arises again to life."[16]

This is the ground on which alone we can preach. The foolishness of preaching is the foolishness of God. The Word of God can become flesh in us because the Word of God has become flesh in Jesus Christ. The Word of God can be read in historical Scripture because Scripture is the witness to the Word made historical in Christ. It looks intrinsically foolish to the philosopher. To the debater it seems impossible to defend. To the comedian it appears laughable. But the possibility of God is determined not by what we think or argue or mock it to be, but by what God actually reveals it to be. Can God become human? Can God suffer? Can God break the bonds of sin and death from within? Of course not. It makes no sense. Unless the reality of Jesus Christ is as the New Testament says it is. But if it is, the foolishness of preaching might just be the wisdom of God unto salvation.

---

[16] Ibid.

Part II

Experience and God

4

Unless You Become as Little Children

Theology and the Uses of Childhood

Wisdom directs us to childhood—not only to the immortal wishes
of childhood for the substance of things hoped for, but also to the
failure of childhood for the cause of our disease.[1]

—Norman O. Brown

I want to explore the issue of childhood, or to be more precise, our "uses of childhood," in religion and theology.[2] Childhood, or at any rate the idea of childhood, is a slippery commodity. It is impossible to deal with it *per se*—as if every age and culture lives and interprets childhood in the same way, a sort of Tillichian universal infant humanity, so to speak. Childhood, as we in the modern and postmodern West have understood it, is a comparatively recent discovery, we might even call it "invention," going back in the first instance to Rousseau in the eighteenth century but owing most to Freud who made childhood a major preoccupation of our own times.[3] It is *our* uses of childhood I want to explore theologically. Others may and will have other perspectives.

One of the reasons, though not the only one, why this is an important question is the current horrified fascination in Church and society with what is now called the *abuse* of children. Stories of incest and child sexual molestation are a regular feature of our daily news. Some of the experiences that are being told, personal and institutional, are terrible. But some of the ramifications, perhaps unintended, are also distressing. A nagging suspicion now hovers over men, especially in their role as fathers,

---

[1] Norman O. Brown, *Life Against Death: The Psychoanalytic Meaning of History* (Middletown, Conn.: Wesleyan University Press, 1959) 110.

[2] I have taken the phrase from Graham Little's essay, "Using Childhood," *Eureka Street* 4/7 (September 1994) 28–32.

[3] Ibid. 29.

whether in the family or as priests in the Church, that is alarming and destructive. This is clearly going to be a major focus of justice and pastoral care as we enter the new millennium. My concern here is not with this matter directly, but with the use we make of childhood in our *theological* constructs. The two are connected, however.

The question of childhood is not unlike Martin Kähler's question about "the so-called historical Jesus."[4] It has to do with the past, but a past that also lives in the present. The nineteenth-century dream of finding the "real" Jesus of Nazareth, rescued from the distortions of a theological tradition that has lived an "infinite passion" in relation to him (Kierkegaard), still lingers on—but hardly in terms of its original hopes. The Christ of passionate faith abides in the community (and the believing soul) with immediate consequences, as Schleiermacher eloquently demonstrated. Archaeological expeditions that set out to uncover the bones of the man Jesus loosed from the clothing of his resurrected (i.e., contemporary) significance find that they must dig through the time-sedimented layers of the self and its communities on the way. The dust of that excavation clings and shows up in the results even of the most careful of practitioners.

Likewise with childhood. We all lived through it. The faded photographs, the dog-eared books, the school reports, the scars on elbows and knees bear witness to the journey. But the child we were is also the child we have become. The autobiographer's "quest for the historical childhood" is inevitably caught in the constantly changing relationship between the self that remembers and the self that is remembered.[5] We use our remembered childhood in a variety of ways, from the Cinderella-style self-excuse—"it's not my fault, look at the way my (step)mother treated me"—to the Augustinian-style self-reproach—"of course I'm no good, I've been stealing pears since I was five." And much in between. Graham Little sums up the living significance of childhood in these words:

> I have come to think of "childhood" as a thing we carry about in our grown up heads, a thing we are constantly polishing or editing and even rewriting, a set of worry beads, a ticket of leave from adult guilt, a narrative that *places* us. In this sense, childhood is selective and open to revision, a construct shaped by who we are and what we are about in the here and now. It belongs as much to the present as to the past, is active and as we play the game of *pro vita sua* it is the joker in every hand.[6]

The thing to note here is the fluid quality of childhood, its interactive character in the process of continuous self-creation, the narrative that

---

[4] Taken from the title of his book, *The So-called Historical Jesus and the Historic Biblical Christ*, translated by Carl E. Braaten (Philadelphia: Fortress, 1964; original German publication 1896).

[5] Little, "Using Childhood," 29, quoting the words of Richard Coe.

[6] Ibid.

"places us" in the turmoil of the "who we are and what we are about in the here and now." This orientational use of childhood has some degrees of freedom attached to it. It can be edited, that is, renegotiated to a certain extent according to need—worry bead or ticket of leave.

It is no secret that childhood is a vital presence in religious life and consequently in the theological reflection that goes with it. The enigmatic saying of Jesus, "whoever does not receive the kingdom of God as a little child will never enter it" (Mark 10:15), would probably be enough of itself to put the issue on the agenda. But the evidence is much thicker. Believers are regularly styled "children of God." The gospels overwhelmingly indicate that Jesus' preferred title in reference to God is "father" or (especially in John) "my father." Some commentators make much of the Aramaic word *Abba* that seems to be embedded in the earliest of Jesus material. Even if we don't go all the way with Joachim Jeremias' view that this is the height of filial intimacy, the equivalent of the child's "daddy," it certainly seems to have connotations of personal familiarity—God perceived as a loving parent.[7] Paul makes this designation integral to his understanding of faith as a life in which the Spirit draws the believer into an *Abba* relationship with God (cf. Rom 8:15; Gal 4:6). The summary theological import, however, is the doctrine of the Trinity itself. Here the father/son relationship is imported into the being of God itself. "The only Son of God, eternally begotten of the Father, God from God, Light from Light," says the creed. Childhood's apotheosis.

Freud: Religion as Illusion

If ever this theological use of childhood was unproblematic, it certainly no longer is. The rot starts in earnest with Freud, though the whiff of over-ripeness is detectable much earlier in the writings of Nietzsche and Jean Paul Richter. For Freud religion arises out of the fundamental vulnerability and ultimate helplessness of the human condition, especially in primitive times. The crushing power of natural phenomena, the capriciousness of fate, and the inevitability of death conspire to terrify and condemn. Human beings clump together in groups to ward off the threats. The gods are conceived in this psycho-social context of fear. And the womb from which they spring is childhood: first the childhood of the race, then the childhood of the individual.[8] The ultimate helplessness of

---

[7] See Joachim Jeremias, *The Prayers of Jesus,* translated by John Bowden et al (London: S.C.M. Press, 1967) 11–65.

[8] "Thus a store of ideas is created, born from man's need to make his helplessness tolerable and built up from the material of memories of the helplessness of his own childhood and the childhood of the human race." Sigmund Freud, *The Future of an*

the adult—Schleiermacher would have said "absolute dependence"—in face of the threatening boundaries of finitude has its origins, or at least its memory echoes, in the helplessness of the child. But, and this is the crucial point, the possibility of solution lies there also. In the words of Freud:

> This situation [i.e., of helplessness] is nothing new. It has an infantile prototype, of which it is in fact only the continuation. For once before one has found oneself in a similar state of helplessness: as a small child, in relation to one's parents. One had reason to fear them, and especially one's father; and yet one was sure of his protection against the dangers one knew.[9]

Childhood lives on in our adult heads, and punches a ticket of leave from adult fears. But it bears the shape of its origins—a saving god made in the image of the father.

> When the growing individual finds he is destined to remain a child forever, that he can never do without protection against strange superior powers, he lends those powers the features belonging to the figure of his father; he creates for himself the gods whom he dreads, whom he seeks to propitiate, and whom he nevertheless entrusts with his own protection.[10]

In short, one of the uses to which our childhood is put is the creation of God.[11] This God performs the functions of a human father, but without flaw or limitation. The overwhelming powers that be are personalized. The caprices of fate become expressions of a hidden but trustworthy providence. Death is not extinction, but sleep before reunion with that greater life. Good will be triumphant. Evil will be punished. Suffering will be compensated. And all this provided the almighty father is obeyed, respected, propitiated—in short, worshiped.

Famously, Freud regarded this theological use of childhood as immature and illusory. It is a childish response—Freud called it "infantilism"—motivated by the wish that things in the wide world were the way they used to be in the nursery. There, despite the fears of the night, we knew all was well because on the other side of the darkened door a light gleamed and daddy kept watch to ensure that "hobgoblins and foul fiends" were put to flight. Bunyan's hymn sets it out—an adult's comforting nursery rhyme in which Pilgrim makes it through the dark wood

---

Illusion, translated by W. D. Robson-Scott, edited by James Strachey (London: Hogarth Press, 1973) 14.

[9] Ibid. 13.

[10] Ibid. 20.

[11] For an interesting description of the psychological dynamics of this process of construction see Ana-Maria Rizzuto, *The Birth of the Living God: A Psychoanalytic Study* (Chicago: University of Chicago Press, 1979).

of the world with the "master's" help.[12] The problem is it flies in the face of harsh reality. Growing up means learning that what once was the case in terms of security no longer is. Worse, in fact: It means recognizing that what, as children, we thought was security is also an illusion. The world intends to kill us from the moment of birth. In the end there is nothing daddy or mummy, prince or princess can do about it. Like St. Paul, though with very different intention, Freud argues that in becoming adult we must "put an end to childish ways" (1 Cor 13:11). Human beings come of age must have done with the consolations of religious illusion. In doing so:

> They will have to admit to themselves the full extent of their helplessness and their insignificance in the machinery of the universe; they can no longer be the centre of creation, no longer the object of tender care on the part of a beneficent Providence. They will be in the same position as a child who has left the parental house where he was so warm and comfortable. *But surely infantilism is destined to be surmounted. Men cannot remain children forever; they must in the end go out into "hostile life."*[13]

Freud is under no misapprehension that transcending a neurotically relived childhood is easy. Religion is tenacious in the human spirit precisely because it provides a way of justifying what we want most but in fact cannot have, the denial of death. Genuine adult humanity—we might say in theological terms "salvation"—lies in facing the truth. We are orphans in the world, thrown on our own resources. Such help as is available to defend against "outrageous fortune" is found in an ever-developing science. And where against the great necessities of fate there is no help, courageous resignation is the one clear-eyed disposition. Life is strictly "do it yourself," as the famous closing lines of *The Future of an Illusion* make clear. "No, our science is no illusion. But an illusion it would be to suppose that what science cannot give us we can get elsewhere [read "in religion"]."[14]

Here then is a classic analysis of the use of childhood in religion. The core of it is that religion prolongs the state of childhood past its appropriate term, projecting it into the age of maturity. We remain daddy's

---

[12] *Hobgoblin nor foul fiend*
  Can daunt his spirit:
He knows he at the end
  Shall life inherit.
Then fancies fly away,
  He'll fear not what men say.
He'll labor night and day
  To be a pilgrim.
[13] Freud, *The Future of an Illusion* 45 (italics added).
[14] Ibid. 52.

boys and girls long after daddy has in fact departed the scene and by his death revealed the ultimate vulnerability of the entire human condition, his and ours. The way in which childhood works this magic is complex, but includes at least four elements. (1) Projection. The memory of the interaction of dependency and security experienced in childhood in relation to the parent(s) is projected, or "thrown out," of the unconscious depths of the self onto the infinitely wider cosmic context of being. (2) Personification. The superior powers of destiny, the forces of life and death, which seem uncanny, overwhelming, and dangerous are "tamed" somewhat by being given a nature and disposition like our own. (3) Placation. Though in fact we are still defenseless before the powers that be, by personifying them they no longer seem utterly alien. They can be placated, appeased, cajoled, and trusted as the child does with the stronger parent. (4) Protection. As a result of the former mechanisms the religious person can rest easy with the world. God, who has the characteristics of the father, will in his great mercy "defend us from all the perils and dangers of this night."

In summary, infantilism, the neurotic use of childhood in religion, results in an oppressive, but ultimately illusory image of God as father almighty. This functions in turn to create a dependent kind of human existence. It is an existence that is ultimately inauthentic in that it covers deep-seated fear with wishful illusion. It is an existence that is ultimately immature in that it refuses to make use of its own freedom to act or think, but instead turns in blind obedience to the authority and guidance of the God/father. It is an existence that is potentially fanatical in that it perceives any critique of its foundations (i.e., critique of God) as a radical attack on its security. This in turn threatens to unleash the elemental forces of fear that religion is designed to disguise. Therefore it is likely to be resisted with all the energy of a life and death struggle.

Feminism: Religion as Collusion

A more contemporary critique of the use of childhood in religion, a critique that often sees Freud as more a part of the problem than the solution, comes from feminism. Like the Freudian critique, feminists target the father/son language of theology for analysis.[15] But it is now the gender issue, the maleness of the image, rather than the protective relationship that is at the focus.

[15] It goes without saying that diversity marks feminist thought as much as any other these days. In what follows I am concerned with feminist *theologians*, and only a selection among them. Common themes are detectable. But I am not suggesting that this is the only feminist perspective on the market.

A significantly different interpretation of the functioning of theological language is evident in a comparison of the two perspectives. For Freud the language of childhood and the experience it embodies are used as a way of interpreting a newly emerging, but (apparently) emotionally parallel experience, namely adult helplessness before the superior forces of nature and society. Unfortunately the problem is that while the feelings of helplessness may be similar, the realities they presuppose are not. The helplessness experienced within the harbor of childhood, at least as far as the child comprehends it, is held within the controlling power of the parent. What lies outside the child's control lies within the father's. Father knows best. Consolation and protection are therefore reasonable hopes. This is not the case on the open ocean of adulthood. The threats of nature and fate are the ultimate forces. There is no superior power behind them to hold them in check or bend them finally to human hopes and wishes. But the experience of helplessness remains even when the language of the heavenly father has been exposed for the illusion it is. This experience must then, according to Freud, be reinterpreted in terms of the stark realism of a scientific picture of a cosmos indifferent to the aspirations of human hearts. A corresponding shift in disposition occurs from placation to defiance, from consolation to resignation. Courage and truth, not faith and hope, are its virtues. Nature, not God, is reality *causa sui*. This is childishness put away.

The uses of childhood are many, however. For feminism helplessness is not so much a given experience in search of an interpretive language, but the reverse. The language of childhood, understood in a patriarchal way, is used to engender and perpetuate feelings of helplessness and dependence, especially in women, while at the same time reinforcing a sense of power and dominance in men. In the words of Catharina Halkes:

> The image of God as the patriarchal Father has established itself so firmly in men's imagination that it has not only confirmed the status quo of the patriarchal society, but has also become the *cause* of the legitimation and even the sacralisation of the domination of men over women in accordance with God's plan and dispensation.[16]

The causal rather than merely expressive use of language of childhood is evident in this statement. The circumstance of helplessness is brought about, rather than relieved, by the use of this language. Indeed, that is its intended outcome. Freud's hermeneutic is a contribution to the process.

A second difference in the two perspectives lies in feminism's concern with gender asymmetry. The image of God the father does not function with the unifying force Freud assumed. God as father places some

---

[16] Catharina Halkes, "The Themes of Protest in Feminist Theology against God the Father," *Concilium* 143, (1981) 103 (italics added).

people, namely women, in a position of dependency. But the same language established others—men—in the position of power and control. This dynamic is only reinforced by Christian concentration on Jesus as Son of God, "eternally begotten of the Father." A thoroughly male-oriented view of childhood is thus articulated. The parent's power and goodness (father almighty and holy) and child's security and recognition ("this is my beloved son") are depicted through the male. In this theological family, to be female is to be invisible. Cinderella never had it so bad. Far from keeping men in a prison-house of extended infancy, as Freud argued, God/father language founds male power and supremacy. Mary Daly's famous sentence rings the changes. "If God is male then male is God."[17] This is not religion as illusion. It is religion as *collusion*. A link—as it turns out a fraudulent link—is established between God and the male. In a vicious dialectic, worship of God as father reflects and reinforces the domination of the father in family life, patriarchal rule in the state, and father/priest power in the Church.[18] The payoff of this collusion is the oppression of women in all three spheres of life.

But feminism pushes its critique of the use of childhood in religion further. The question is not only power but punishment. Freud was aware of this aspect of the question with his emphasis on fear and the effort of the human child to placate the divine father: a cosmic oedipal struggle, no less. Childhood in the accusative case is shot through with the realities of disapproval, guilt, punishment, and possibly reconciliation. Classic atonement theology relives and restates its dynamics on the cosmic stage. Humanity is at enmity with God through disobedience to the divine command. We are dependent on the generosity of the God/father to create a way of restoring the relationship with him on which our well-being is founded. On the cross Jesus, the perfect son, takes the consequences of this estrangement and, as a result, a divine-human shield is placed between us and destruction. This "sacrifice" is often conceived in penal terms. The father punishes the innocent son—who is also an extension of himself—in order that forgiveness may be granted the rest of us (Anselm). Rita Nakashima Brock suggests this is the classic "this-hurts-me-more-than-it-hurts-you" theory of punishment often argued by the parent to the child, the school teacher to the pupil. In less overtly brutal forms of the theory (say, Moltmann's) the father *allows* rather than inflicts the suffering of the beloved son out of respect for human freedom, albeit free-

---

[17] Mary Daly, *Beyond God the Father* (Boston: Beacon, 1973) 19.

[18] It is instructive to note that in the 1920 Lambeth Conference Resolution 9 it is advised that the office of bishop should, among other things, "more truly express all that ought to be involved for the life of the Christian family in the title Father-in-God." I am indebted to Alan Cadwallader for drawing this reference to my attention.

dom gone terribly wrong. In this way suffering is taken into the being of God and finally conquered by his superior love. As we might imagine that famous father saying to the prodigal son as he packs his bags, this is the "I-can't-stop-you-from-doing-what-you-want-but-whatever-it-costs-I-will-be-there-when-you-discover-you-need-me" theory. Brock sums up her critique:

> Such doctrines of salvation reflect by analogy . . . images of the neglect of children or, even worse, child abuse, making it acceptable as divine behavior—cosmic child abuse, as it were. The father allows, even inflicts, the death of his only perfect son. The emphasis is on the goodness and power of the father and the unworthiness and powerlessness of his children, so that the father's punishment is just, and children are to blame.

Following Freud's theory of projection, Brock believes that this religious use of childhood recaptures in adult life the ambivalent memory of the child who projects onto the parent the ideal image of love and goodness, but who must also take from the parent frustration and punishment whether it is right or wrong. "Such projection helps the child manage a sense of rage about being denied love, being hurt, and being made wrong."[19] And so does the memory of childhood, now projected on a divine canvas, help the adult struggling with a sense of guilt or worthlessness to manage.

Beyond Illusion and Collusion

It is clear that these two critiques of the use of childhood in religion, focused in the image of God as father, are insightful and persuasive. They have uncovered important ways in which religion and its language function. Freud sees the issue basically as one of protection, or rather overprotection. God/father theology is powerful, but distorting, because it speaks of and to the neurotic wish for an ultimate defense against the threats of life. The faithful are forced into the passive role of dependents who have not come of age, who cannot cope with the truth of life nor decide its values for themselves. The cure he recommends for the disease of infantilism is therefore the abolition of religion. The God/father must die for human beings to live.

Feminists emphasize oppressive control. Freud's reading of authority, they argue, is blind to its patriarchal bias. It is not merely that "father knows *best*," so we don't grow up, but "*father* knows best," so women

---

[19] References are to Rita Nakashima Brock, *Journeys by Heart: A Christology of Erotic Power* (New York: Crossroad, 1992 [first published 1988]) 55–56. I am indebted to Marie Louise Uhr for drawing this reference to my attention.

are not allowed to be grown up.[20] God/father theology is powerful, but distorting, because maleness is conceived as an essential character of the divine being and hence women are by gender excluded from what is fundamental to power and prestige in life.[21] The solution proposed in this instance is not, or at least not necessarily, to do away with the idea of God altogether. That may be only to play further into the hands of male dominance. If there is no divine power beyond the political powers of society, Church, and family to which to appeal by way of critique, then protest against patriarchal structures and abusive actions of fathers toward children may lose a valuable ally. The task is rather to do away with the God/father by reinterpreting divinity in the feminine gender (God as mother, queen, sister), or at very least in gender inclusive ways (God as creator, redeemer, reconciler).

Either way God as father is deeply suspect. The countervailing argument is for "growing up." The ties of a childhood oppressively conceived and then illegitimately extended into adulthood by means of ecclesiastical (and political and familial) language and practice must be broken. In Norman Brown's terms this is the "failure of childhood for the cause of our disease" uncompromisingly put. But what of the other part of Brown's dictum, "the immortal wishes of childhood for the substance of things hoped for"?[22] Can we say more about that? Perhaps. But it is a big job, beyond the scope of a single essay. So then a few pointers only.

The first thing to acknowledge is that the idea of God reflected in the image of the child/father relation seems to touch something fundamental in the human condition. According to Luther, Kant, and Freud, the genealogy of any authority reveals its source as ultimately grounded in the power and prestige of the parent vis à vis the child, especially the standing

---

[20] Of course Freud is not alone in this analysis of authority. In his comments on the fourth commandment (to obey father and mother) in the "Greater Catechism" Luther notes, "For all of us authority has its root and source in parental authority." Cited by Jürgen Moltmann, *History and the Triune God: Contributions to Trinitarian Theology*, translated by John Bowden (London: S.C.M. Press, 1991) 7.

[21] Kant's critique of government conceived in terms of "fatherly rule" draws similar conclusions in one astonishing sentence. "A government which was established on the principle of good will towards the people like that of a father towards his children, i.e. a paternalistic rule *(imperium paternale)*, one where the subjects are compelled to behave in a merely passive way as children who have not come of age, who cannot distinguish what is truly useful or harmful for them, so that, if they are to be happy, they must look only to the judgments of the chief head of the state and, be he so willing, merely to his goodness, is the greatest conceivable despotism (a constitution which deprives subjects of all freedom, so they have no rights at all)." Cited by Moltmann, *History and the Triune God* 9. The original reference is from Immanuel Kant, *Werke*, edited by Wilhelm Weischedel. 12 vols. (Frankfurt: Suhrkamp, 1956–64) 6:145.

[22] See n. 1.

of the father.[23] This judgment appears to be borne out not only by the fact that the father image is used powerfully in traditional theology, as we have seen. Even the debates between atheist and believer, spelled out in the long line that runs from Jean Paul Richter through Kant, Feuerbach, Marx, and Nietzsche, to Freud, Bonhoeffer, Moltmann, and Mary Daly, make reference to it continually, with language about humanity reaching its majority, the "world come of age," and the like. The idea of being "grown up" makes no sense without the presupposition of the child that has grown. And child presupposes parent. This suggests that the theological use of "father" (or parent) in relation to God is not accidental or arbitrary. It is not easily replaced. In Tillich's terms, "father" is a genuine symbol of God, that is, an image that grasps something essential in the reality it symbolizes, rather than merely a sign, which is a conventional label used to point to the reality indicated but has no intrinsic connection with it, and hence can just as easily be replaced by some other sign.[24] I think we are probably stuck with the symbol of parent/father, for the time being anyway.

Can we do something with it that is positive? As I noted at the outset, our use of childhood in religion is selective and open to revision in relation to where we find ourselves presently placed. Father/child relations *may* all too often include overprotection and abusive control. Where this happens in family, Church, or theology it stands urgently in need of the kind of deconstruction the critics offer. But this is not the only option. Parenting is not necessarily smothering or abusive. I want to argue that the irreducible point of the father symbol for theology lies not so much in the question of protection or control, but in the significance of generativity. To be a child means to know yourself irreducibly derived from another. Or, to put it in the negative, the essence of childhood is not to be *causa sui*. Just this is the long shadow of childhood over which we can never jump, even as adults.

The intriguing question of origins is obvious in the child's insistent question: "where did I come from?" In the first instance this is a question about sexuality. But more is at stake. The question really opens the issue of personal identity. Because I am a derived being, one who is not self-creating, who I am depends on where I have come from. Every child at some point wonders about its parents. Do I really belong to them? Or was I adopted, taken over from some other family? Many adopted children, to say nothing of those who have been orphaned, come to the point

---

[23] See nn. 20 and 21.

[24] See Paul Tillich, "The Nature of Religious Language" in Robert C. Kimball, ed., *Theology of Culture* (New York: Oxford University Press, 1959) 53–67; *Systematic Theology* (London: James Nisbet & Co., 1964) 1:318–21.

where they want to know who are the parents of origin, the womb from which they were taken. Lurking within these immediate concerns lies the deeper ontological question: what is the final ground of our human life? From what reality have we sprung? To whom do we really belong? Once again identity, but this time species identity—what does it mean to be human?—hangs on the answer to these questions.[25]

This generative relation is never outgrown, as the overprotective or abusive relation should be. We are fundamentally derived beings. Adult identity is born out of childhood identity. "Father" is an issue, like it or not. I hope it is clear that in saying this I am not dismissing the feminist critique of this language. The case that much of the tradition about the fatherhood of God has expressed and perpetuated a patriarchal perspective on the world and the Church is, in my opinion, comprehensively proven. New ways of imaging and speaking of God must be minted, including the use of feminine symbols. But in the theological use of childhood, "father" has been the classic symbol and I only have space to work on that. It is possible to speak of the child/parent relationship. If that helps the reader, I certainly have no objection to its substitution. What follows if we work on the question of generativity as the essence of the father/parent image?

1. *To believe in God the father is to understand that as human beings we are, in the **final analysis,** "at home" in this world.*

Whatever the threats and dangers of life, fundamentally we belong here. If God is understood to be our ultimate origin, then those qualities that we feel express our humanity most intimately, that make us what we are as distinct from other beings—self-consciousness, thought, love, courage, hope, and the rest, in short all that is included under the umbrella term of "spirit"—are thereby affirmed to be grounded in the heart of the world. In other words, these human qualities are at least as much a part of the world and a clue to its deepest meaning as the fundamental forces with which the physicists play—electricity, gravitation, strong and weak nuclear force, and so on.

Freud could never affirm this. Precisely this view, he held, is the "parental house" from which the child must go out into a "hostile world." In the core of our humanity—Freud called it summarily "mind"—we are not really children of this universe. We are more like orphans or adoptees. What we thought was our home and lineage in fact is not. The true source and meaning of being lies in another genealogy altogether. Blind

[25] For an interesting discussion of the theological significance of adoption see the essays of Tom Frame, "'Born not of blood . . . but of God': human identity and adoption," and Lynlea Rodger, "Thrice Born: theological reflections on adoption," *St Mark's Review* 170 (Winter 1977) 7–12 and 13–18 respectively.

mechanical nature is the real "father." Freud expressed this sense of alienation in a poignant letter to Oskar Pfister:

> I can imagine that several million years ago in the Triassic age all the great
> -odons and -therias were very proud of the development of the Saurian race
> and looked forward to heaven knows what magnificent future for them-
> selves. And then, with the exception of the wretched crocodile, they all died
> out. You will object that . . . man is equipped with mind, which gives him
> the right to think about and believe in his future. Now there is certainly
> something special about mind, so little is known about it and its relation to
> nature. I personally have a vast respect for mind, *but has nature?* Mind is
> only a little bit of nature, the rest of which seems to be able to get along
> very well without it. Will it really allow itself to be influenced to a great ex-
> tent by regard for mind? Enviable he who can feel more confident about
> that than I.[26]

This perspective drove Freud toward an adversarial view of human life in
relation to the world at large. Mind, as he saw it, is adrift on the vast sea
of a mindless cosmos. To be sure nature is bountiful and nature is beautiful, but it is also terrifying and lethal. Fire, earthquake, famine, flood,
pestilence, and plague—the horsemen of the apocalypse—ride the earth
and strike with devastation, unexpectedly and often, indifferent to human
aspirations and unmoved by human sensitivities.

> Against the dreaded external world one can only defend oneself by some kind
> of turning away from it, if one intends to solve the task by oneself. There is,
> indeed, another and better path: that of becoming a member of the human
> community, and, with the help of technique guided by science, *going over to
> the attack against nature* and subjecting her to the human will.[27]

For all the reasons Freud enumerates, this view of ourselves and the world
is certainly plausible. Much theology has accepted it as given and sought
to maintain faith in God by a focus on individual salvation in a heavenly
realm "beyond" the world.

   To affirm God as father is to revision all this. Happily we seem to be
in a time congenial to such revisioning. A new ecologically driven science
is retelling "the universe story" with revolutionary results.[28] The so-called

---

   [26] Quoted in Ernest Becker, *The Denial of Death* (New York: The Free Press,
1973) 121–122 (italics added). The original is taken from the collected letters of
Freud and Pfister.
   [27] Freud, *Civilization and Its Discontents,* translated by Joan Riviere, edited by
James Strachey (London: Hogarth Press, 1973) 14 (italics added).
   [28] Cf. Brian Swimme and Thomas Berry, *The Universe Story: From the Primordial
Flaring Forth to the Ecozoic Era—A Celebration of the Unfolding Cosmos* (San Francisco: HarperCollins, 1992). See also J. D. Barrow and F. J. Tipler, *The Anthropic Cos-
mological Principle* (Oxford: Clarendon Press, 1986).

"anthropic principle," if I understand it aright, argues that the universe is delicately poised, from the moment of its emergence in the "big bang" some fifteen billion years ago, through its mysterious expansion ever since, to permit (intend?) the appearance of life, including human life, within its bounds. In short, the world seems to be put together in such a way that all beings, including human beings, are intimately related and meaningfully connected with each other. We belong. "We are not tourists here. . . . We are at home in this world because we were made for it."[29]

In itself this does not establish the reality of God as independent creator and director of the world, of course. Not many would want to re-construct an old Paley-style natural theology on the grounds of the new cosmology. Ultimately a faith stance confronts us here, as it always has. But nonetheless, this gathering cosmic vision has deep moral and philo-sophical implications. It argues for a new ecological ethic, a sense of re-spect, courtesy, even love for the created order, in contrast to the adversarial and exploitative view articulated in much of the history of modern tech-nology. Theology too has the chance, perhaps unequalled since the Re-formation, to rethink the doctrine of creation, of God as "father of us all," so as to envisage the world as "a community of subjects rather than a collection of objects,"[30] and to act accordingly. The new creation spiri-tualities of writers like Matthew Fox, Thomas Berry, and Sally McFague, explore how the God-world-human relationship can be reinterpreted in ecologically responsible ways. In one sense this is a re-mapping of our childhood. And the genealogy points to belonging. We trust that that which grounds the world means well by us.

2. *To believe in God the father is to understand that as human beings we are, in the **penultimate analysis,** not at home in this world.*

A sense of belonging is fine. But one of the problems with the new ecological imagination, both in science and theology, is that it tends to imbed our humanity rather too comfortably in the context of the cosmic process. The difficulty is this. If we interpret the symbol of God the father exclusively in terms of being "at home" in the world, the critical distance between God and the creation becomes blurred. Unhappy with theol-ogy's tendency to center revelation (i.e., the divine self-disclosure) in merely verbal forms such as the Bible and preaching, Thomas Berry ar-gues that a creation-centered perspective must "perceive the *natural world*

---

[29] Mary Midgley, *Beast and Man: The Roots of Human Nature* (New York: Cor-nell University Press, 1978) 194–95, quoted in Sallie McFague, *The Body of God: An Ecological Theology* (London: S.C.M. Press, 1993) 111.

[30] The phrase belongs to Thomas Berry. I heard it first during an interview with Berry conducted by Paul Collins and broadcast on the Australian Broadcasting Com-pany "Insights" program in November 1993.

as the primary mode of revelation of the divine, as primary scripture, as the primary mode of the numinous."[31] At-home-ness indeed. But the view of God becomes correspondingly vague. Is God the creative force of evolution, or cosmogenesis itself, or some mystery that grounds the creative process, but is itself permanently hidden and unknowable? If the processes of the world, from our genetic coding to the business of galaxy formation, are the primary revelation, how are we to determine what in fact lies at the heart of God and identifies the true divine essence? For in cosmogenesis, as Freud so eloquently said, processes of death seem at least as present, powerful, and all-pervasive as processes of life. Why are the latter (i.e., processes of life and creation) to be taken as more the clue to divine nature than the former (i.e., processes of death and destruction)? For all we can tell from simple observation, single-minded pursuit of self-interest, rather than a common march toward a "universal community of subjects," is the basic drive of all living entities. Why not, then, propound a God of "the survival of the fittest" and let the devil take the hindmost? Modern fascisms of various stripes, including patriarchy, have adopted this credo to great effect.

The agonized protest of women (and others who experience life from the margins) rightly gives voice to the enormous abusive realities of history, of society, and of Church. Our existence, for all its immersion in the great self-creative movements of the universe, is also distorted by fate, hedged about by meaninglessness, and suffused with suffering, guilt, and death. What are we to make of this hurt in creation? What of the victims of the process, human and non-human? What of the waste and loss and cruelty of evolution and politics? Any God/father theology that ignores, or worse, reinforces such structures by implying, however indirectly, that we should feel "at home" in them is worse than useless. It is demonic. On this the feminists are surely right.

If the symbol of the God/father is to mean something more nuanced than the sum total of movements of energy in the cosmos (or in politics or the Church), it seems we must grasp some particular manifestation, some outcropping of the divine that imposes itself upon us as definitive, in the sense of manifesting the essential nature of God in the midst of the deep ambiguity of the world. The experiences of hurt that fuel the drive for such a vision seem inevitably to pose the question to which christology has traditionally been the answer. According to this answer God is not concerned merely with the "fittest," with those who remain victorious in the latest moment of the cosmic process, rising to their (no doubt temporary) ascendancy over the bodies and beings of others

[31] Thomas Berry, *The Dream of the Earth* (San Francisco: Sierra Club Books, 1988) 104 (italics added).

that have gone before. If the biblical witness is to be noted as revelation, God is also, and especially, the God of the victims, of the "unfit" ones, of the world's discards, if I might use that phrase. God intends to reclaim what is lost or crushed or oppressed in the process of creation, with its apparent drift toward distortion that we see all about us. "The fundamental criticism of biblical faith," writes Walter Brueggemann, "is against voicelessness, against a society in which speech about power and powerlessness is banished and in which social power is so concentrated that it need no longer listen and is no longer capable of hearing."[32]

There is no way of knowing this just by looking at the way things run in the world. The God who is present in the animal stall of Bethlehem and on the executioner's tree at Calvary and beside the empty rock tomb in the garden is needed to qualify and illuminate the God who is present in nature's great cosmic movements. If there is to be justice in history and fulfillment of the natural order, that is, if we are finally to be "at home" in the world, somehow, somewhere God, the ground from which we have sprung, must acknowledge, resist, and bear the uproar of creation and society as we presently experience them. Otherwise loss, fate, waste, the tears of women and children, and the unfulfilled sighs of creation are the last word, the final disclosure of the meaning of the process. A theology of the cross and resurrection (or something like it) is needed if God is to be understood and experienced as "parent/father" in the midst of sin and oppression.

Feminist thinking, along with other kinds of liberation theology, is re-visioning this aspect of God/father symbolism. The outlines of this work are still emerging. And there is not always agreement. This much is clear, though: there can be no future for a theology that interprets the generativity of God as founding and legitimating the plausibility structures and strictures of unjust ideologies. Cinderella may be condemned to the cellar by (step)motherly decree while her more favored sisters dress in finery for the prince's ball. But not so the children of God—anyway not if God is understood as God of the Exodus and even more as "the Father of our Lord Jesus Christ." The doctrine of the Trinity ("childhood's apotheosis" as we called it earlier) not only divinizes Christ, "it 'christifies' God, since it draws the Father into the destiny of the Son."[33] This destiny is a compassionate attention to the hurts of the world and a passionate (unto death) commitment to the healing of the world. Belief in God as *this* father is an act of powerful social critique. For this God

[32] Walter Brueggemann, *Old Testament Theology: Essays on Structure, Theme, and Text,* edited by Patrick D. Miller (Minneapolis: Fortress, 1992) 92.

[33] Moltmann, *History and the Triune God* 22. The first two essays in this volume are attempts to interpret the fatherhood of God in non-patriarchal ways.

grounds and nurtures a new vision of things, a dream that dismantles the absolutist claims of the status quo. If God is parent/father, then "the dream is understood as certified from heaven, and as that dream is certified from heaven, it has enormous credibility in the life of the community on earth. The dream of liberation and justice has credibility theologically because to deny it is to deny everything" biblical faith knows about the God of the Exodus and the cross.[34]

These are a few of the issues theology needs to explore in the future, so it seems to me. I would like to think that in face of the Freudian critique we can find constructive and mature rather than destructive and immature uses of childhood in faith. After all, we are derived beings. And that is no bad thing. It should be possible to speak of God as father in heaven in a non-infantile way, as grown-ups. On the other hand, I would like to see a new interpretation of masculinity that is not intrinsically oppressive: one that can joyfully assert (in the words of Moltmann) "there is nothing wrong with becoming and being a father."[35] Though both Freudians and feminists will probably feel I am drawing a long bow, maybe the time will come when we will learn new languages and discover new actions that will allow us to feel that there is nothing essentially wrong with talking about God as father in heaven. Such talk might even assist us in being better fathers and mothers on earth. And this includes father and mother "in God."

---

[34] Walter Brueggemann, *Revelation and Violence: A Study in Contextualization* (Milwaukee: Marquette University Press, 1986) 20. The quotation actually concludes with the words, ". . . everything Israel knows about Yahweh, the Lord of the Exodus." I have broadened it beyond the Old Testament reference.

[35] Moltmann, *History and the Triune God* 4.

5

Yahweh Doesn't Show His Face in Reproductions

Seeing Is Believing

Robert Hughes was a rookie art critic in Australia in the 1960s. Wrapped in the mantle of an antipodean cultural cringe and cut off by the Pacific Ocean from the great temples of abstract expressionism in far away New York, Hughes was dependent upon reading about such figures as Barnett Newman and Willem de Kooning. But there was no way of entering into what was claimed for these new titans, much less criticizing it, for the originals were inaccessible. Hughes writes:

> The copy of *ARTnews* would arrive and we would dissect it, cutting out the black-and-white reproductions and pinning them on the studio wall. One was, say, a Newman. You had just read one of Tom Hess's discourses on how Newman's vertical zip was Adam, or the primal act of division of light from darkness, or the figure of unnamable Yahweh himself. How could you disagree? On what could you base your trivial act of colonial dissent? A mere reproduction, two inches by three? But Yahweh doesn't show his face in reproductions. He shows it only in paintings. And if you got to see the paintings, what if you still didn't see it? Did that mean that his terrible and sublime visage was not there either? Of course not; it meant only that you had a bad eye; or that Yahweh doesn't show himself to goyim from the South Pacific.[1]

Hughes is talking art, not theology. The face of Yahweh for Hughes, that "terrible and sublime visage," is not the face of the living God that Moses sought, cowering in the cleft of the rock halfway between Egypt and the promised land and covered by the divine hand.[2] It is a matter of experiencing whether a painting, a Newman or a de Kooning, has that mysterious quality of depth that enables us to see in it some manifestation of the true stuff of life, the unmasked nature of ourselves or our world. You

---

[1] Robert Hughes, *Nothing if Not Critical* (London: Collins Harvill, 1990) 5.
[2] See Exod 33:12-23.

can't know that, says Hughes, unless you can see the original, and perhaps not even then. "Yahweh"—meaning the truth or essence of things—doesn't show his face in reproductions. Too much of the textured immediacy of the original is lost in the copying process.

But the demilitarized zone between art and theology may be narrower than we think. The Yahweh of Hughes and the Yahweh of Moses may not be so far apart after all. Anyway, the declaration "Yahweh doesn't show his face in reproductions" is as true of theology as it is of painting. A good deal of what passes for God-talk looks like reproduction. It feels thin and scaled-down, less revelation than reports of revelation supposedly received elsewhere and by others: *ARTnews* de Kooning, not the thing itself. As Gustavo Gutierrez says, only involvement in real pastoral situations creates new theology. From *reading* theology you only get new theology books. I take it this is not a blanket condemnation of all attempts to speak of God. The observation "you talk like a book" may not sound like much of a compliment. But it all depends on *which* book is in question. There is nothing secondhand about a book like *A Theology of Liberation!*[3]

But the problem is a real one. Speaking credibly about God in the contemporary world is no matter of course. It is not only a question of that shift in human consciousness variously labelled secularization, demystification, the hermeneutics of suspicion, or what have you, about which liberal theology was so concerned. It is also, and more importantly, the matter of suffering. Fifty years after the liberation of Auschwitz it is impossible to forget the massive pain and death that has been and still is so terrible a feature of the twentieth century. Nor will the voices of those who have been pushed aside in less dramatic ways—the forgotten, the exploited, the oppressed—be silenced. In these circumstances many people find it difficult to make sense of God-talk. They wonder if God-experiences and God-words refer to anything real on the "slaughter bench of history."[4] It is not just that we are in a period of "the worldly non-necessity of God."[5] That seems too bland. We are in a period when the sufferings

---

[3] Gustavo Gutierrez, *A Theology of Liberation: History, Politics and Salvation*, translated by Sister Caridad Inda and John Eagleson (London: S.C.M. Press, 1974). See the interesting essay by Eberhard Jüngel, "You talk like a book. . . ." in his *Theological Essays II*, edited by J. B. Webster, translated by Arnold Neufeldt-Fast and J. B. Webster (Edinburgh: T & T Clark, 1995) 20–34. The phrase is taken from one of the dialogues in Kierkegaard's *Philosophical Fragments*, where Climacus is accused of talking "like a book." And the observation is sharpened: "'indeed, you talk . . . which is unfortunate for you, like a very specific book'—the *Bible*" (pp. 28–29).

[4] The phrase is David Tracy's. See *On Naming the Present: God, Hermeneutics, and Church* (New York: Orbis, 1994) 63.

[5] Eberhard Jüngel, *God as Mystery of the World*, translated by Darrell L. Guder (Grand Rapids: Eerdmans, 1983) 20.

of the world seem a living demonstration of the death of God. God-talk goes on, especially in the churches. But is it mere reproduction?

How does one test that? Presumably Hughes knows how he might test it in the case of art: get to New York and look at the originals. But where is New York for the theologian? Where hangs the original theological canvas on which we may gaze to see the face, or detect the absence, of Yahweh? That is a major question. And there is certainly no agreement as to its answer. I want to argue that unless God-talk has significance in the context of *ordinary human experience*, especially the experience of suffering, it is artificial. The face of God must show up in the history of people living their lives, in the actions they choose and the accidents they suffer. The theologian, if he or she is not simply "to talk like a book" in the worst sense, must attend to traces of transcendence—I will call them "moments of grace"—in human experience. The noting and nurturing of such moments in no sense guarantees that God-talk refers to a reality beyond our own psyches. But it does connect our talk about God with real experiences. And theology may then appear original rather than reproduced.

Grace is a word that needs to be freed from its religious captivity. The poet Les Murray and the historian Manning Clark both refuse to leave the term to the mercies of the Church and its theologians. Murray describes the motivation and meaning of his poetry as waiting for and giving expression to the mystery of grace. Manning Clark calls the second volume of his autobiography *The Quest for Grace*.[6] For these writers "grace" refers to something of fundamental significance in common human experience. It has to do with the wonder and terror that confront us in living. It marks the gift-like quality of being itself. Grace has nothing to do with sentimental optimism. For Clark the flaws and anguish of life are sometimes the surest conduits of grace. The quest for grace is the quest for *meaning* in the midst of it all. The words of Dostoevsky that Clark puts at the head of his book sum it up. "But the little sticky leaves, and the precious tombs, and the blue sky, and the woman you love! How will you live, how will you love them? . . . With such hell in your heart and your head, how can you? . . . I want to be there when everyone suddenly understands what it has all been for."[7] The longing to understand what it has all been for, in spite of and in face of the suffering of life, is integral to the task of life. It is part of any process of initiating change for the improvement and healing of life. This is an operation of grace.

The determination to search for grace in the gallery of pictures that is ordinary human experience is controversial. The powerful critique of

---

[6] Manning Clark, *The Quest for Grace* (Ringwood, Vic.: Viking, 1990). Murray's comment was reported in a newspaper article but unfortunately I have mislaid the publishing details.

[7] Clark, *The Quest for Grace*, facing page; cf. also p. 19.

Karl Barth dogs the progress of such plans. In matters theological, Barth argued, looking at the human canvas guarantees you a reproduction in the Hughesian sense. "You cannot speak about God by speaking about man (*sic*) in a loud voice," was his famous jibe. Searching for God in human experience is like playing blind man's buff with divinity. It inevitably confuses God with human vitalities and winds up calling God what is not God and not calling God what is.[8] This delivers theology lock, stock, and barrel into the hands of Feuerbach and his hermeneutical successors. God-talk is surreptitiously converted into human-talk, and probably *man*-talk at that. The only sure defense against this reductionism, according to Barth, is to attend to God's own self-disclosure. The original in which the "terrible and sublime" image of God is perceptible in the midst of so many reproductions is Jesus Christ. God's self-declaration in Christ is "theological New York," the place where discrimination of true from false in theology and idol from God in faith is possible. Theology, to be faithful to its object, must work from here. And the world will have to make do.

This critique puts a finger on a manifest danger of our approach. Perhaps I will fall into it. But the approach is not entirely without defense, even in Barthian terms. Let me take as an example the debate between the Jewish philosopher Emmanuel Levinas and the Christian theologian Eberhard Jüngel. Levinas argues that an irreducible element of transcendence, a sense of the divine, breaks into human experience in the "face of the other person." It is not that God's presence makes the nearness of the neighbor a call upon me that necessitates a responsive and responsible action on my part. Rather it is the call of the near presence of the other person, the neighbor, that makes transcendence, the near presence of God, possible and perceptible to me. Jüngel comments, "for Levinas . . . another human astonishes me to such an extent that there is an interruption of my being in the world and my being as a self: an interruption which as such is the condition of possibility for the Word of God, for God's nearness." Jüngel is a defender of an essentially Barthian view of revelation. Genuine knowledge of God, as far as he is concerned, arises when "God as the mystery of the world comes nearer to the world than the world is able to be to itself," namely in Jesus Christ, and *not* via some human path from the world toward God. Consequently Jüngel feels that Levinas' view of the Word of God risks being somewhat empty and insubstantial, giving rise, as he puts it, to "a ghostly kind of speech." But even so—and this is the important issue—Jüngel is prepared to concede that "God still allows himself to be testified to adequately in apophatic statements which bring *something*, and thus in this respect, *world* to speech, namely in par-

[8] Cf. Carl E. Braaten, *Our Naming of God* (Minneapolis: Fortress, 1989) 22.

ables. *The world which is elementally interrupted becomes a parable of God.*[9] This is all that is required. Within the Christian understanding of God it is simply a mistake to believe that the farther we move away from all things human the closer we are to God. God's nearness fulfills rather than diminishes the human.

We might agree (as I would) with Barth and Jüngel that the incarnation of God in Jesus Christ is unique. God was in the humanity of Jesus Christ not merely as a vague presence but, in a non-trivial sense, as an identity. *Homoousios* was the word used by the ancient creed. Jesus is of "one substance" with the Father. Not anything human, but *this* humanity manifests the divinity of God. Much that is human is anything but divine, indeed is actively in opposition to God. We don't need Barthians to tell us that. To this extent the fear that an emphasis on human experience threatens the "otherness" of God, the God-ness of God, is justified. Unless there is something more than human in the quest for grace, then it seems to be only human, and perhaps all too, too human. This being said, though, it remains true that the particular presence of God in Christ points up the intention and action of God in general. God declares divinity to humanity in and through things human. How else could such a declaration be made to us? The paradox of incarnational theology is that we humans cannot be *truly* human unless something more than the *merely* human informs our *being* human. If we must speak here of parable rather than direct speech, so be it.

But this is all too general, reminiscent of the style of the theological unifiers who talk of an abstract humanity.[10] It needs to be grounded. Where? Among the theologies of liberation—Aboriginal, Asian, Latin American and feminist—there is a rough consensus. If God is to be found at all, God must be found in the concrete history of suffering. It is well to argue that "talk about God either concerns everybody or nobody."[11] But that cuts both ways. Unless talk of God can make sense in those human contexts where everything seems an affront and mockery to God it can make sense in no situation at all. For liberationists this means "the central theological question today is not the question of the nonbeliever but the question of the nonperson—those forgotten ones, living and dead, whose struggle and memory are our history."[12] It is a time for the voices of those who have been voiceless to speak. It is a time for those who have spoken too much and too confidently to be silent. And I certainly cannot place myself in the first group. Therefore, if the conversation

---

[9] Eberhard Jüngel, *Theological Essays II*, 98–99 (italics in last sentence added); the whole section pp. 91–99 is relevant to this argument.

[10] See above pp. 5–8.

[11] See above p. 11.

[12] Tracy, *On Naming the Present* 64.

is to go on at this point it needs to be paying attention more than making comment, listening more than speaking. What follows, therefore, will be very much an attempt to let others speak.

I want to do two things. First, I want to try to describe *how* one might pay attention. What stance or attitude is appropriate to a careful listening to or—since I am working basically with a visual metaphor—*seeing* another person? Second, I want to illustrate through a concrete example how suffering in human experience can be read, and in its own terms, as a living canvas on which the terrible and sublime face of Yahweh can be seen, and not as mere reproduction.

Paying Attention

Hughes wondered anxiously whether if he got to see those much vaunted New York originals he still might not detect the face of Yahweh. What then? Did that mean the sublime visage was not there? No, he replies, though there may be irony in his words, it means only that you—insignificant critic from the South Pacific—have a "bad eye." You are blind to the deeper truth accessible to more sensitive observers. My guess is that Hughes' irony consists in the suspicion that the reverse may be the case. Those who rhapsodically claim to see greatness in this art may themselves be the blind ones, reading the face of Yahweh into places where manifestly it is not. This, too, is a theological, not only artistic, dilemma. If I claim to read the canvas of human experience as transparent to the reality of grace do I see it because it is there, or because my stance makes it necessary for me to see it? Is divinity, like beauty, in the eye of the beholder?

Whatever the answer to that may be, one thing is pretty clear: it is possible to have a "bad eye" in reading human experience. Then we will certainly not see any trace, not even, as with Moses, the "back side" of Yahweh.[13] So what is a "good eye" in this instance, an eye that sees deeply and sees what is really there? In a word I would call it *respect*, an absolute regard for the mystery of human life. In matters of attention disrespect is the "bad eye." Disrespect will never see the face of Yahweh. It can only ever look upon reproductions of its own image. Dostoevsky goes a step further. His term is love. "How will you *love* them? . . . With such hell in your heart and your head, how can you?" That puts Dostoevsky squarely where the New Testament says any genuine engagement with God in the gallery of human originals must begin. "Whoever does not love does not

---

[13] "And the Lord continued, 'See, there is a place by me where you shall stand on the rock; and while my glory passes by I will put you in a cleft of the rock, and I will cover you with my hand until I have passed by; then I will take away my hand, and you shall see my back; but my face shall not be seen'" (Exod 33:21-23).

know God, for God is love." And again, "those who do not love a brother or sister whom they have seen cannot love God whom they have not seen" (1 John 4:8, 20). If this is right it means that the business of seeing Yahweh is not a matter of the cursory glance. Indeed, that terrible and sublime visage is not visible directly at all. It can only be seen through the canvas of the other, and then only if that canvas is approached in love.

I am aware that this has the potential for turning into sentimental claptrap. Should we be in danger of forgetting it, the comedians are there to remind us. So I want to turn to work that is serious and unsentimental. One of the most underrated of "theological non-theologians" on the contemporary scene is the neurologist Oliver Sacks. Sacks is a person with the "good eye," because of a respectful heart. The quality of respect is evident in all his books. I first came across it in his famous series of case studies entitled *The Man Who Mistook His Wife for a Hat,* and again in a marvelous autobiographical piece *A Leg to Stand On.*[14] But here I want to look at the work that has been most widely influential because of the film based on it, namely *Awakenings.* In speaking of originals and reproductions, good though the film is, and brilliant though Robert De Niro is in playing the part of the stricken patient, it is nevertheless a reproduction in comparison with the book. To feel the impact of the truth and grace in the experience of the people Sacks deals with you have to read his biographies, the stories of their lives as he tells them, since they are unable to speak for themselves. And you have to read them through the "good eye" of his profound respect for their humanity in its awful constriction and suffering. Even then, Sacks would say, you are still looking at a reproduction: his reproduction of the truth of the experience of his patients. Really to see "Yahweh" in those extraordinary canvases, according to Sacks, you have to live with them, know them, respect them. What I am going to do, therefore, is at best to present a reproduction of a reproduction. Where Yahweh might be in that . . .

Briefly the story is this. In 1969 Oliver Sacks took up a position as neurologist at Mount Carmel hospital on the outskirts of New York. It was then a hospital for the chronically ill. There was a particular ward in the hospital that was home for a group of "human wrecks," survivors of the so-called sleeping sickness, *encephalitis lethargica,* which swept America in the 1920s. For thirty or forty years these people had been stuck in various states of physical and mental immobility, immured in bodies that would no longer work as mediums of life in any normal sense. "Extinct volcanoes," one writer called them. Sacks tells the story of his twenty-year relationship with these people. He is especially concerned with the re-

---

[14] Oliver Sacks, *The Man Who Mistook His Wife for a Hat* (South Yarmouth, Mass.: J. Curely, 1986); *A Leg to Stand On* (London: Picador, 1986).

vealing moment when the administration of a new drug, L-dopa, precipitated a rehabilitation, a reawakening to life for the patients. The tragedy of the story is that the reawakening was not sustained and eventually the sufferers fell back into their former state of tribulation and frozen frenzy. I will not attempt to tell the stories as Sacks does. They must be read for themselves. It is his *stance* or attitude I want to examine.

At the outset, Sacks reports, he was positively discouraged from committing himself professionally to these patients. The current medical literature as well as his own medical training stressed the hopelessness of the situation. "Chronic hospitals—you'll never see anything interesting in *those* places," he was told.[15] But it turned out to be a question of point of view. Meaning was not there for those who looked only at the surface: the apparent stillness, darkness, emptiness of arrested and frozen lives. People of the abyss, no more. Perhaps not real people at all. In time, however, Sacks found another dimension, completely at odds with the reports given by his advisers. In terrible abnormality he found an invitation to reevaluate what the so-called "normal" means, and to find how often it, that is, the "normal," appears as a shrunken caricature of itself. To observe, to care, to attend in this strange place was, he found, to be forced to scale the heights and depths of what being human means. It was to see *people* struggling to survive.

> "The physician is concerned (unlike the naturalist) . . . with a single organism, the human subject, striving to preserve its identity in adverse circumstances" (Ivor McKenzie). In perceiving this, I became something more than a naturalist (without, however, ceasing to be one). There evolved a new concern, a new bond; that of commitment to the patients, the individuals under my care. Through them I would explore what it was like to be human, to stay human, in the face of unimaginable adversities and threats. Thus, while continually monitoring their organic nature—their complex, ever-changing pathophysiologies and biologies—my central study and concern became identity—their struggle to maintain identity—to observe this, to assist this, and, finally to describe this.[16]

The struggle to be human and to stay human; the quest for identity—the coherent unity and uniqueness of a human person, an "I" to itself, a "Thou" to the other—that is what Sacks saw. And he understood that his task as physician was to facilitate and protect that endeavor. But it could only be done in the context of care expressed as respect or love.

Sacks contrasts this call to care with much that characterizes medical action and, indeed, human relationships in general, in our technological civilization. The determination to see disease as mechanical, chemical,

---

[15] Oliver Sacks, *Awakenings* (London: Picador, 1991) xxix.
[16] *Awakenings* xxviii–xxix.

and physical malfunction of the machine-like body or computer-like mind dominates our perspective. Quantities, locations, durations, classes, functions are clear-cut and finite. They allow precise definition, measurement, and estimation. But they cannot see the self, much less Yahweh. Not that this way of looking is wrong. It has brought immense gains to healing and to our dealings with the world. It is just that we seem to have made it the *only* or the primary way of attending. It is a looking that demands detachment from the observer and objectification of the observed. That is its strength—and weakness.

> Folly enters when we try to "reduce" metaphysical terms and matters to mechanical ones: worlds to systems, particulars to categories, impressions to analyses, and realities to abstractions. This is the madness of the last three centuries, the madness which so many of us—as individuals—go through, and by which all of us are tempted. It is the Newtonian-Lockean-Cartesian view—variously paraphrased in medicine, biology, politics, industry, etc.— which reduces men to machines, automata, puppets, dolls, blank tablets, formulae, ciphers, systems, and reflexes. It is this, in particular, which has rendered so much of our recent and current medical literature unfruitful, unreadable, inhuman, and unreal.[17]

Stance is crucial if we want to be fruitful, readable, human, and real. The stance that sees, or has the chance of seeing, is the stance that respects the human being as one, whole, unified, and living. Health is *ours*. Disease is *ours*. Reactions are *ours*. They cannot be understood in themselves, but only in reference to *us*. Thus an adequate view of the human canvas would, ideally, embrace all that happens to a person, all that affects or is affected by that person. In the end, therefore, a human life is only held in its completeness in the eye of God. On earth biography, a detailed history of the person in concrete immediacy, is the place from which personal truth may be glimpsed. It is an effort to see in part as God sees whole. Hence the heart of Sacks' book is a series of superb case histories of people in their struggle with disease.

The desire to see clearly must be on guard against what Sacks calls reductionism, which is the temptation to see the whole in terms of a part. It is of interest to note his word. We try to reduce "metaphysics" to mechanics, he says. The questions "How are you?" or "How are things?" are the basic medical questions. Clinical data is needed to answer them. But before that they are human questions. They have to do with the human condition as a whole. "They are at once exact, intuitive, obvious, mysterious, irreducible and indefinable."[18] The terrors of suffering, of sickness, of death, of losing our powers and with that losing our world, are among

---

[17] *Awakenings* 228.
[18] *Awakenings* 224.

the most intense and elemental feelings we know. So too are our longings for recovery and rebirth, of the hope of being somehow restored to that sense of what essentially we were meant to be. Thus the concrete circumstances of illness raise in us the fundamental issues of being and well-being. In Sacks' words:

> For all of us have a basic, intuitive feeling that once we were whole and well; at ease, at peace, at home in the world; totally united with the grounds of our being; and then we lost this primal, happy, innocent state, and fell into our present sickness and suffering. We had something of infinite beauty and preciousness—and we lost it; we spend our lives searching for what we have lost; and one day, perhaps, we will suddenly find it. And this will be the miracle, the millennium![19]

Clearly this is not medicine of the everyday sort. It is of another kind. "Something deeper, older, extraordinary, almost sacred"—the search for well-being; medical "metaphysics." If it is not theology in the normal sense it is at least the exploration of a pre-theological dimension implicit in the telling of the full story of a human life. It takes little imagination to see that Sacks is talking about matters that parallel what classic theology has called creation and its goodness, the fall and its corruption, reconciliation and its renewal—in short, the quest for grace. The human is not fully human unless it reaches beyond the human in becoming human. Most of our readings of ourselves and each other are too pallid—a skimming of the skin of being—to see what Sacks calls the "forces below the surface of consciousness, forces below the surface of the world, powers beyond powers, depths beneath depths, extending into the infinite depths of our world-home, the cosmos."[20] But only the person who takes the difficult stance of attentive regard—the regard that senses the outrage, not merely the pity or inutility, of the suffering of the beloved—can see the terrible and sublime visage that hovers over and in it all. The temptation, says Sacks, using the words of the poet John Donne, is that in dealing with the struggle of the human self we all too easily confuse the "Apothecaryes shope" and the "Metaphoricall Deity."[21]

---

[19] *Awakenings* 29.

[20] *Awakenings* 232, n. 111.

[21] *Awakenings* 30. Eberhard Jüngel makes a similar point concerning the attitude society has to people who are in situations of helplessness. "Only if we experience those who cannot yet or can no longer do anything for their existence as a *blessing*, only if we respect their dignity instead of asking about their—fluctuating—value, will our worship radiate the gospel into the everyday world in such a way that our achievement-oriented society may deserve to be called humane." See *Theological Essays II*, edited by J. B. Webster, translated by Arnold Neufeldt-Fast and J. B. Webster (Edinburgh: T & T Clark, 1995) 258.

Homo homini lupus?

The second and more difficult task is to illustrate how the human canvas can be read so that "the terrible and sublime visage" of Yahweh can be seen. I have chosen the story of Guiseppe Pardo Roques (Pardo for short) as told in a moving book by the psychiatrist Silvano Arieti entitled simply *The Parnas*.[22] Arieti explains why he wrote the biography:

> This is a story of suffering and fear, but it is also more. It is the account of a discovery I made by means of that suffering, one that has deeply affected my life and work. . . . the discovery concerns the nobility and greatness that are at times hidden within mental illness. Yes, I have come to believe that mental illness may hide and express the spirituality of man.[23]

It is this "spiritual reading" of a human story that interests me. Clearly it arises from the same, or a very similar, stance to Sacks'. It is the *discovery*—not the *a priori* assumption of—a theological depth in human experience that the unsuspecting do not see. Such a depth is often hidden in and expressed through adversity. Arieti calls it the "spirituality of man." Sacks refers to it as the "metaphysical question."

The basic narrative can be sketched briefly, although the full life and color of the experiences Arieti describes are obviously lost in such compression. Pardo was the parnas, or chief elder, of the Jewish community in Pisa in the 1930s, in the period leading up to and including the catastrophe of the Second World War. Arieti, the author, a young man in 1939, was an admirer and protegé of the parnas, who was then sixty-four years old and held in high esteem in the city for his wisdom, his compassion for the poor, and his courage in the face of mounting evil. When it became clear that Mussolini intended to reduplicate in Italy the full horrors of Nazi Antisemitism under Hitler, Arieti, along with many other Jews, fled to safer shores. He went to New York to study psychiatry. Pardo stayed, partly to shepherd the ever-diminishing flock of the Pisa synagogue and partly from phobic compulsion, about which more in a moment. In the summer of 1944 Pisa was hopelessly partitioned. The Germans occupied the city north of the Arno, where Pardo lived. The Americans held the south. An uneasy stalemate prevailed. Meanwhile increasingly violent pogroms were carried out in the Nazi sector against the Jews—murder, ostracism, incarceration. Strangely Pardo, though well known, was left untouched. On the night of July 31, 1944 six other Jews, mainly elderly, took shelter in his house. Word came that renewed terror was raging in the city. The parnas tried to persuade his friends to leave for safer places. But they would not abandon him and he would not abandon his house.

[22] Silvano Arieti, *The Parnas* (New York: Basic Books, 1979).
[23] Ibid. 4.

He would not leave because he *could not* leave. Since his teenage years Pardo had suffered a crippling phobia, a desperate fear of animals. He lived in a constant state of horror that animals would come after him, pounce on him, bite, torture, or even kill him. Dogs, especially those that reminded him of wolves, were the most terrifying. Try as he would he could not conquer such fears, nor could he understand them. Medical help came to nothing. Cruel people exploited his weakness, creeping up behind him and suddenly yelping like dogs, then watching with malicious enjoyment the terror that flooded him and his desperate effort to maintain human dignity. His friends tried for the most part not to mention the illness, aware of his sensitivity to it and his deep shame in face of it. It was for this reason that he could not leave. He felt safe only in the area near his house. The thought of traveling to unknown places was more than he could bear. Thus he felt a guilty responsibility for those who chose to stay with him despite the fact that they, one and all, assured him they were staying not to keep him safe, but rather the reverse. They felt safe because they were in his presence. Much of the book is about the debate that took place between the friends on that night.

On the morning of August 1 the Nazis came. They ransacked the house for valuables, then herded everyone except Pardo, eleven souls in all—six more people having come to the house—into the pantry. They threw a hand grenade in after them.

"We know who you are," the officer in charged snarled. "The rich Jew who hates dogs. The Führer loves dogs and hates Jews."[24] He laughed. They tormented Pardo, beat him mercilessly and finally put out his eyes with the barrel of a rifle. Then the Nazi paused for a second.

"We are about to kill you, Jew. Think hard with the last thoughts of which you are still capable; think hard about everybody you can and tell me: Can you think of anyone who, at this very moment, is worse off than you?"

"Yes," said Pardo at once. *"You."*

The man reacted in rage. "You are about to die and you know it, dog-hater. We are kind to you. Because of us you will not worry any more about dogs or other animals. You will never see them again. You are blind."

"I see as never before," said Pardo.[25] And then with a loud cry he gave voice to the inner sight that now dawned on him and in whose light the deep puzzle of his life became suddenly clear.

> "I see all of you around me. I am encircled not by men, but by animals. *You* are what I feared throughout my life, and what now I can finally face, you who have accepted evil and become the bearers of evil and evil itself.

---

[24] *The Parnas* 134.
[25] *The Parnas* 138–39.

You no longer wear the image of God. You have become wolves. You are the animals of my fears. Now I know! I know! I know! . . . *You are animals.* Your voice is the barking of hounds, the howling of wolves. In each of you I see a snout, fur, four claws, and a tail."[26]

Then silence.

Many things no doubt can be seen in such a story. I am interested in its theological dimension. This dimension is not some special aspect of the story that can be separated off from the rest. It is not a part of the story alongside other parts so much as the *depth* of the story in all its parts, to use a Tillichian image. It is the metaphysics of Sacks' question, "How are you?" in a concrete case. In the life of the parnas of Pisa the visage of Yahweh is glimpsed primarily in an indomitable quest for meaning in the face of chaos within and appalling evil without, a marking with blood of the boundary between light and darkness. This quest for meaning—for grace—is the single identity that is Guiseppe Pardo Roques.

Let me try to illustrate. In the course of his discussion with his guests on the night before the fateful day Pardo confided in his friend Ernesto his struggle to grasp the meaning of his illness. "I do agree," he says,

> that my illness has a meaning. What has to such a large extent shaped my life cannot be just an aberration of my mind. It must have meaning, at least for me, the prisoner and bearer of this affliction. . . . I must consider my illness as something I must hold on to, observe, and even respect, until the time comes when I can understand it fully or be sure of its meaning.[27]

To this point the closest he had come to finding any meaning in his affliction was in Freud's famous analysis of little Hans. As is well known, little Hans developed a desperate phobia of horses. Freud interpreted it as an effort by the boy to cope with the unbearable tensions of the Oedipus complex. Hans loved his father yet, at the same time, hated him as a rival for the love of his mother. He feared deeply that his father would find out about his feelings and punish him accordingly. Thus he threw up a curtain covering what made him unhappy and confused. He repressed his sexual desire for his mother and displaced the fear of his father onto horses. Horses stood for the dangerous father. Thus Hans could go on loving the good father by being concerned only with the avoidance of horses.[28]

Pardo found the sexual interpretation unconvincing in his case. But the idea of displacement did provide a clue. Thinking back over his

---

[26] *The Parnas* 140.

[27] *The Parnas* 87–88.

[28] Cf. *The Parnas* 84–85. For Freud's original study see Sigmund Freud, *Case Histories I: "Dora" and "Little Hans,"* edited by Angela Richards, translated by Alix and James Strachey. The Pelican Freud Library 8 (Harmondsworth: Penguin Books, 1977) 169–306.

adolescence, Pardo recalled that at the time he had slowly become aware of the problem of evil. He read the history of the sufferings of the Jewish people from Old Testament times to his own. He could not understand how so many innocent people had been scapegoated, blamed, destroyed by others. How could this terrible thing be? Then he remembered.

> One day in high school the Latin teacher was making us translate the Latin proverb *Homo homini lupus*, and in a stubborn way I said to myself, "This proverb is false. Man does not act like a wolf to a man." I refused to accept that concept. And then—Ernesto, I do remember now what happened. I instantly became afraid of wolves. Freud is right. I did what he explained so well; I displaced. I became afraid of wolves, and then of dogs, which resemble wolves, and then of all animals.[29]

This statement is the hinge on which the whole question of meaning in Pardo's experience swings. But it is a door that swings two ways. It connects two levels of meaning. As Arieti comments, "he had reached the point at which the mysteries of life require a metaphysical, not a psychological explanation."[30] Clearly it *is* a psychological pattern of meaning, the mechanism of displacement. But it is not merely a matter of the defense of the self under threat. And that "*not merely*" raises the theological dimension. It has to do with the question of good and evil.

The young Pardo found the reality of evil too much to bear. It not only threatened him personally. It threatened his whole understanding of human existence in the world. His phobia was a way of protecting himself but, as Arieti puts it, "also of protecting the human image of humankind."[31] He had to transform the *Homo homini lupus* (man acts as a wolf to man) into *Lupus homini lupus* (a wolf acts like a wolf to man). To preserve his disposition to love human beings and to respect human dignity he displaced his deep awareness of evil onto non-human sources. Not until the end, when he faced the reality of evil incarnate in the Nazi troops, did he see at last that the animals he had been afraid of stood for humans, humans who bring horror and terror into the world. "That momentary epiphanic vision," writes Arieti, "which could last no longer than his last instants on earth, was lived by him as a permanent truth and revealed that his illness was an inherent and genuine part of him, bespeaking the truth of his life."[32]

And what was the truth of his life, the truth that found expression in the whole history of his being, the truth that made and was his identity? Simply put, it was the faith that life counts, the conviction that there is

[29] *The Parnas* 86–87.
[30] *The Parnas* 103.
[31] *The Parnas* 159.
[32] *The Parnas* 159–60.

meaning in the depth of this strange journey of being. In his conscious mind Pardo expressed it in terms of radical hope. At one point in the evening one of the fated friends in his house had pressed a question on him. "I can perhaps understand the callousness of the government in its cooperation with the Nazis," Angelo said, "even perhaps the silence of the Pope. But what about the silence of God?" Pardo struggles to answer, but cannot. Who could? At last he blurts out:

> But I cannot believe that the forces of dissolution will prevail forever. The love I have for people like you and for what God has created makes it impossible for me to accept an ultimate futility in everything. To believe in nothingness is worse than to believe in power, it is more tragic than Hitler. . . . I stopped believing in a friendly universe. What I believe now is that we must make it friendly.[33]

This might sound like pious posturing, except that it is the utterance that makes sense of a man's whole existence and is the ground of an immense courage in the face of torment. Here is the terrible and sublime visage of Yahweh in the texture of this canvas. It is present not only in Pardo's conscious actions, his efforts to support the needy, to shelter the outcast, to encourage the young, to resist the powers of darkness. It is also significantly present in the contours of his illness. Pardo's fear of man-the-wolf was built on his sensitivity to the threat that evil human beings posed to the foundation of his life, namely faith in the friendliness of the universe. His refusal to buckle under to that fear and his determination to stand for the humanity of the human, despite the threats against it, is the measure and expression of his courage to live the faith that he must help to make the universe friendly or deny his own self. The moment of grace that broke in on him at the end like a flood of freedom was that he *had* lived the meaning of his being. At last he saw the fear for what it was—the fear of genuine evil. Moreover, he saw that he had fought it in his life, consciously as best he could, unconsciously in a terrifying awareness of the strength of evil that he felt he could not face and so displaced. And yet when that evil really did confront him inescapably, face it he did and defy it in the name of goodness. "Can you think of anyone worse off at this moment than you?" "Yes, *you.*" Human dignity may be destroyed, but it is not conquered by *homo lupus.*

Of course the real test of the presence of that terrible and sublime visage in the canvas of a human life is not seen in a discussion like this. This is mere reproduction. The point is, as Hughes said, can you see it in the original? Arieti thinks he can. His whole book is testimony to his seeing. But he has first hand witnesses to back up his claim. In their debate

---

[33] *The Parnas* 73, 75.

in the house on the last night of their lives the friends argue about why they decide to stay rather than leave, despite the danger and Pardo's pleas that they should go. Finally, what they all felt is put into words by Ernesto. We stay, he said, because you (Pardo) give us security: "Because of the Shekinah that rests in you!"[34]

The Shekinah is the name for the Divine Presence, the immanence of God in the world. When applied to individuals it means the person in whom God's presence and grace abide: in short, the face of Yahweh in a human form. The six friends agreed that they saw that face in the face of Pardo. Indeed, they bet their lives on its reality. The next day they died because of that wager. Were they wrong? Who can tell? It doesn't prove God. It doesn't prove goodness, at least not the victory of goodness. It doesn't disprove ultimate futility. But it does pose the theological issue in flesh and blood, where it belongs. It does show, for those who have eyes to see, that the questions "How are you?" and "How are things?" pose more than a technical problem. It does show that when we look at originals, at least when we look at them with love, the possibility is that the face of Yahweh will be seen. That at any rate is my hope. In the end that is why I think it worth being a believing soul in the world—and I mean in the worldly world, not merely the world of the Church.

---

[34] *The Parnas* 45.

6

God and Jesus

Saying what it means to be Christian is not easy. Is there such a thing as "Christian identity," of which Moltmann speaks so decisively?[1] If so, my grip on it is decidedly fragile at times, and when I look at what some others seem to regard as Christian identity for themselves, I am further unsettled.[2] There is some comfort in history, however. If we look back to the beginning we find the early Christians also struggled to express what it was they were on about—why it was that they were who they were and were as they were. Their endeavors took many forms, but most characteristic, and of greatest subsequent influence, was the form of narrative. They told the story of Jesus. And they told it in a number of different ways. There are four gospels in the canon. They are not identical. That fact has become increasingly significant in a situation of postmodern pluralism. The drama of the story of Jesus, and hence its meaning, apparently needs a variety of expressions if the full character of truth is to be grasped in different situations. Story theology turns out to be a more flexible witness to the Christ figure than creeds or doctrines, which tend to become set, tied to particular concepts, forms, and words.

[1] See Jürgen Moltmann, *The Crucified God*, translated by R. A. Wilson and John Bowden (London: S.C.M. Press, 1974) ch. 1, especially 18–25.

[2] The idea of "identity" is not easy to pin down. It means different things in different contexts. I am using the term in roughly the sense set out by Hans W. Frei: "When a person's intentions and actions are most nearly conformed to each other—and further when an intention-action combination in which he plays a part is not merely peripheral to him but is of crucial importance, involving his full power in a task—than *[sic]* a person gains his identity." In short, identity is a matter of self-understanding expressed in crucial, that is, life-committing action. Christian identity might thus be characterized as a fundamental faith in God as revealed in Jesus Christ (as love) expressed in (loving) actions in daily life. See his *Theology and Narrative: Selected Essays,* edited by George Hunsinger and William C. Placher (New York: Oxford University Press, 1993) 63; also *The Identity of Jesus Christ: The Hermeneutical Bases of Dogmatic Theology* (Philadelphia: Fortress, 1975).

One of the first and most creative of thinkers to develop the notion of "narrative theology," H. Richard Niebuhr, put it in these words:

> The preaching of the early church was not an argument for the existence of God nor an admonition to follow the dictates of some common human conscience, unhistorical and super-social in character. It was primarily a simple recital of the great events connected with the historical appearance of Jesus Christ and a confession of what had happened to the community of disciples. Whatever it was that the church meant to say, whatever was revealed or manifest to it could be indicated only in connection with an historical person and the events in the life of his community.[3]

No doubt the early believers got into arguments about the nature and existence of God. There is the New Testament example of Paul debating the Epicurean and Stoic philosophers in the Agora (Acts 17:16-33). But at the end of the day such philosophical issues were not at the center of his preaching. Even in this recorded encounter Paul winds up his case with direct reference to God's self-disclosure "by raising him (i.e., Christ) from the dead" (v. 31). The young Church also found itself involved in questions of morality and the appropriate rules of behavior. But this was not central either. As Niebuhr argues, it was not some common conscience that bound them together and made them who they were. It was the story of Jesus and the reality of the Spirit that story mediated in their midst. Hence a good deal of New Testament ethical argument includes, at some point in its development, a direct appeal to the Jesus story. (See, for example, 2 Corinthians 8 on the ethics of generosity).

In this history of encounter with the person of Jesus the first witnesses were faced, so they believed, with God in a new and unsettling way. In the life of Jesus and the events that surrounded it they felt themselves confronted by a presence and addressed by a word that they could acknowledge and respond to only as the presence of God and the Word of God. Their story was not a utopian vision of what might one day be possible. It was a story of actual happenings. This became the basis for their understanding of possibility itself, of what *could* happen in human experience and human history. Hence their insistence on the utterly human reality of Jesus as the Christ against any tendency to spiritualize or idealize him. "That which was from the beginning, which we have heard, which we have seen with our eyes, which we have looked upon and touched with our hands . . ." says John, *that* we proclaim to you (1 John 1:1).

Of course a claim that telling the story of Jesus was the preferred mode of self-identification of the early Church sets rather than solves the

---

[3] *The Meaning of Revelation* (New York: Macmillan, 1960 [first published 1941]) 43–44.

problem. The question arises, as it always has: What does the story, and the history, of Jesus amount to? What does it say to us and to the world? What reality does it reveal? These are large questions. And there is no agreement on the answers, any more than there is agreement as to what the story of Hamlet means. The full significance of the story of Jesus only the whole history of the Church and its mission in the world can unfold. Even then it will not be complete until the end when, as Paul says, we come to know as we are known (1 Cor 13:12). In the meantime we are faced with the challenge of what answer we will give to the meaning of the story in our lives and world. What do *we* say this story comes to?

We cannot hope to answer that question alone, of course. A lot of people have attempted interpretations before us. We need to take our bearings from their efforts. In this chapter I want to explore some of the implications of what became a classic—though controversial—interpretation. According to this reading the story of Jesus commits us to a highly distinctive view of God, namely that God chose to become present in history in the life of a particular person. This is the *incarnational* interpretation of Christian faith. It found definitive expression in the Chalcedonian statement of 451 C.E. which declared Jesus to be "truly God" *(vere deus)* and "truly human" *(vere homo)*. The life of Jesus properly understood, according to this view, is the self-expression of the supreme Reality in history. Jesus Christ is the decisive disclosure of who God is and who we are in relation to God. Incarnation is an affirmation—about as strong an affirmation as could be conceived—of the fundamental *belonging together* of God and the world.[4] In telling the story of its life the early Church found that it was unable to speak of God without at the same time speaking of Jesus as the Christ, and conversely it could not say what it had to say about Jesus without speaking about God. A mutual and inescapable entailment connected the two.

In passing, it is important to note an obvious consequence of this conviction. If, as faith confesses, God has drawn near in *this* particular human being, then Christian identity is inextricably linked to what can be known about him. The gospel story is therefore of a different kind from the story of Hamlet. However profound an analysis of human experience the play might be, it makes no claim to be anything other than fictitious, *just* a story. I have spoken thus far about the "story of Jesus." But since the time of Reimarus and Lessing (late eighteenth century) the critical distinction between story and history, event and report of event, has

---

[4] Cf. the words of Gerhard Ebeling: "The nearness of God in Jesus is . . . understood in terms of the togetherness of God and humanity." *(Dogmatik des christlichen Glaubens II* [Tübingen: Mohr, 1989] 456; quoted by Eberhard Jüngel, *Theological Essays II*, edited by J. B. Webster, translated by Arnold Neufeldt-Fast and J. B. Webster [Edinburgh: T & T Clark, 1995] 110, n. 56. Jüngel comments in detail pp. 109–110).

become entrenched in common consciousness. The long and unfinished "quest of the historical Jesus"[5] appears to have demonstrated fairly convincingly that we do not know with certainty many personal details about the figure who stands behind the gospel stories, not enough anyway to write what might today be regarded as a satisfactory biography. Nevertheless a consensus prevails among scholars that the history of Jesus—Jesus as he actually was—bears, or at the very least *permits*, the basic shape that the gospel narratives place upon it. "They are the portrait of a person and not a series of characteristics or changing circumstances."[6] To defend this conclusion in detail has been the work of a generation of investigators. I am simply going to assume it. In what follows I am concerned with the interpretation of the *story* of Jesus as given in the gospels.

The assertion of the fundamental togetherness of God and humanity in Jesus Christ has always been controversial. Even if it is true, there remain the tantalizing questions of what sort of togetherness it is and how it is achieved. The history of the early Church, including that part of its history reflected in the New Testament, is full of the debate. But since the time of the Enlightenment a distinctive kind of challenge has emerged. The link between these two subjects—God and Jesus—has been seriously questioned from both sides. On the one hand the rise of modern atheism brought about by, among other things, the collapse of the ancient worldview in face of the rising power of the new natural sciences, rendered "the God in heaven homeless."[7] Hegel was one of the first to sense the changed theological circumstance and stamp it with the famous verdict, "God is dead." But if there is no God, what is left of this Christian "togetherness"? If God is dead, who is Jesus, "theologically" speaking? To put the question another way: Can Jesus be "God" if *God* is dead?[8] On the other hand, an attack comes from modern historical skepticism concerning miracles and reports of miracles. Since the time of Reimarus and Hume critical doubts have been raised about miracles in general, but

[5] Albert Schweitzer, *The Quest of the Historical Jesus* (London: S.C.M. Press, 1981 [first published 1906]).

[6] Frei, *Theology and Narrative* 50. For a skeptical assessment of the fruits of historical research into the life of Jesus and its implications for theology see Van A. Harvey, *The Historian and the Believer* (Philadelphia: Westminster, 1966). A more positive reading, including a perceptive critique of Harvey, is given in Keith Ward, *Religion and Revelation: A Theology of Revelation in the World's Religions* (Oxford: Clarendon Press, 1994) 232–258, especially 247–51.

[7] The phrase is Hans Küng's, taken from his discussion of Hegel's christology. See *The Incarnation of God: An Introduction to Hegel's Theological Thought as Prolegomena to a Future Christology*, translated by J. R. Stephenson (Edinburgh: T & T Clark, 1987 [German original 1970]) 164.

[8] This question was put as the subject of a recent debate at the Australian National University. It set me thinking along the lines that follow in this essay.

most far-reaching have been questions about the central miracle report in the story of Jesus—the resurrection. If there is no resurrection of Jesus what does that do to the claimed "togetherness"? To put the balancing question: Can God be God if *Jesus* is dead? I want to look at these questions in turn.

Can Jesus Be God if God Is Dead?

The togetherness of God and humanity in Christian faith classically interpreted means, among other things, that faith and worship, which otherwise can only be appropriately directed toward God, are now *also* directed toward the figure of Jesus. "It is fitting," writes Clement, "that you should think of Jesus Christ as of God."[9] Such a sentence makes a certain kind of sense in a tradition that already acknowledges the reality of God and is searching for ways to describe what it believes to be a new and unprecedented action of God in human history. But what happens when such a presupposition no longer holds? Can Jesus be thought of as "God" if God is dead?

On the surface the question looks merely rhetorical. If God is dead, Jesus is certainly wrong; wrong in his speaking and acting, for example, because he definitely speaks about God and acts as if the purposes and intentions of God were to be taken with utmost seriousness. He is also mistaken in his dying because it is in pursuit of what he calls "the will of God" that his journey to the cross comes about (cf. Matt 26:39 *parr.*). So he is *wrong* if God is dead. But he can hardly *be* God.

If the term "God" means what traditional Christianity, or even traditional theism, has usually meant by it: that is, if the term God points to a living and personal reality that transcends human existence, and the existence of everything finite, in such a way that this reality [God] is understood to be the mystery that grounds and determines all being; if this is God and this God is real and living, *then* it may make some sense to say, as Clement insisted, that Jesus is profoundly united with God, in fact so at one with God that it is possible to say that God is *in* Christ, or even to say that in dealing with Jesus we are dealing with God. With this kind of presupposition it is quite possible to speak of Jesus as God, if we are careful. A lot of people have done so and still do.

On the other hand, it is hard to think of going the other way. Suppose God is dead. What could this mean? It seems to imply that God was once alive, but eventually, like all living beings—and some would say

---

[9] 2 Clement 1.1 in *The Ante-Nicene Christian Library I*, edited by Alexander Roberts and James Donaldson (Edinburgh: Clark, 1867) 55; quoted by Jüngel, *Theological Essays II*, 85, n. 7.

quite recently—ceased to be.[10] This is hard to imagine if God is as we have described above, since it could only mean that what grounds all other beings, and hence gives them such reality as they have, has ceased to be, which presumably means that they (the other realities) cannot *be* either. And that would include commentators on the death of God!

More plausibly it might be claimed that in saying God is dead we mean there never was any reality that answered to the description of the word given above. Those who use the word God in this sense may have an idea in their heads of what they intend by it, but in fact nothing answers to that intention in reality. To believe otherwise is to labor under an illusion. So if we mean by saying God is dead that there is no personal reality that is ground and mystery of all being, that nothing now is or ever was that answers to that description, then it does not make sense to speak of Jesus as God. If there is no reality that is the ground and mystery of the world other than, say, some non-personal basis of things in energy, matter, superforce, or what have you, then whatever else Jesus may be, he is certainly not God. So if God is dead, meaning unreal in this ontological sense, the answer to our question is no. Jesus is not God.

That is all very well. But more is at stake here than a game of definitions, however important it may be. The Jesus question may look rhetorical in form. But its substance, what it is feeling for, touches something in us that is more significant than playing with the meaning of words. The phrase "the death of God" certainly points to something of great seriousness in our contemporary culture (and perhaps in our own hearts), when this is compared, say, with the culture that existed in the West two hundred years ago. In his famous parable of the madman in the marketplace who announces to an amused audience that "God is dead! God remains dead! And we have killed him!"[11] Nietzsche, in the midst of the nineteenth century, was not so much arguing a case about the reality or unreality of a transcendent being called God. He was reporting the spiritual condition of the *human* world he found himself in. God in the sense of the divine other—"our maker and our judge," as the prayer book puts it—seemed to be effectively absent from the souls of many of his contemporaries. God no longer played a significant part in the ordinary lives of people as had once been the case. In that human sense God was dead, whatever might be the case about a divine reality "beyond."

What do we do with this? A figure as significant as God cannot just vacate the stage, and the players (i.e., us) go on as if nothing has hap-

---

[10] Thomas J. J. Altizer in an early work appeared to make the claim that the death of God is an objective event of cosmic significance that occurred in the death of Jesus. See *The Gospel of Christian Atheism* (Philadelphia: Westminster, 1966) 62–92.

[11] Friedrich Nietzsche, *The Joyful Wisdom*, translated by Thomas Common (New York: Frederick Ungar, 1960) 168.

pened. Who fills the role of God? As Nietzsche put it, how do we know now which way is up and which way is down? How do we know what is the purpose of human life, the goal toward which it is oriented, since one of God's primary functions, as far as we humans are concerned, was to determine exactly that? Who says where the horizon is now—that is, the direction we ought to go in to make our lives worthwhile? If God is dead what is right and what is wrong? Is Dostoevsky correct that in the circumstances of God's death anything goes?

The problem is that when God dies—that is, disappears from the process of founding and forming human selves—the functions God once performed within the human realm still have to go on. Humans still have to ask what is up and what is down, what is truly worthwhile and what is not. But now a crucial way of answering such questions has disappeared. This is where the figure of Jesus emerges again in connection with God, at least for some people. But the connection is with God absent. "Can Jesus be God if God is dead?" now means: Can Jesus stand in for God in performing those necessary human functions that formerly God fulfilled but now, *post mortem dei*, no longer can?

There is a poignant expression of the link between the death of God and the continuing significance of Jesus in our human struggle given by Jean Paul Richter in his famous tract, *Speech of the Dead Christ from the Universe, that there is no God* (published 1796). In his story Jean Paul has Christ, after his descent into death, come before the great company of the dead to report the findings of his experience.

> Now a lofty and noble figure with an everlasting sorrow descended from the heights on to the altar, and all the dead cried out, "O Christ, is there no God?" He answered, "There is none." . . . I voyaged through the worlds, I climbed into the suns and flew along the Milky Way through the wastes of heaven; but there is no God. I climbed down as far as the shadow of being is cast, peered into the abyss and cried out, "Father, where are you?" But all I heard was the eternal storm which no one governs, and the shining rainbow from the west hung over the abyss without a sun to make it, and rain fell from it. And as I looked up at the immeasurable universe to find the divine eye, an empty and bottomless socket stared back at me; and eternity lay upon chaos and gnawed at it and chewed upon it . . . and everything grew empty. Then came a heartrending sight. The dead children who had come to life in the graveyard came into the temple and cast themselves down before the lofty figure at the altar, and said, "Jesus, have we no father?" And he answered, his face streaming with tears, "We are all orphans, I and you, we are fatherless." . . . Then, as great as the highest finite being, he raised his eyes towards the nothingness and the empty immensity, and said, "Dumb, unbending nothingness! Cold and eternal necessity! Senseless chance! . . . How solitary everyone is in the vast tomb of the universe! I am alone with myself—O Father! O Father! Where is thine

everlasting bosom, that I may rest upon it? Ah, if every self is his own father and creator, why cannot everyone be his own avenging angel?"[12]

Of many things that might be said about this amazing utterance I want to note just two. Clearly there is here a deep feeling that the old appeal to a transcendent God, personal and protective—the "Father, O Father"—is no longer possible. The immensity is devoid of any such life. The universe is a vast tomb. Death, not God, is the ultimate reality. And Jesus, who in the past had been seen by many as the clearest manifestation within our human arena of the nature and reality of God in this old sense, is the one who now reports from beyond the grave the terrible truth. There is no God. We are cosmic orphans. And he, the so-called Son of God, is son without parent.

No longer can Jesus be understood as God in the sense of participating in, and so making manifest, the Being of a transcendent and loving Creator. However, Jean Paul will not, for that reason, have done with him. Jesus towers still amid the awful wreckage of a failed theological vision. "A lofty and noble figure," he calls him, "as great as the highest finite being." He may have lost the old aura and power of infinite cosmic divinity. But he is still recognizable as the greatest *finite* being. Lord of *all* being he is not. But he remains, among our experience of finitude, the greatest example of love and most reliable guide to truth. If we can say with Anselm that God is "that than which none greater can be conceived," then perhaps, in the new God-less situation, it is not nonsense to say Jesus is the greatest expression of human being that we have or could hope to have, and in this sense he takes over the role of "God" for us, albeit in a kingdom much reduced in scope.

Such a claim has often been made both in theory and in practice. The death of God theologians of the Sixties are a vivid example of it.[13] But they merely brought into the open a wider, though less explicitly stated, reality. In various ways the humanity of Jesus, or the teaching of Jesus, or the example of Jesus, or the story of Jesus, are used as a profound moral and spiritual resource from which to determine what is a truly worthwhile life. In short, Jesus' *humanity* is regarded as normative. He provides, as it were, that needed center of gravity from which what is up and what is down can be reckoned. God is dead. But precisely this gives opportunity for Jesus to be—functionally—"God." Christian identity is then determined by a commitment to live in the light and power of this example.

---

[12] Quoted in Heinz Zahrnt, *The Question of God: Protestant Theology in the Twentieth Century* (London: Collins, 1969) 125.

[13] The best discussion of the whole movement to my knowledge is that of Langdon Gilkey, *Naming the Whirlwind* (Indianapolis: Bobbs-Merrill, 1969).

There are problems with this position, of course. Perhaps the most conspicuous of them is that, while ascribing almost unsurpassable greatness to him, this view doesn't seem to take Jesus himself seriously. Jesus' whole life, teaching, and death seem utterly centered on God. The story depicts him as one who in his own person represents the authority of God's kingdom (or rule) in dynamic action in the world (Luke 11:19f). He teaches with an affronting personal authority and sets his own edict—"but I say unto you"—above the law of Moses which, in faithful Jewish circles of the day, was regarded as the Word of God (Matt 5:21-48). He assumes the authority to forgive sins, prompting the criticism, "who can forgive sins but God alone?" (Mark 2:5-11). And he claims that final destiny is determined according to the decision human beings make for or against not his teaching, but his own person (Luke 12:8-9; Mark 13:26-27). In short, the kingdom of *God*, the rule of *God* on earth, is enacted in the intention and activity of Jesus. This *is* his identity.

Of course we could reply to this by saying that Jesus' talk of God is merely an expression of his cultural context. He lived in a time when the old theological vision was still alive. That was the framework in which human life was interpreted and experienced. But the God-talk is not the central issue. It is the humanity of Jesus that is normative. He embodies, as no other figure does, the conviction that a truly human life must be lived on the basis of self-sacrificing love: "Jesus the man for others," as Bonhoeffer called him. It is this incarnation of virtue that is Jesus' importance. The talk of God can be quietly dropped without injuring this truth. We might note, of course, that a whole range of other virtues has also been detected in Jesus and held up as the heart of his normative humanity: Jesus the man of faith, of hope, of freedom, of justice, of humility, even of femininity. And so on.

There is something in this. But the question remains whether we can quite so easily sever the humanity of Jesus from his passionate concern with God the transcendent Father. Love *per se* was never at the center of his action and teaching. It was always love of *God* and of neighbor in *God*. And it was the God-element in his love that shaped his life and determined his destiny on the cross. The same is true of his hope, his freedom, his justice, or what have you. It was not in this world, and certainly not in himself, that he found the source of these virtues. Though expressed powerfully in the world his life seems, at its center, to draw its being and authority from beyond itself. If he himself is to be believed, it is drawn from the God whom he called Father. "Why do you call me good?" he says. "No one is good but God alone" (Mark 10:18). *Jesus is not himself apart from God.*[14] To cut the nerve of "togetherness" with God from the

---

[14] *"Jesus is not himself apart from God.* That is how he understood himself. That is how one must understand him if one is to do justice to what can be known historically

center of Jesus' existence makes it much more difficult to claim a general, still less a universal authority for his humanity. I am not saying it is impossible to do this. But I am inclined to agree with Pannenberg that "anyone to whom Jesus' message concerning God no longer means anything would do better to look around for other exemplary figures of humanity, towards which the self-realisation of man in the world can be more securely orientated than Jesus."[15]

The second point I want to draw from Jean Paul's imaginative drama is less precise, a mood rather than an idea. It has to do with what we might call the "tragic dimension" of the story of Jesus and the death of God. There is a kind of robust matter-of-factness about the view I have just put. "God is dead" means the scene has changed drastically. But all is not lost. Perhaps some important things are gained. We are no longer able to look to a transcendent reality to determine our values and to protect our life against the various threats that lower over it.[16] But we can at last take our human responsibility and freedom seriously. Within the restricted realm of finite human freedom *we* must decide what we will do and where we will go. We can take heart, however, because there are great figures in our midst—like Jesus—who provide us with the guidance and example we need to adopt this new autonomous stance. And if it is within this life only we have to operate, so be it. Much human good and joy can be created in the span of our three score years and ten. So let us joyfully grasp our responsibility and stop gazing toward the heavens. A robust and admirable courage marks this disposition.

But it leaves something out—a sense of injustice, almost outrage. The Markan account of the passion has the crucified Jesus utter that terrible cry of dereliction at the moment of death. "My God, my God, why have you forsaken me?" (Mark 15:34). Jean Paul interprets this to mean that at the final moment Jesus discovered the life he had lived on the basis of the active presence of divine love was totally illusory. There was no such love. But surely that discovery is not merely the disclosure of a personal mistake, which can be rectified by the simple expedient of writing off the theological dimension of Jesus' life and reinterpreting it without remainder in ethi-

---

about Jesus' self-understanding." Jüngel, *Theological Essays II*, 102. Cf. Ward, *Religion and Revelation* 235–40.

[15] Wolfhart Pannenberg, *Basic Questions in Theology* (London: S.C.M. Press, 1973) 3:103. Cf. the words of Hans Frei: "The unity of his [i.e., Jesus'] personal being in the Gospels . . . is not to be seen directly, by adumbrating the personal excellences discernible in him and then choosing the most noticeable in comparison to the others as the first. That unity is seen more nearly indirectly as the shaping of all his personal qualities in conformation to his mission or aspiration in obedience to God." *Theology and Narrative* 51.

[16] Cf. the discussion of Freud's arguments in ch. 4 above.

cal, this-worldly terms: love for our fellows, the pursuit of justice, and so on. The discovery of the "eternal storm that no one governs," the "empty and bottomless socket" staring blankly in the place of the divine eye, precipitates, for Jean Paul, not merely an ethical reinterpretation of theological language, but an "everlasting sorrow," a cosmic grief.

The impact of this grief is given powerful expression in the image of the "heartrending sight" of the dead children who crowd about the altar where Jesus, now merely the highest of finite beings, has the terrible responsibility of delivering a negative answer to their question: "Have we no father?" And this negation has to be made in the teeth of the unconditional affirmation that Jesus (in the story) gives to children prior to the cross. "Let the little children come to me; do not stop them; for it is *to such as these that the kingdom of God belongs.*" (Mark 10:14, italics added). Dead children raise the question of justice and meaning in its acutest form. Dead children have been cut down before ever they had a chance to live what, without God, and hence without some hope of a life beyond this historical existence, is the only life they can ever have. The call to live a life of selfless love or compassionate freedom in emulation of the highest example given in Jesus has been cruelly snatched from them. They could not, and cannot, reach fulfillment, not even finite fulfillment, since they were never given the chance. And there is no redress. "Dumb, unending nothingness. Cold and eternal necessity. Senseless chance": such ultimates don't give a damn about the children. All the love that we, or the fatherless Christ, may feel for them cannot rescue them, or comfort them, or make good the promise their young lives once had. Where is the kingdom that supposedly belongs to them?

It seems to me that the question: Can Jesus be God if God is dead? uncovers here a deep poignancy. Without God as understood in the traditional sense Jesus, however great, or anybody else—or any combination of others for that matter—can do nothing for the dead children. That fact opens a tragic dimension to the question that ethical reinterpretation does not really touch. I am not suggesting that the sense of "everlasting sorrow," however keenly felt, is reason in itself to cling to belief in God for the comfort it brings. Atheism is a long, tough business, as Sartre said. But it may be true. If so, then so be it. But if so, then there is more to the question of Jesus in a godless world than the ethical model expresses. If the cry of dereliction from the cross means what Jean Paul's story has it mean, I for one would want to see in the new, de-divinized Christ something more than an example of a loving life, however great. I would also want to see an element of tragic courage—an ultimately futile but, nonetheless, unbowed defiance of the dumb, unending nothingness that produces children only to see them crushed. I would want to see in the cross something of the attitude expressed by Senancour. "Man is perishable.

That may be; but let us perish resisting, and if it is nothingness that awaits us, do not let us so act that it shall be a just fate."[17] I would hope that, even had he come to the awareness before the cross that there was no transcendent Father whose will he pursued in the journey that took him there, Jesus would still, and with passion undiminished, have taken the same way, if only to make abundantly clear that the fate of the children was no just one and, as such, was cosmically unacceptable even in the very moment when he saw it to be cosmically unavoidable. Thus he might become, within the limits of a wildly unequal contest with cosmic death, "his own avenging angel."

As it happens I don't think this is our only option. The story of Jesus insists that it was not only death that took Christ into itself, but also God in Christ who took death into divinity. In the light of the essential togetherness of God and Jesus it is thus possible to speak meaningfully of "the death of God," but not in a way that death is shown to be the triumphant ultimate in a realm of senseless chance. Rather, that death itself is overcome, and the life that God created finds its true destiny—for the children and the whole created order—in God. This leads to our second question.

Can God Be God if Jesus Is Dead?

The togetherness of God and Jesus in the gospel story includes the startling claim that even death did not break the living bond between them. The cross was a brutal reality. Jesus died a tortured death. And if the cry of dereliction is taken seriously we must accept that his suffering included the experience of utter loss, including the severing of relationship with God. He entered the darkness of godforsakenness. But this state did not prevail. Shortly after the burial, reports circulated of his re-emergence into the network of living relationships, not as one who had merely evaded for the time being the finality of death by whatever process of revivification, but as one who had come through death to a new kind of life in relation to which death itself was now past and done with. Only one kind of life has such a quality: the eternal life of God. The witness of the story is that God raised Jesus into God's own divine vitality. Jesus "was declared to be Son of God [i.e., participant in the life-being of God] with power according to the spirit of holiness by resurrection from the dead" (Rom 1:4; cf. Acts 2:32–36; 5:31-32).

In a recent discussion John Macquarrie has called this the "conventional ending" or "happy ending" to the story.[18] It is the ending accepted

---

[17] Quoted in Miguel De Unamuno, *The Tragic Sense of Life* (New York: Dover Publications, 1954) 263.

[18] John Macquarrie, *Jesus Christ in Modern Thought* (London: S.C.M. Press, 1990) 403.

by most New Testament writers and by the creeds and liturgies of the Church. Certainly the first Christians gave only one answer to the question of the existence and motivation of their new communal life, namely that Jesus Christ had risen from the dead and was alive among them. But, as Macquarrie rightly observes, "for post-Enlightenment mentality, resurrection is a very difficult idea to accept."[19] Influenced deeply by David Hume's argument that one should always believe the lesser miracle, this modern mentality has found it easier to interpret the reports of resurrection as the outcome of an understandable process of rationalization in dealing with profound disappointment. It is no wonder if, unhappy with the terrible conclusion to a life of exemplary virtue, "some people began providing smoother endings, including appearances of the risen Christ and the affirmation that he had been taken up to heaven and seated at the right hand of God."[20] Most of us can sympathize with this process. "We all have the happy ending syndrome."[21] It arises from the kind of moral outrage expressed by Senancour to which we referred above. We long for goodness to be crowned with power, for virtue to be conjoined with happiness, for the murderers not to triumph finally over their victims.

But the need to be absolutely honest compels us, Macquarrie thinks, to look at an alternative scenario, a more "austere ending" to the story.

> Suppose in our account of the career of Jesus we had felt compelled to draw the bottom line under the cross? Suppose we omitted the "joyful mysteries" that traditionally came after the cross? Would that destroy the whole fabric of faith in Christ? I do not think so, for the two great distinctive Christian affirmations would remain untouched—God is love, and God is revealed in Jesus Christ. These two affirmations would stand even if there were no mysteries beyond Calvary.[22]

This reading of the story works in the reverse way to Jean Paul Richter's. In Jean Paul's account the dead Christ enjoys a kind of *post mortem* life to the extent that he "journeys" through the realm of the dead to bring back the terrible news that there is no God and "we are orphans." This is a poet's way of saying that the disastrous ending to the life of Jesus demonstrates the godlessness of the world for all to see. Jean Paul makes no bones about it. If God is dead the Christian vision of life is profoundly altered, probably altogether destroyed. By contrast, Macquarrie's austere ending has Jesus simply dead, with no mysterious life

---

[19] Ibid. 406.

[20] Ibid. 404–405.

[21] Ibid. "Even that very austere moralist, Immanuel Kant," Macquarrie notes, "believed that the *summum bonum* or highest good must include not only moral goodness or virtue, but happiness conjoined with it."

[22] Ibid. 412.

"beyond Calvary." But *God* lives and relates to us in love. Macquarrie is well aware that the omission of the "joyful mysteries" leaves a "major gap" in the conventional story. And given the interrelated nature of the Christian vision, the "knock-on effect, so to speak, would be pretty drastic."[23] Even so he believes the heart of faith, the "great distinctive Christian affirmations," remain *untouched*. God *can* be God if Jesus is dead.

No doubt God can. If it is possible, without essential contradiction, to say (1) that God exists and (2) that human beings die and stay dead—as it seems to be—then there is no *a priori* reason why it cannot be said that God lives and Jesus remains unresurrected. That does no more than put Jesus into the same fundamental situation of finitude before God's infinity as the rest of us. If we do not wish to take Christ out of history altogether, such a placing seems unavoidable. Moreover, it is in line with the classic readings of the story: "he had to become like his brothers and sisters in every respect," says the writer to the Hebrews (Heb 2:17). To this extent, then, the "austere ending" is both honest and plausible. But Macquarrie is *not* speaking *a priori*. He argues that the "great distinctive Christian affirmations"—that is, the theological conclusions derived from an interpretation of the life and destiny of Jesus—are essentially unaffected by drawing "the bottom line under the cross." This is a good deal less plausible.

For the sake of argument let us agree that the distinctive Christian affirmations are as Macquarrie indicates: God is love and God is revealed in Jesus Christ. Is it true that the meaning of these summary statements remains essentially unchanged for Jesus resurrected as for Jesus dead? It is certainly correct to say that Christian faith believes God is revealed in Jesus Christ. But *who* is Jesus as revealer? What does he *do* in order to manifest this revelation? And what is the *revelation* that comes to light in his action? It is not enough simply to say Jesus reveals that God is love, for then the question arises: What kind of love is revealed? Is God's love like that, say, of a shepherd for the sheep—protective, but within the framework of an arrangement in which the shepherd intends to use, or even kill the sheep for his own purposes? Is it like the love of a parent for a child—creative and supportive, but finally impotent in face of the ravages of time and the "slings and arrows of outrageous fortune"? Is it like the love of a naturalist for the truth—an abstract concern with cosmic structure and law-governed interrelationships? It could be argued that Jesus used all these images in his teaching (cf. John 10:1-30; Luke 15:11-32; Matt 6:25-33). How are their various implications, which are clearly quite different, to be assessed and applied to God and our human response to God?

---

[23] Ibid. 406.

The classic readings of the Jesus story have a specific answer. "God's love was revealed among us in this way: God sent his only Son into the world so that we might live through him" (1 John 4:9; cf. John 3:16). The divine intention (to give life) and divine action (sending the Son) through which God's love is revealed are manifest in the being and action—that is, in the *identity* of Jesus.[24] The love of God is defined by a particular kind of togetherness of God with Jesus. All other images of love find their determinate meaning here. Hans Frei has argued cogently that *who* Jesus is is established most realistically in the gospel story in the dramatic transition from cross to resurrection. As nowhere else, at this juncture the "one and unsubstitutable individual" we recognize as Jesus defines himself in the story.

> In the story up to his death it was right and proper to say of Jesus that his identity was embodied in the activity of his passion. . . . Here he was most of all himself. He *was* this transpiring of circumstances in action. It is equally right to say of his resurrection that here his identity is most fully *manifest*. In the resurrection he is most sharply revealed and attested not as a mythological figure but as the human Jesus.[25]

So strong is this literary link that Frei is forced to a kind of Anselmian logic in his interpretation of the narrative. In terms of the story, to speak of a non-resurrected Jesus is simply not to speak of Jesus at all. It is like speaking of a non-neurotic Hamlet or a pacifist Hitler. Jesus' identity as *narrated* is such that to be himself *is* to be alive. To conceive Jesus as simply dead is not to conceive *him* at all.[26] Hence the Johannine logic, "I am the resurrection and the life" (John 11:25).

Moreover, we have to ask what resurrection means. It is not merely a happy ending to an otherwise terrible story, an ending that leaves the identities of the major protagonists—God and Jesus—basically unaffected. The resurrection lays claim to being the manifestation of a *unique* togetherness of God with *this* human being. The relationship that exists or might exist between God and Jesus if Jesus is unresurrected is radically different in kind from that which *must* exist between God and Jesus if Jesus is resurrected. The idea of resurrection is an affront to post-Enlightenment minds in part because it can *only* be understood as an act of God. What is revealed in the resurrection is not the way Jesus is related to ultimate Reality (God) but the way ultimate Reality (God) is related to

[24] See n. 2 above.

[25] Frei, *Theology and Narrative* 76.

[26] Ibid. 85. Note Frei's qualification (p. 83): "This does not mean that his resurrection *is* conceivable, any more than saying that God is that than which a greater cannot be conceived means that he *is* the greatest conceivable, or than saying that God cannot be conceived as not existing means that his existence *can* be conceived."

Jesus. Without God to raise him Jesus would be, as Macquarrie's austere ending has it, simply dead. But *if* he is raised it is revealed that Jesus receives his being totally and completely from God. This is his identity *as* the revealer of God. The oldest christological tradition sees the resurrection of the crucified Jesus as a disclosure of Jesus' divine sonship. It is the event in which Jesus is "defined" as the Son of God, Lord, and Christ (Rom 1:4; 10:9; Acts 2:36).[27] In short, the togetherness of God and Jesus resurrected is a togetherness of the divine reality in unity with this historical figure. The revelation *of* Jesus is identical with the revelation that *is* Jesus. "This is not the belief that God *tells* humans what God is like or what the Divine purposes or laws are. It is not even that God *shows* what the Divine nature is like, as if there were one thing which somehow modelled another. It is rather that God makes the Divine reality itself present in a particular historical form."[28]

If this is true at the level of narrative analysis—and the burden of proof is on those who argue otherwise—Macquarrie's claim that Jesus unresurrected is the revealer of God is highly questionable, for *that* Jesus simply isn't the Jesus of the story at all. The togetherness of God with Jesus dead is radically different from the togetherness of God with Jesus raised. Of course Macquarrie can reply, as he does, by saying in effect, "so much the worse for the story." It is a matter of real, not narrated events, of history, not story. This brings us back to the question of how closely the narrative tells what "really happened." As I said previously, that aspect of the debate is beyond the scope of this investigation.[29] The point at issue here is simply that the *narrative* claim that Jesus was raised by God is not *theologically* neutral. It matters in how we understand the identity of the revealer and his relationship to the God he reveals.

It matters also in understanding what the revealer *does*. According to the story the fundamental task of Jesus as revealer of God is to undertake a work of healing or salvation on our behalf, a work that comes to its climax in his death on the cross. This is variously expressed. According to Mark "the Son of Man came not to be served but to serve, and to give his life a ransom *for* many" (Mark 10:45). Matthew's Jesus speaks of his impending passion as "my blood of the covenant, which is poured out *for* many for the forgiveness of sins" (Matt 26:28). Paul argues that in the death of Jesus we have all undergone death: "we are convinced that one

---

[27] Cf. Jüngel, *Theological Essays II*, 113.

[28] Ward, *Religion and Revelation*, 193.

[29] On the question of narrative, history, and theology in relation to the resurrection witness see, for example, Wolfhart Pannenberg, *Jesus—God and Man*, translated by Lewis L. Wilkins and Duane A. Priebe (London: S.C.M. Press, 1968) 53–114; *Systematic Theology*, translated by Geoffrey W. Bromiley (Grand Rapids: Eerdmans, 1994) 2:343–362; Paul Avis, ed., *The Resurrection of Jesus Christ* (London: Darton, Longman

has died *for* all; therefore all have died" (2 Cor 5:14). The cross is interpreted as a radical identification with our human situation of need. Jesus
participates in the sin that distorts our humanity and death that destroys
it. By this identification and participation he is said to bring healing *for* us
that we cannot bring for ourselves. But a question refuses to be silenced:
In the final analysis is the redeemer himself redeemed? If he is not, how
is his failure to be redeemed to avail as health and salvation for us?[30]

It is clear how Macquarrie means to answer this in the context of his
austere ending.

> If the highest virtue is the kind of love which the New Testament attributes
> to Jesus, then it seems to me that his victory over evil was already won in
> the agonizing hours before his death, and that it would remain decisive
> even if there were no subsequent events of resurrection and ascension.[31]

The "victory" of Jesus in these circumstances can only mean his
courageous defiance of evil to the bitter end. Presumably the giving of his
life so utterly to the cause of love is itself the thing of decisive saving value
for us. Since there is no subsequent event beyond death, language about
resurrection can only be understood as a symbolic way of speaking about
the significance of the cross. Bultmann's famous sentence, "faith in resurrection is really the same thing as faith in the saving efficacy of the
cross," meets with Macquarrie's approval.[32] But how is the cross effica-
cious? As far as I can see the answer must be in terms of moral and religious influence. In his life and death Jesus provides the model for us to
follow. Where this differs from the godless Christ of Jean Paul's poem is
that Macquarrie's Jesus relies on the love of God to reach his death-
crowned victory. God's will is that love should resist hatred in this world
even if it is defeated in the process. The unbowed struggle *is* the victory.
In face of this great demonstration we can take heart and try to do the
same. But the "for us" of Jesus' death is definitely the "for us" of exemplary behavior, not the "for us" that amounts to the creation of a "new
and living way" (Heb 10:20) whereby we are enabled to do and be what
previously we were not able to do or be.

I have no wish to challenge the idea that Jesus' struggle against evil
is of great, and maybe unique exemplary value. But again it is a question
of whether that is all, or even the most important thing to be said of it.

& Todd, 1993) *passim*; Thorwald Lorenzen, *Resurrection and Discipleship: Interpretive Models, Biblical Reflections, Theological Consequences* (Maryknoll, N.Y.: Orbis,
1995) Part II, 115–190.

[30] See Frei, *Theology and Narrative* 58–59.

[31] Macquarrie, *Jesus Christ in Modern Thought* 412.

[32] Ibid. 413. The original comes from Hans-Werner Bartsch, ed., *Kerygma and
Myth* (London: S.P.C.K., 1957) 41.

In terms of the story, Jesus on the cross is placed in solidarity with us in a position of godlessness. And yet by the grace of God he is brought through death and evil in the power of the resurrection. Obviously resurrection is *not* an example we can be called upon to emulate. Resurrection is the work of God or it is nothing. But *if* it is given by God in the case of Jesus it cannot but be seen as the central feature of the revealer's achievement and of the benefits he thereby bestows upon humanity. "The chief article and foundation of the gospel," according to Luther, "is that before you take Christ as an example, you accept and recognize him as a gift, as a present that God has given you and that is your own."[33] The "for us" of the narrative is the "for us" of a gift, an action that effectively changes the possibilities we confront in our human lives. A christology that interprets the achievement of Jesus as exemplary only reduces the significance of his role to that of hero or saint. His sacrifice might appeal to our moral endeavor, but it can hardly be regarded as a "victory" over the desperate human circumstances we face, especially the finality of death. A christology of example can make no sense of the affirmation: "I am the resurrection and the life. Those who believe in me, even though they die, will live" (John 11:25).

It may be that exemplary christology is all that is possible in a post-Enlightenment world. But if so, Macquarrie's austere ending faces us with a radically revised account of the achievement of Jesus on our behalf. It may still make sense to say that "God is revealed in Jesus Christ." But the practical consequences that flow from that affirmation are hard to distinguish from the ones implicit in the reading given by Jean Paul Richter's "dead Christ."

If the identity and achievement of the revealer are radically affected by reading the story of Jesus with "the bottom line under the cross," the same is true of the substance of the revelation given. The fundamental theological question: Who is God? is answered by Macquarrie in terms of love. God is love. And Macquarrie is content to let the story of Jesus' life and destiny determine the kind of love intended. But a great deal hangs on what his destiny actually is. The love of God—and hence, if Macquarrie is right, the *being* of God—revealed in the event of a story that concludes with Jesus simply dead is different, not merely in degree but also in kind, from the love, and hence the being of God, revealed in a story of Jesus truly raised. In other words, the nature of God and not simply the meaning of the cross is implicated in resurrection language.

In word and action Jesus proclaims that God, the final reality with which we have to do in life and death, is trustworthy and loving, and so deserving our total commitment. "Therefore I tell you, do not worry

---

[33] Quoted by Jüngel, *Theological Essays II*, 170.

about your life . . . . Look at the birds of the air; they neither sow nor reap nor gather into barns, and yet your heavenly Father feeds them. Are you not of more value than they?" (Matt 6:25-26). But what is revealed about this "Father" if the human life in which divinity supposedly manifests its love with unprecedented nearness ends in rejection, futility, and a sense of utter godforsakenness? If this is the end how can it reveal anything but that love in this universe is finally mocked? If divine love exists, as Macquarrie insists, and if this is its true destiny in the world, what conclusion can we honestly draw except that this love is an order of magnitude weaker than the forces of darkness and hatred arrayed against it? The God revealed in the cross is a God who suffers a father's loss of a child, just as Mary at the foot of the cross suffers a mother's loss. Both loves are real—and both impotent. Evil has the victory, though the love of "father," mother, and child has each suffered defiantly to the end.

The case is quite different if the "bottom line" in Jesus' life is not the cross but the resurrection. Only if resurrection is actual can "the life of a crucified man . . . show, not just that self-sacrifice has a certain tragic, useless nobility, but that Being itself is to be trusted, since death, however cruel, is not the end."[34] God did not abandon Jesus on the cross or even "suffer silently alongside" as Mary did.[35] The resurrection reveals the unique and inseparable togetherness of God and Jesus. In turn this means that the cross is not something God *observes* but something God *does* and *undergoes*. God's togetherness with Jesus in not broken by death. What is revealed by his death is that God takes suffering, tragedy, and death itself into the heart of the divine life. All that alienates from God, hatred, sin, violence, death—godlessness itself—is shown to be a moment endured *within* the being of God and not somehow "far from it." What is manifest as absolute negation, the triumph of death over life, is transformed. The negation is itself negated, the annihilating power annihilated, releasing thereby the possibility of new life in the world. The story refers to this new possibility as "the power of the Holy Spirit." All this is the *being* of God. This is who God *is*. God takes the godlessness of the world and unites it to divinity in the death of Christ, without self-contradiction. The essence of God revealed in Christ resurrected is therefore that God endures the negation of life and love without contradicting God's self as love or losing God's self as life. In so doing God is revealed to be the one "who gives life to the dead and calls into existence the things that do not exist" (Rom 4:17).

[34] Ward, *Religion and Revelation* 252.

[35] Cf. the remark of Peter C. Hodgson: The cross "reminds us that God will not rescue us from history or provide miraculous victories. Rather God suffers silently alongside us, so silently that we may not know that God is there." *Winds of the Spirit: A Constructive Christian Theology* (London: S.C.M. Press, 1994) 264.

A doctrine of the Trinity lurks in such sentences about God. For God to be God as the indestructible ground and source of all being, and for God to be God in the place of destruction, that is, in the godlessness of evil death, and for God to be God in the victory of life over death—then God must be God in a complex way, not as an undifferentiated unity beyond change and suffering. As creative ground of the world God also enters the world at a particular point to draw it back toward the deathless (because divine) love that is both its origin and its goal. This is a unique kind of love. It cannot be defined without the narrative assumptions of incarnation (God was in Christ) and cross (God underwent death in Christ) and resurrection (God's indestructible life re-presented in the Spirit of Christ risen).

Can God be God if Jesus is dead? Our answer has been yes and no. If God is not together with Jesus in any way significantly different from God's togetherness with others, then God can be God and Jesus simply dead. In such circumstances God can still be love. But it will be love understood on the model of the suffering love of Mary, a love that stands alongside and endures the sight of the cross but ultimately is silent and submissive and impotent. This, however, is not the God of the "great distinctive Christian affirmations." Those affirmations see God uniquely present in the history of Jesus. The suffering of Jesus can therefore be called the suffering of God in a direct and not merely an empathetic way. In that case the cross is not simply a shining example of self-sacrificing resistance to evil that we are called to emulate. It is God's deliberate entanglement with the realm of godlessness. And the outcome is resurrection, where the victory won means death itself is defeated. God cannot be God in *this* sense if Jesus is dead.

Christian identity, we said at the outset, is bound up with telling the story of the togetherness of God and Jesus. But everything hangs on the way this togetherness is understood. If God is dead, Christian identity is a courageous following of the way of Jesus, aware that the cross is a tragic revelation of the cosmic insignificance of love. But since it is nothingness that awaits us, let us, like Jesus, "so act that it shall not be a just fate." If Jesus is dead, then Christian identity is a courageous commitment to the way of Jesus, knowing that the cross is the call to resist lovelessness to the end in the strength of a divine love that suffers alongside us and, beyond our (individual) death, remains to sustain the struggles of future generations. This is the victory of God over evil that Jesus "won in the agonizing hours before his death." If Jesus is resurrected, then Christian identity is a courageous participation in the way of Jesus, interpreting the cross as the love of God that undergoes with us the violence of death, but through it all maintains the divinity of God, and rises anew to make way for our participation in a deathless life. Jesus Christ is "the resurrection and the life."

Part III

Life and Christ

7

Mrs. Vicar

I have argued that Christian identity is tied up with interpreting the story of Jesus. But not just any interpretation will do. Christian faith interprets Jesus of Nazareth as the Christ of God. In other words, it sees in Jesus the one in whom God's grace and truth are made concretely present in history and accessible "for us." Christology—that is, the study of the "Christ-character" of Jesus—tries to express in the clearest way what is entailed in the conviction that Jesus is of central importance for the right ordering of the complex relationship that human beings have with God, the final mystery that grounds and encompasses their lives.[1] The previous chapter focused mainly on the kind of "togetherness" that holds between God and Jesus, if this faith conviction is valid. Now I want to turn to the other side of the story. Instead of concentrating on God's relationship with Jesus Christ, I want to explore God's relationship to *us*, as that relationship is shaped and mediated through the figure of Jesus as the Christ. What follows, therefore, is mainly concerned with *soteriology*, that is, the affirmation that God's salvation, or healing grace, is given to the world in Christ. What difference does this claim actually make in human affairs?

This is a large question, or nest of questions. I can only touch on a few aspects of it. But I intend those aspects to be thoroughly practical, to do with the way our ordinary lives are lived. The heart of this section is a real-life drama. It is the story of Susan, the vicar's wife, as told in Alan Bennett's television drama, *Bed Among the Lentils*. Susan is not real in the sense of being a living person. She is the creation of Bennett's imagination. But she is real in the sense that her story could be the story of any number of people, women and men, in the Church today. Susan struggles to make sense of what goes on in the Church. But she feels more hurt

---

[1] In this study I intend to confine myself to the dynamics of Christian faith. The place of Jesus Christ in relation to other religious traditions is a different, though related, question that I cannot go into here.

than helped by its message of salvation in Christ. Why? I want to analyze the kind of theology, especially the view of Christ, that operates in Susan's life. Then, in the three chapters that follow, I will argue that a better, more robust christology is needed if anything like "salvation" is to be experienced in Susan's circumstances. But before introducing the story in detail let me make a brief theoretical digression.

Two Types of Christology

In a famous letter to Eberhard Bethge, written in 1944 from his prison cell on death row, Dietrich Bonhoeffer said: "What is bothering me incessantly is the question what Christianity really is, or indeed who Christ really is, for us today."[2] Ambiguity haunts Bonhoeffer's use of the word "really." On the one hand we could take it *descriptively*. Then the question who Christ really is for us today means: What kind of place does Jesus Christ actually occupy in our day-to-day experience? What sort of impact does he have in our thoughts and feelings? What difference, if any, does that name, and the one who bears it, make to the way we act in or interpret the world? I will call this *functional* christology. Who Christ really is in *this* sense for, say, a modern secularist, might be little more than a swear word for stressful occasions, or perhaps a hazy figure of ancient times referred to in the Bible and heard of in church. This is who Christ really is to such a person in the functional sense. It is not very much. Certainly it is not what the Council of Chalcedon or the Gospel of John meant in referring to Jesus as the Christ of God. But functional christologies are vitally important. They are the visions of Christ that people actually live by—or live without. The images and meanings of Christ that take root in consciousness and emotion shape the Christian existence, which means the human existence, of believers. They also strongly influence what those who do not share the faith see and feel about Christ, God, and the Church. The real Christ, so understood, is the actual Christ that men and women relate to, whether centrally or marginally. The data to be investigated by functional christology are the living experiences of people, the images, words, attitudes, and outlooks they work with, often unconsciously, in reference to religion in general and Jesus in particular.

The other sense of the word "really" is normative rather than descriptive. Its reference is ontological not functional. Who Christ "really" is in this case means who he is in his own being: Not Christ as he is imagined by the secularist with irreverent indifference, nor Christ as he is pictured by the pietist with warm sentimentality, nor Christ as he is decoded

---

[2] Dietrich Bonhoeffer, *Letters and Papers from Prison* (London: S.C.M. Press, 1971) 279.

by the philosopher as the charismatic moralist, not any of these or a thousand other views that operate in the world and the Church. The normative Christ is Christ as he is in God's determination, so to speak. Who is *this* Christ for us? That is the other side of Bonhoeffer's question. Its concern is *revelation*—the Word *God* speaks in Christ. One of the fundamental tasks of theology is to attend carefully to the Word of God in this sense. *Normative* christology (as I will call it) flows from this attention and stands in critical tension with all functional views of Christ. The poor and often distorted images of Christ that empirically operate in the Church and the world need to be confronted with the Christ of revelation in whom the reality of God is truly embodied.

This is too simple a picture, of course. I have set the problem up as if the functional Christ (my working image of Christ) and the normative Christ (God's revelation in Christ) are as easily distinguishable as, say, the mountain is distinguishable from its shimmering reflection in a lake. Just as we can check, and if need be correct, the image in the lake by looking up at the real mountain, so, the argument seems to be, the functional Christ can be critically checked and corrected by reference to the normative Christ. If only the task were so easy! Unfortunately there is no "reality without quotation marks" in theology. All our data are theory-laden.[3] The only way in which we can receive Christ at all is through the images, impressions, feelings, and language that make it possible for us to grasp him. From the beginning these words and images have been notoriously slippery. We can see the conflict well under way in the New Testament itself. The gospel story is already a debate about the "real" Jesus Christ. In Pilate's view Jesus "called" the Christ is a political troublemaker, scarcely more than a failed "king of the Jews" (Mark 15). For the religious establishment Jesus is no Christ at all but a dangerous religious reformer preaching false, if not blasphemous doctrine (Luke 22:66-71). Peter at one time seems to have regarded Jesus as a muddle-headed messiah, hell-bent on a cross he needn't have (Mark 8:27-33). Matthew understood Jesus as a kind of second Moses bearing a renewed Torah (Matt 5:17-48). In the Gospel of John, Christ is the eternal Logos, the Word of God made flesh in the man Jesus (John 1:14). And so on.

No matter how far we go back in history, we never get to a place where the reception of Jesus as the Christ is not also an interpretation of Jesus as the Christ. The ideal of an uninterpreted Christ, the real Christ

---

[3] Cf. David Tracy's description of positivism as a dream of discovering "a reality without quotation marks: a realm of pure data and facts." We simply have to accept, he argues, "the fact that 'fact' means not an uninterpreted 'already-out-there-now real,' but a verified possibility," and "that all data are theory laden and all inquiry is interested." *Plurality and Ambiguity: Hermeneutics, Religion, Hope* (San Francisco: Harper & Row, 1987) 47–48.

in the naked revelational sense, is just that: an ideal. It is unrealizable and so unreal. Chalcedon's dream of the theological Christ, truly God/truly human, doesn't give it. It is an abstraction that seems to ignore the life of flesh and blood of the man from Nazareth. Luther's dream of the biblical Christ doesn't give it. Contemporary exegesis has demonstrated a diversity of views in the New Testament itself. The nineteenth century's portrait of a historical Jesus stripped bare of all dogmatic encrustation doesn't give it. As the long quest for the Jesus of history demonstrates, it is impossible to get behind the texts to Jesus as he actually was, independent of what his witnesses thought about him. And anyway, as Kierkegaard argued, even if we knew every last detail of Jesus' daily behavior it wouldn't give what faith requires, which is not "objective" detail at all, but the presence of the new creation of God.[4] Schleiermacher's view of the inward Christ of the heart doesn't give it. Of all the Christs that present themselves for consideration, the inward Christ is perhaps most vulnerable to distortion, susceptible of being confused with the unconscious desires of individuals and groups.

There is no easy way out of the dilemma set by Bonhoeffer. The real Christ is both the functional Christ of our actual living and the normative Christ of God's revelation in human history. These two are always in tension with each other. Christologies that try to avoid the tension are doomed and dangerous: doomed because the struggle of normative and functional christology is unavoidable; dangerous because if we think we can avoid it we are likely to wind up affirming solutions that are unreal. The two extremes, objectivism and subjectivism, are equally discredited. The objectivists claim to possess the true image of Christ, Christ as he really is in himself, "without quotation marks." They claim to know Christ with the mind of God. Of such stuff religious fundamentalism and even idolatry is made. The subjectivists despair of knowing the "really real" and opt for the view that seems most appealing. Of this stuff the corruption of faith is made. If Christ is merely what appeals to me or my group, then I am left with the limits of my own broken humanity as the boundaries of the possible. I meet myself (largely) in this Christ and not the new creation of God. Those who are familiar with the history of modern theology will recognize here the echoes of the debate that continues between the disciples of Barth and Schleiermacher.

The real situation is more complex. Christology is always in a process of what might be called "transitional dialogue." By this I mean the kind of thinking that aims not to reach a solution that is absolutely correct,

---

[4] Søren Kierkegaard, *Philosophical Fragments or A Fragment of Philosophy*, translated by David F. Swenson and Howard V. Hong (Princeton: Princeton University Press, 1962) 68–88, especially 74–75.

timeless, and universal—the mind of God. Rather, it seeks through critical conversation to move from a given comprehension of Christ, acknowledged as partial and fallible, to a new comprehension judged superior *relative* to the former position, at least in some respects. In other words, christology always has to do with comparative perspectives. We debate our various views of Christ drawing on all the factors that have been found useful in the history of worship and theology—Bible, tradition, creed, history, reason, experience, practice, and prayer. In the process of discussion we find that our sense of things has shifted. We become convinced that a view we once held is really no longer satisfactory because it neglects or distorts some aspect of traditional meaning, or it fails to take account of emerging problems in contemporary experience, or it appears to be significantly undermined by criticism from an alterative point of view. We struggle for a new interpretation that takes account of the difficulty. And we sense that the new position, if we find it, is superior to the old, because we have lived through the transition from one to the other, and so can judge between them.

To use the phrase of Charles Taylor, the transition is an "error-reducing one." It leads to a deeper, less flawed apprehension of the truth we are seeking. Such transitional thinking is committed to what Taylor calls the BA, or "best account," principle.[5] Theology is always groping toward a more satisfactory statement—a better account in a given situation—of the meaning of revelation. We are not left in absolute relativism where every functional view of Christ is deemed as good (or bad) as every other. But neither do we claim possession of final truth, the reality of Christ as God is embodied in him. "Relativism of authority does not establish the authority of relativism: it opens reason to new claimants."[6] The Christ of revelation remains a critical goal toward which our functional christologies, the christologies we actually live by, move through dialogue, discussion, and the joy and pain of living. The Church as a whole in its liturgy, prayer, and praxis, not merely in its specific theological endeavors, is involved in such movement. It trusts that the Spirit of God will be its guide and guard in the process.

The christology of transitional dialogue can be seen in the great controversies of the Church. The question of whether to understand Jesus Christ in incarnational terms, as the Word made flesh, the embodiment of Divinity in a particular human being, is a time-honored case in point. The issues at stake are central to the christological debates of the ancient Church, as illustrated in the classic struggle between Athanasius

---

[5] See Charles Taylor, *Sources of the Self: The Making of the Modern Identity* (Cambridge, Mass.: Harvard University Press, 1989) 71–74.

[6] Gillian Rose, *Love's Work* (London: Chatto & Windus, 1995) 129–130.

(c. 296–373) and Arius (c. 250–c. 336).[7] The Arians argued that a realistic understanding of God as the absolutely transcendent source of all created being makes an incarnational christology impossible. How can it sensibly be claimed that the uncreated source of all creation (God) is now a part of that creation (the man Jesus), a claim that incarnational views of Christ must make? How is infinitude to be encompassed by finitude? How can eternal self-sufficiency be linked with temporal contingency? Worst of all, how can the immortal be embroiled in the crisis of mortality? How can God and the cross be thought together? For Arius and his followers these questions were basically rhetorical. Merely to ask is already to answer them. There can be no possibility of the mingling of the "uncreated" with the "created." God cannot actually be *in* Christ. Therefore the eminence of Christ must be honored by interpreting him as the first-born of God's creation, the greatest and best of all that is made, infinitely superior to us, but firmly on *this* side of the creator/creature divide. It is a good argument. We can see its logic and feel its persuasive force. So strong is the case that Arian christology remains to this day a powerful *functional* reality in the Church.

Athanasius contested the point vigorously. *If* salvation comes from God alone; *if* we human beings are unable to save ourselves, that is, overcome the sinful distortion that mars our personal and social existence, and conquer the suffering and death that consumes us all; and *if* salvation that can overcome these threats is found in Jesus Christ, *then*, said Athanasius, the only solution to the question of the Christ is that he must be one with, indeed the very expression of, the reality and power of God.

> . . . no one else could bring what was corrupted to incorruptibility, except the Saviour himself, who also created the universe in the beginning from nothing; nor could any other recreate men in the image [of God], save the image of the Father; nor could another raise up what was mortal as immortal, save our Lord Jesus Christ, who is life itself; nor could another

---

[7] What is known of Arius is based largely on scraps of information about him handed on mainly by his opponents, of whom Athanasius was the chief. The attempt to reconstruct a clear picture of his views is therefore somewhat speculative and open to dispute. I do not intend to enter into the detailed historical debates. It is the basic outline of the controversy over incarnation that I wish to use in the chapters that follow. For detailed discussions see R. P. C. Hanson, *The Search for the Christian Doctrine of God: The Arian Controversy 318–381* (Edinburgh: T & T Clark, 1988); Jaroslav Pelikan, *The Christian Tradition: A History of the Development of Doctrine*, Vol. I, *The Emergence of the Catholic Tradition (100–600)* (Chicago: University of Chicago Press, 1971) 193–205; Robert C. Gregg, ed., *Arianism: Historical and Theological Reassessments* (Cambridge, Mass.: Philadelphia Patristic Foundation, 1985); Rowan Williams, *Arius: Heresy and Tradition* (London: Darton, Longman & Todd, 1987).

teach about the Father and overthrow the cult of idols, save the Word who orders the universe, and who alone is the only-begotten Son of the Father.[8]

God is in Christ. Without this togetherness there is no God-grace in Christ but only the same human-grace we all already share by virtue of our common humanity, but that we all already know, through suffering and death, is without ultimate redeeming power. A human Christ, no matter how great, cannot be the new creation we need. History is not and cannot be its own redeemer.

On the other hand, the God-grace that is in Christ must be present and powerful *in* our human realm, because if not it is not us, not our humanity, that is touched and transformed by that grace.

> In the beginning, when nothing existed at all, only a nod and an act of will were necessary for the creation of the universe. But when man had been made and the necessity arose to heal, not the non-existent, but what had come into being, it followed that the healer and Savior had to come among those who had already been created to cure what existed. Therefore he became a man and used the body as a human instrument. . . . For it was not the non-existent that needed salvation so that a command alone would suffice, but man, who had already been made, was corrupted and perishing.[9]

For these reasons, Athanasius argued, Arius' view that he does Christ an honor by making him infinitely superior to us only undermines further the possibility of real salvation in him. God comes to us in Christ. It must be God or no salvation. But it must be us, also, or no salvation. The presence of God is right in our history, not somehow separated from it.[10]

Athanasius consistently maintained that the Arians were mistaken in their basic approach to theology. They assumed a concept of God from the outset without taking into account the mystery of the incarnation and the historical event of salvation accomplished through it. They then tried to interpret Christ in terms of this assumed doctrine of God. But the appropriate operation of Christian theology is the other way around. God alone is able to say what God may do or be. On what grounds can it be maintained that God *cannot* become a part of, or one with, God's creation? Where does such unchallengeable theological knowledge come from? It comes, in fact, from a particular view of God as immaterial, unchangeable, and beyond suffering: in short, a Greek view of God. But

---

[8] *De Incarnatione* 20, edited and translated by Robert W. Thomson (Oxford: The Clarendon Press, 1971) 183.

[9] *De Incarnatione* 44, p. 245.

[10] "The ultimate outcome of the Arian system was a Christ suspended between man and God, identical with neither but related to both; God was interpreted deistically, man moralistically, and Christ mythologically." Pelikan, *The Christian Tradition: A History of the Development of Doctrine* 1:198.

what if the truth of God is not exhausted by such a description? What if God declares that God will become human, will enter creation, and will undertake a recuperation of history from within its own borders and bounds? If God were to engage in such an undertaking, are human beings in a position to "correct" it because they presume to know better? The Christian revelation proclaims precisely this: God has made divinity manifest in the man Jesus. "Whoever has seen me has seen the Father" (John 14:9). Incarnation is possible for God because incarnation is real for God. Reality determines possibility in this instance, not possibility reality. Such is the essence of Christianity according to Athanasius.[11]

The clash between Athanasius and the Arians in the fourth century is the *locus classicus* of the debate. But variations on the theme can be found in different guises in, to take a random selection, the epistle to the Hebrews, Anselm's interpretation of atonement, Karl Barth's critique of liberal Protestantism, John Hick's restatement of christology without "the myth of God incarnate," and Daphne Hampson's post-christian feminism.[12] The previous chapter is a minor contribution to the same dialogue. It tried to argue the case that incarnation is a "better account" of the figure of Jesus than the modern and postmodern alternatives represented by Jean Paul Richter and John Macquarrie.

There is no magical adjudication between the antagonists in these dialogues. Each person has to argue the case as best he or she can within the limits of language, tradition, experience, and the rest. The Church on the whole, at least since the time of Chalcedon in 451 C.E., has judged the weight of truth to lie with Athanasian incarnational (Christ the God-man) rather than Arian inspirational (Christ the inspired prophet) positions. For all that Arius seemed the more rational, Athanasius captured the sense, the "idiom" or interior rule, of Christianity and the Christ it worshiped more fully and profoundly.[13] Salvation in Christ, the ancients agreed, depends upon the unity of Christ and God. As Kenneth Leech puts it: "The belief that the Word of God, the eternal self-manifestation of the Creator of the universe, took to himself human nature is so basic to orthodox Christian-

---

[11] Cf. "Athanasius of Alexandria and the Foundation of Traditional Christology" in Charles Kannengiesser, ed., *Arius and Athanasius: Two Alexandrian Theologians* (Hampshire: Variorum, 1991) VI, 103–113, especially VI, 112.

[12] Anselm, *Why God Became Man and The Virgin Conception and Original Sin,* translated by Joseph M. Colleran (New York: Magi Books, 1969); Karl Barth, *Church Dogmatics* I, 2, translated by G. T. Thomson and Harold Knight (Edinburgh: T & T Clark, 1956) 122–202; John Hick, ed., *The Myth of God Incarnate* (London: S.C.M. Press, 1977), and *The Metaphor of God Incarnate* (London: S.C.M. Press, 1993); Daphne Hampson, *Theology and Feminism* (Oxford: Basil Blackwell, 1990).

[13] Cf. George A. Lindbeck, *The Nature of Doctrine: Religion and Theology in a Postliberal Age* (Philadelphia: Westminster, 1984) 79–84.

ity that without it the entire edifice crumbles and falls."[14] The belief that God is love; the belief that God is in essence a dynamic energy of *eros/agape* that overflows the boundaries of isolated divinity in reaching out to the world, first in the act of creating and sustaining it and then, more specifically, in the shaping of human history by the power of the divine Spirit manifest in prophecy, community-building, and the struggle for justice; the belief that this outgoing personal energy, which St. John calls the Word *(logos)*, has taken up residence in our place, in flesh of our flesh and bone of our bone, and has done this without reserve, without special pleading or special protection; the belief that this God-love lived our human life and died our human death in Jesus of Nazareth is the central and definitive mark of orthodox Christian truth. Incarnational theology, the Logos one with Christ and Christ one with us, became the church's BA—best account—position. It has remained so in the mainstream tradition until modern times. Without it Christianity, in the historical sense of the mainline classical view of Christ, crumbles and falls.

This does not mean that different sorts of christology did not flourish alongside the classic view. They did and still do. The New Testament itself presents a variety of "christological permissions."[15] As we have noted in previous chapters, since the Enlightenment incarnational christology has been under heavy challenge. We seem to be in a period when significant groups within the Church feel that the BA solution is no longer with Athanasius and consequently, they argue, both creed and worship in the Church need to be significantly changed. If the classic view were to "crumble and fall" it would not necessarily mean that Christianity itself would lose viability. New and different accounts are emerging that might well prove more creative in the postmodern world. As Julie Hopkins, John Hick, and others have argued, in a situation of increasing religious pluralism it is vital to allow for "a plurality of saving human responses to the ultimate divine Reality."[16] This is well said and I have no wish to dissent from it. But I want to pursue the classic line, for this reason: There are strong functional views of Christ alive and well in the contemporary Church that are in fact variations on Arian-like themes. Bennett's Susan, as we shall see, is an example. I want to challenge these views since, in my opinion, they are doing us no good. Incarnational christology is one powerful counterattack. It is not the only one. But it is still worth exploring. I also have a personal reason for adopting this approach. An incarnational understanding of Christ has been central to the tradition in

[14] Kenneth Leech, *True God: An exploration in spiritual theology* (London: Sheldon, 1985) 236.

[15] I think the phrase was coined by Dietrich Ritschl.

[16] Julie Hopkins, *Towards a Feminist Christology* (London: S.P.C.K., 1995) 24; cf. John Hick, *A Philosophy of Religious Pluralism* (London: Macmillan, 1985) 28–45.

which my own faith took shape. I am keen to explore the extent to which it has continuing relevance to me, and perhaps not to me only. Whether I can make a convincing case remains to be seen.

Bed Among the Lentils

Enough theory. I want now to examine a specific example of functional christology, the way one person perceives "who Christ is for us today." Alan Bennett is again the conversation partner, this time not in the role of comedian but of playwright. In 1987 BBC television presented six monologues written by Bennett under the general title *Talking Heads*.[17] They were shown on several occasions on public television in the early nineties. In each program a single speaker is alone with the camera and in fifty minutes tells the story of his or her life. It is riveting drama, although nothing but "talk" happens on the screen. All the action is mediated through the narration itself.

As is true with most autobiographers, these "talking heads" don't tell the whole story. The events and characters that make up their lives are all seen and discussed solely from the point of view of the speaker. Perhaps it is misleading to use the term autobiography at all in this instance. It has connotations of formality and premeditation. Bennett intends his narrators to be artless. They talk as they would to an intimate friend, not as they would in a book. We overhear them relating tales "to the meaning of which they are not entirely privy" [7]. *Bed Among the Lentils* is the second in the series of monologues. The "talking head" in this instance is known simply as "Susan." She is a vicar's wife. C. of E., naturally. In the original series the part was played brilliantly by Maggie Smith. Bennett admits that much of the feeling for the Church and its theology evident in the play comes from his own childhood experiences. With disarming candor he notes: "The disaffection of Susan, the vicar's wife, I can trace to opening a hymn book in the chapel of Giggleswick School and finding in tiny, timid letters on the fly leaf, 'Get lost, Jesus'" [8].

At this point the best thing would be to stop and watch a video of the play. Next best would be to read the original script in its entirety. For those unable to do either I will briefly sketch the character of Susan and then go on to analyze the images of Christ that she lives with. In Susan— "Mrs. Vicar," as the bishop in the story calls her—Bennett has captured a truth about contemporary Christianity. It is not the whole truth. Some of it is caricature. But Susan is real. Her experience is there in the world and the Church. I want to look at that experience and ask: what is the

---

[17] They were subsequently published: Alan Bennett, *Talking Heads* (London: BBC Books, 1988), and have since run through many editions. Other page references to this work will be given in brackets in the text.

functional christology that Susan lives by? Who is the real Christ in the sense of the Christ she actually sees and knows? Later I want to challenge this functionalism with a more normative, in this case incarnational, reading of the Christ. But first an outline of her story.

Standing by the kitchen stove in the vicarage, Susan kicks off her *apologia pro vita sua* with the line: "Geoffrey's bad enough but I'm glad I wasn't married to Jesus" [30]. Given what we learn about Geoffrey in the course of the story, this is an ominous comparison. Geoffrey is vicar of "St. Michael and All Angels," a nondescript parish somewhere in the Diocese of Ripon. The vicar and his wife are a couple in their early middle age—forty-something. Susan is thin and nervous and self-doubting. She drinks too much. In fact, as the story unfolds we discover that, despite her best efforts to hide it, the whole parish knows she is an alcoholic. She is even reduced to filching communion wine from the vestry until Geoffrey, "white-faced . . . and practically in tears," discovers the loss while preparing to celebrate Holy Communion, and subsequently puts a lock on the cupboard door [37]. Discreet meetings are held in the parish to pray for her "problem." As far as Susan is concerned the marriage is empty. She bluntly avoids intimacy with her husband when at one point he awkwardly hints at it.

Geoffrey is ambitious. He is preoccupied with running the parish. This means attending to the demands of what Susan calls the "fan club"—those over-zealous church folk who think "they love God when they just love Geoffrey"—and trying to catch the eye of the bishop. Rumor has it he is "shopping around for a new Archdeacon" [38; 32]. Susan tries to fill the role of dutiful vicar's wife. But she is not much good at—and perhaps not much interested in—what is expected of her. She delivers the parish paper, attends services, visits the sick and organizes fetes. In a wonderfully funny sequence she (drunkenly) sets flowers in the church in company with Mrs. Shrubsole, Mrs. Belcher, and Miss Frobisher of the fan club. The whole enterprise turns into a debacle of decorating one upmanship. In the process of criticizing Mrs. Shrubsole's altar arrangement— pompously called "Forest Murmurs"—Susan loses her balance, falls down the steps of the sanctuary, and almost knocks herself out on the communion rail. "If you think squash is a competitive activity," she tells the camera as she relives the tale, "try flower arrangement" [34].

The deep questions of faith bother her. But she struggles to believe what Geoffrey preaches. And she wonders whether he actually believes much of it either. Perhaps God really is just a job like any other. "You've got to bring home the bacon somehow" [31]. But no discussion of the matter takes place. Religion is a man's game. It never crosses Geoffrey's mind (or the bishop's or anyone else's) to draw her out on serious questions of theology. It is simply taken for granted that, as the vicar's wife, she goes along with it all.

A dark secret slowly comes to light. In the course of her frequent visits to the Off License where she buys her wine, Susan strikes up a relationship with the proprietor, a young Asian man called Mr. Ramesh. To her own (and our) surprise she has a brief and passionate affair with him on a "bed of lentils" in the back of the shop. For the first time in a long time—perhaps ever—she feels noticed, appreciated, and even loved. Ramesh eventually persuades her to seek help with Alcoholics Anonymous. It takes Geoffrey "all of three weeks" to notice "that Mrs. Vicar is finally on the wagon." When he does, he immediately claims credit for the change, attributing it to the work of God "moving in his well-known mysterious way" [40]. Mr. Ramesh meanwhile sells the shop and moves away from the area, so Susan loses contact with him.

Both AA and the congregation work to restore her to the fold, though they really don't know the half of it. Geoffrey starts to tell her story around the diocese. He goes so far as to pretend that the "problem" belongs to an anonymous parishioner. Then, when he has them all well and truly taken in, he springs the surprise. "Friends, I want to tell you something. . . . That drunken flower-arranger was my wife" [40]. The bishop is suddenly interested. Here is a vicar who has "looked life in the face" and "come through with flying colors," someone who's "been there." Susan feels doubly trapped—by a Church that doesn't understand her struggle and an AA group that sees her as a case to be cured. She finishes her story bitterly. "I never liked going to one church so I end up going to two. Geoffrey would call it the wonderful mystery of God. I call it bad taste. And I wouldn't do it to a dog. But that's the thing nobody ever says about God . . . he has no taste at all" [41].

The Christological Question

The theory runs like this. Faith is about what it means to live a human life, especially what it means to live a human life in the face of the terrible possibility of *mis*-living it. Athanasius was right to put the argument in terms of salvation. The question of Christ is the question of the possibility and reality of salvation. Through the grace of God our broken existence, personally, socially, and ecologically is made whole. Christ comes as the divine response to the anguish of self-estrangement in our existence.

Susan knows all about the question and the anguish. Her life is anything but whole. She maintains throughout a sense of ironic, sometimes bitter humor, which is a mark of her unwillingness simply to capitulate to the life others demand of her. But there is scarcely anything that could be called happiness, much less joy in her lot. In the congregation she is more role than person. She feels forced to be a part of the religious ritual, but it seems false and unreal to her. "One of the unsolved mysteries of life, or the unsolved mysteries of my life, is why the vicar's wife is expected to go to church at all. A barrister's wife doesn't have to go to court, an actor's wife isn't at every performance, so why have I always got to be on parade?" [31]. Geoffrey uses her battle with alcoholism as an illustration in a sermon on "Prayers Answered" [40]. But he lays claim on her behalf to a reality of healing grace she knows full well is not hers, at least not in the way he represents it. Such work as she is given to do is trivial and boring—housewife at home, flower arranger at church. She recites the words of the wonderful prayer: "Almighty God unto whom all hearts be open, and from whom no secrets are hid, cleanse the thoughts of our hearts by the inspiration of thy holy spirit that we may perfectly love thee and worthily magnify thy glorious name." According to this theology love and glory are supposed to enter the human lot, borne on the wings of grace. But they don't for Susan. And she sits in her car in a rest area on the Ring Road on a Sunday afternoon, trying to avoid a loveless sexual encounter with Geoffrey, watching other people go by and "wondering what happened to our life" [31]. Meaninglessness, lovelessness, boredom, and living through others are how she experiences life.

She is not entirely without spunk. Cast down to be sure, but not quite destroyed. As I said, in her humor she mocks the situation and to that extent rises above it. When Geoffrey preaches on sex and marriage he concludes with the admonition that as "we put our money in the plate it is a symbol of everything in our lives we are offering to God and that includes our sex." Susan looks into the camera. "I could only find 10p," she says [31]. It would be going too far to say she seeks salvation in alcohol, but there is at least consolation. Inebriation dulls the pain. There is genuine courage, in fact a touch of defiance, in the sexual affair with the Hindu grocer, Mr. Ramesh. Susan knows full well the affair would be unacceptable on every count to her entire circle at home and church. But at least it makes her feel something—feel some*one*. She longs that her life might count, maybe not for something eternal, but at least count in the good memories of nice people she imagines coming away from her own funeral in a country church on a fine winter's afternoon saying, "Well, she was a wonderful woman" [33].

In theological terms the human longing Susan gives expression to in word and deed *is* the christological question. Is there a grace in history that can renew a life deeply hurt by the cruelty of fate and the guilt of failure? If so, where is that grace? Susan doesn't find it in the Christ of the Church she is a part of. The reverse is nearer the truth. The Christ she confronts sitting in the pew of Geoffrey's worship services is remote and oppressive. Although she knows the official line is that Christ is her only hope, the truth is that the Christ she meets there is a Christ she needs to be redeemed *from*, not a Christ she can be redeemed *by*.[18] Her functional Christ is at log-gerheads with the theological theory. She is forced to turn elsewhere for hope. Healing grace is not in Christ as she knows him. "Get lost, Jesus!"

Who is the Christ she knows? What is Susan's functional christology? It can be sketched quickly in four or five points. They are simple and easily recognizable in today's world. At the same time they paint a devastating picture. This Christ is wimpish, stern, unattractive, and ethereal. He is largely powerless to address any real questions of making and keeping Susan's life human. If this is "real" christology, we are in serious trouble.

Susan's Functional Christ

1. *The Immaterial Christ*

The functional Christ of Susan's world is an immaterial Christ. At first I was tempted to say "spiritualized" Christ. But that does injustice to the word "spiritual." If by "spirit" we refer to the unity of vitality *(dynamis)* and meaning *(logos)* in divine and human life, then it is far too important a term to concede to this kind of christology. It is better to speak of "etherealness," by which I mean the sort of being that is wraithlike, thin, and insubstantial. This ethereal Christ wafts somewhere above the blood and bone of real life, above the solid flesh of our humanity. The official doctrine is there. "Jesus was made man," says Geoffrey, "so he smiled and laughed and did everything else just like the rest of us." But it is mere words. And Susan knows it. "If Jesus *is* all man I just wish they'd put a bit more of it into the illustrations," she mutters, giving expression to a genuine piece of incarnational christology [37].

And it matters because matter matters.[19] The crucial point is sex. We are sexual beings in body and, as Freud taught us, also in soul. Sex is the great indicator of our materiality and our mortality. We cannot *be* without sex. Yet sex reminds us relentlessly that we are embodied beings. Our deepest spiritual experience, the experience of the love and passion of another person, is reached through physicality, and the extraordinary antics of the sexual act. This blend of the material and the spiritual—a meaning-filled vitality—is a fearful paradox of human existence. Moreover, sex is

---

[18] Cf. "Ah, that someone would redeem them from their Redeemer!" Friedrich Nietzsche, *Thus Spoke Zarathustra*, translated by R. J. Hollingdale (Harmondsworth: Penguin, 1969) 115.

[19] I have taken the phrase from Paul Collins, *God's Earth: Religion as if matter really mattered* (Melbourne: Dove, 1995). His whole discussion of Gnostic dualism and its impact on Christian tradition is relevant to this section: see ibid. 96–110. See also James B. Nelson, "On Doing Body Theology," *Theology and Sexuality* 2 (March 1995) 57: "Matter matters to God."

inseparable from death. From sex comes the new generation that will replace the one that, through sexuality, brought it to birth. Sex highlights the joy we have in our own uniqueness. This is *my* love, *my* ecstasy. At the same time it remorselessly informs us of our dispensability. The life of the race is the objective of sex. As individuals we become the disposable means to that impersonal end.[20]

Susan's Christ can't cope. He is above it all. Rather, he is *embarrassed* by it all. This Christ is sexless and against sex, at least in any full-blooded sense. He would rather not know it was there. Somehow it is not quite *nice*. As we noted at the outset, given what we know of Susan's marriage it is damning indeed that she opens her whole discussion of life with the line: "Geoffrey's bad enough but I'm glad I wasn't married to Jesus." Her image of sex and the Christian God is all too clear. "Look at me," she says at one point, "the hair, the flat chest, the wan smile, you'd think I was just cut out for God. And maybe I am" [31]. Who else would be interested? Be spiritual because you're no good sexually. And anyway spirituality is better than sexuality. God is without physical passion. Sexlessness therefore seems to Susan a measure of aptitude in relation to God. Of course, the *theory* doesn't say this. "Marriage gives the OK to sex," is the gist of one of Geoffrey's sermons. And "while it is far from being the be all and end all ['you can say that again,' says Susan, staring into the camera] sex is nevertheless the supreme joy of the married state and a symbol of the relationship between us and God" [30]. But it doesn't work out in practice. Repression, denial, judgment, and pretense are what she meets with in the Church. Heterosexual activity is scarcely deemed a fit subject to be mentioned. And as for other expressions of sexuality, the "shamefaced fumblings" Susan suspects "go on between Miss Budd and Miss Bantock," they are altogether beyond the pale [30].

To find herself as a woman, to discover something of the passion for life and human love within her, Susan has to leave the circle of the Church and its Christ. She turns to Mr. Ramesh, whose Hindu gods affirm the sexual and whose fragile humanity acknowledges her own with a quiet dignity, but also with some astonishing surprises. "It's the first time I really understand what all the fuss is about," she says. "There amongst the lentils on the Second Sunday after Trinity." In his traditional clothes—"long white shirt, sash and what not. Loincloth underneath"—Ramesh is "all spotless. Like Jesus. *Only not*" [38; italics added].

The question of Christ and our human materiality, in both its glory and its degradation, is raised by Susan's functional christology. But it is a christology that offers her little in the way of hope or affirmation as a material being.

---

[20] Cf. Richard Dawkins, *The Selfish Gene* (Oxford: Oxford University Press, 1978).

2. The Sombre Christ

The functional Christ of Susan's world is a *sombre* Christ. To put it
bluntly, he is a killjoy. She feels the dead weight of religious seriousness
relentlessly pressing on her. On the screen we can see it in her face and
hear it in her voice. When Geoffrey discovers the missing wine as he is
about to begin the Holy Communion, Susan, who is in the vestry with
him at the time, is sorely tempted to say, "if Jesus is all he's cracked up to
be why doesn't he [Geoffrey] use tap-water and put it to the test?" [38].
But she resists the joke and instead comes up with a practical solution.
Mr. Bland, the organist, keeps a bottle of cough mixture in the cupboard
"in case any of the choirboys gets chesty." Geoffrey almost has a nervous
breakdown at the thought of celebrating the sacrament in Benylin. But as
Susan points out, "it's red and sweet and nobody is going to notice." And
in the event, nobody does. "I see Mr. Belcher licking his lips a bit thought-
fully as he walks back down the aisle but that's all." Susan feels she has
"got it right for once," been of real help in a moment of crisis. But Geoffrey doesn't share the joke. He refuses to speak to her all afternoon.
"So I bunk off Evensong," says Susan, "and go into Leeds" [38]. To the
grocery shop, of course.

Joy is the biblical word for the state of blessedness that marks the ultimate fulfillment of human life. Joy is the experience of coming to one's
true destiny. In theological terms, joy is that completeness of being that
is promised in the eschatological culmination of human life in the beatific
vision of God. Here on earth, joy is the emotion we experience when we
are united to that which completes our life, answers our deepest need,
and brings us in touch with the purpose for which we feel we were made.
That is why joy is associated with work that is well done and with human
love, as well as with religion. Good work well done is the achievement of
deeply felt purposes. In love we are united with the one we long for and
whose being completes and fulfills our own. In true religion our beings
are made whole in union with God.

Susan knows little such joy. Nor can she see its possibility in the
Christ she is confronted with. Talking with Mr. Ramesh about his many
gods, and particularly the little statue on the wall of his shop that seems
to be "getting up to all sorts," she says ruefully: "Looks a bit more fun
than Jesus anyway" [33]. And in a discussion with Geoffrey she mentions
that the pictures of Jesus never show him smiling, much less smirking. To
which Geoffrey replies that she "should think of Our Lord as having an
inward smile" [37]. That is a smile that is not a smile. A smile is a smile
because it is outward. It is *there* imprinted on the flesh for all to see. This
is a Christ who frowns on fun, who can't take a joke, and whose counte-
nance is permanently sombre. This Christ is suspicious of joy and perhaps
outraged by ecstasy.

3. *The Male-gender Christ*

The functional Christ of Susan's world is *male-gender* specific. I am making the distinction here between sex and gender that has been worked out in recent feminist thought. Sex refers to the biological differentiation of men and women and all that belongs to their relationships based on it: the kinds of things we discussed under point 1 above. Gender refers to the roles that society and its institutions place on people. Common male-gender roles in our society include authority, aggression, bread-winning, and the like. Female-gender roles include receptivity, compassion, nurturing, and so on. The Christ of Susan's world is manifestly male-gender specific. Men represent God in this scheme. Geoffrey and the bishop have all the power. They do all the important work. Susan belongs to the margins of the Christian world. "Mrs. Vicar," the bishop calls her at lunch after the service, mercilessly underlining her derivative status. At the time the bishop is probing clumsily to see whether Geoffrey is "Archdeacon material." Ironically, that depends in part on whether, as wife, Susan fits, or at very least doesn't offend, the role. Though the question clearly concerns her life and feelings, the discussion takes place between Geoffrey and the bishop as if she were not there. "How outgoing is Mrs. Vicar?" the bishop inquires, at which "Mr. Vicar jumps in with a quick rundown of my accomplishments and an outline of my punishing schedule." Most of what he says is grossly exaggerated and excessively pious. "The ladies," says the bishop when he has finished. "Where would we be without them?" [32].

The fact of the matter is that Susan arranges flowers and serves meals and fulfills the roles in turn of guinea pig and illustration for Geoffrey's good works. She is not expected to engage in the serious business of theological discussion. The question of her own faith, whether or not she actually believes in God, is never raised. It is simply taken for granted. Her bitter "I'd just like to have been asked that's all" [31]—asked about whether she believes—covers a depth of exclusion that goes to the core of her being. As we noted, she is simply expected to concur with what Geoffrey and the fan club believe, even though she suspects that their faith, too, is shaky. When it comes to the question of the ordination of women Geoffrey once more answers the bishop's questions for her, leaving Susan to express—silently, of course—the full force of her alienation from the whole system. "So long as it doesn't have to be me, I wanted to say, they [the services] can be taken by a trained gorilla" [32].

The Christ figure that lurks at the back of this experience, far from being able to mediate to Susan a sense of hope, healing, and purpose in life, is almost completely alienating for her. This is true not merely at the level of institutional exclusion but at the center of her being, her sense of herself and her most fundamental beliefs.

4. *The Religious Christ*

The functional Christ of Susan's world is a very *religious* Christ. He lives in the Church. And this Church is pretty well insulated from the world outside. The main order of business, as far as Susan can see, concerns competition among the women as to who is the greatest in flower arranging, cultivation of a cloying individual piety among the "fan club" and, most fundamental of all, getting on in the ecclesiastical rat race. When the Church and its Christ do venture into the outside world it is for matters anachronistic or trivial. The bishop rushes from the dinner table where they have been discussing Geoffrey's future "because he's suddenly remembered he's supposed to be in Keighley blessing a steam engine" [32]. Geoffrey attends an interdenominational conference on the role of the Church in (as Susan says) "a hitherto uncolonized department of life, underfloor central heating possibly!" [36]. Both engagements are a complete irrelevance as far as any serious human question is concerned.

Inside the Church the crucial issue is ritual. When the service is late because the communion wine—symbol of the presence of the saving Christ—has been drunk (and we know by whom!), what is at issue between Geoffrey and Susan in the vestry? Appearances. "What does it look like?" he hisses at her. He doesn't mean: what does the suffering and death of Christ look like? He means: what does the interruption in the smooth performance of the rite look like? And not in God's eyes, but in the eyes of the congregation. In short, the question is: what will they think of Geoffrey?

Tragically, the real Christ for Susan is the Christ of these sorts of appearances. This is his annunciation, his incarnation, his ascension. There is little here to challenge the gates of hell in her own heart, much less in the world at large. In this religious context "a God without wrath brought men without sin into a kingdom without judgment through the ministrations of a Christ without a cross."[21]

5. *The Parochial Christ*

The functional Christ of Susan's world is a *parochial* Christ. He is C. of E. Jesus. The Christ represented in her mind's eye is an English, Anglican, middle-class, straight-laced Christ. What possibility is there of this figure being a universal redeemer? What hope for catholicity in this christology? We have seen that Susan's Christ seems powerless to redeem her feminine world since he simply doesn't understand it. We have seen that her Christ is unable to sanctify the world of the flesh since he seems per-

---

[21] H. Richard Niebuhr, *The Kingdom of God in America* (New York: Harper Torchbook, 1959 [first published 1937]) 193.

manently locked in an ethereal world of disembodiment. We have seen that her Christ is alien to the world of fun and laughter, and certainly is ill-equipped to mediate joy. And we see finally that her Christ is unable to cross cultural and religious boundaries. While Susan lies on the bed of lentils in the grocery shop at the time that Evensong is under way at the church—with "Geoffrey praying in that pausy way he does, giving you time to mean each phrase. And the fan club lapping it up, thinking they love God when they just love Geoffrey" [38]—what chance is there that this Christ would have anything to say to Mr. Ramesh with his dancing gods and goddesses? What place does such a Christ have in a pluralistic world, a world of diverse cultures, faiths, moralities, and divinities?

The little statue of a god on the wall of the grocery shop drives Susan to the theological problem of exclusive monotheism. In this place she is confronted with "a god. Not The God. Not the definite article. One of several thousand apparently." Tentatively she raises the issue with her lover. "Safety in numbers?" she asks [33]. But he doesn't take up the challenge. Exclusive theological claims are a Christian, not a Hindu issue. Christianity, for Susan, is the "definite article" faith. Salvation is supposed to come through Christ. So what is she to make of the obvious life, laughter, liberation, and even joy that she has found in the Hindu context, and that stands in marked contrast to her experience in the Church? Is there any possible way Christ can be proclaimed as savior of the *world*? as relevant to all people? as inclusive of all truth? as ground of all divine grace? And does it matter in the end?

Susan can't see that it does. And Mr. Ramesh isn't remotely interested in the point. The boundaries of Christic grace in Susan's functional christology extend no farther than the walls of the church in which that Christ is honored. But it is a fearfully narrow kingdom. To acknowledge the reality of a world wider than Geoffrey can conceive, and a healing grace broader than that known to Mr. Belcher and Miss Frobisher, it is necessary for Susan to leave the Christ of her experience behind. In the end, as we have seen, she is unable cope with the tensions. She doesn't have the strength to break from the religious scene she knows. But she can no longer remotely pretend to accept the theology she has been fed. She is trapped by AA and the parish of Ripon. She feels it is a life without taste. "But that's the thing nobody ever says about God . . . he has no taste at all" [41].

A First Response

There is little doubt that Susan feels acutely the Christ *question*. Her life is fragmented and unfulfilled. She longs for something better. But she feels cheated by her context. Salvation is talked of endlessly yet seems forever out of reach, at least in any form that makes sense to her. The Christ who functions in her experience seems powerless to mediate the healing she wants. Worse, he is part of the oppression that crushes her spirit. As I have already said, Susan seems to need redemption *from,* not *by* this Christ. In desperation she seeks, and partly finds, help elsewhere— in alcohol, with Mr. Ramesh, at AA meetings. I want to argue (much as Athanasius argued with Arius) that Susan's functional christology is deeply flawed. It does not represent the real Jesus Christ in the normative sense of the term—or not very well. This christology is a distortion of the revelational truth of Christ. Because of that it is an ineffective Christ Susan knows, a Christ who lacks saving relevance for her.

Some big issues are at stake here. One of the most important is the charge that this argument is a cop-out. Christianity doesn't work for Susan. That is clear. But then I immediately say, "ah, but that is not *real* Christianity. If she had the real thing she would be okay." This kind of defense has been powerfully and thoroughly challenged. Earlier in our century Bertrand Russell ridiculed it elegantly and on a broad canvas.[22] In more recent times, with the commemoration of the fiftieth anniversary of the ending of the Holocaust, it has again been seriously questioned, especially in the context of Jewish-Christian relations. What has to be faced, says Emmanuel Levinas, "is the fact that, properly speaking, the world was *not* changed by the Christian sacrifice." Nor is that all. "The worse [is] that those frightful things, from the Inquisition and the Crusades [to the Holocaust], were tied to the sign of Christ, the cross."[23] This may well be the most damaging criticism the Church has to face today. Even if I were competent to do so, which I am not, this is not the place to try to respond to the criticism on the massive scale that Levinas outlines. I will confine myself to the small world of Susan's experience, which is the focus of this discussion. In the final analysis, perhaps, the private and the public, the biographical and the sociopolitical, are intimately linked anyway. In discussing one we are implicitly touching upon the other. Be that as it may, for the moment I am concerned with grace at the biographical level.

Throughout what follows I am going to take the risk of following Melanchthon's famous dictum: "To know Christ is to know his benefits."[24] This is not the only test of a good christology, of course. It can collapse into pure pragmatism. What works is what is true. I want to avoid

---

[22] Bertrand Russell, *Why I am Not a Christian and other essays on religious and related subjects* (London: George Allen & Unwin, 1957).

[23] Emmanuel Levinas, *In The Time of the Nations,* translated by Michael B. Smith (London: The Athlone Press, 1994) 162 (italics added).

[24] Philip Melanchthon, *Loci Communes Theologici,* in *Melanchthon and Bucer,* edited by Wilhelm Pauck. The Library of Christian Classics XIX (London: S.C.M. Press, 1969) 21.

that. But it is, for all that, an important test. The real Christ *is* the saving Christ, the Christ who bears God's grace to us and for us. If there is no genuine grace in Christ all the doctrinal sophistication in the world is so much noise. On this Melanchthon—and Russell and Levinas—are surely right. I believe (or do I just want to believe?) there is grace in Christ. And Susan's failure to find it is a failure to know the real Christ. But I am under no illusions that demonstrating it will be easy.

A word of caution to begin with. We need to remember that Susan is telling the story as *she* sees it. It may well be a biased view, for all its truth. We all see things from our own perspective and in our own interests. This means in interpreting her story we should be on our guard in at least two instances. First, Geoffrey, the fan club, and the bishop may not be as bad as Susan portrays them. Almost certainly they are not.[25] And the Christ who lives in Geoffrey's church, and is proclaimed in his sermons, may well be a more profound and liberating Christ than Susan reports. The Church and the clergy come in for a good deal of public criticism these days, not least for exactly the kind of things Susan is on about. Much of that criticism may be justified. But some of it may not be. The real Christ does live in the lives and communities of the Church today, more deeply than we sometimes see or are willing to admit. In seeking justice for Susan we should be careful not to be unjust to Geoffrey, or the Church—or Christ.

The second point is controversial and complex. Susan is a victim of many things, including an oppressive view of Christ. But she may *also* be in part a collaborator in her own unfortunate destiny. As Dostoevsky brilliantly shows in his novels, we all tend to use the freedom we have to build the bars of the prison houses in which we then lock our freedom away. Liberation theology has reminded us that, good or bad, theology almost always serves the special, often subconscious, interests of those who propound it. That is one of the reasons why theology needs to be done in community. My view of Christ is likely to serve my interests. I need your view to challenge it, uncover its self-interest, and help correct it. And vice versa. Western theology looks different from Latin America, and our city theologies, no doubt, look different from a shantytown in Broome. This is what "transitional dialogue" in theology is about.

Susan is very critical of Geoffrey's Christ. She has good cause. But what does *she* get out of the position she adopts? Is she *totally* the victim?

[25] Bennett acknowledges this in his "Introduction" to the monologues. Everything is filtered through the eyes of the narrator. "Geoffrey, Susan's husband, may be a nicer, more forbearing man than her account of him might lead us to suppose . . ." (p. 7). The same goes for the other characters who people her world. And Susan's own *self*-image may not be all that could be said in the summing up of her life. To get a fully rounded picture we would need to hear the story from the others' points of view.

Is the Christ she depicts something completely other than the Christ she wants? What would Geoffrey's response be, if he had the chance to speak? I don't know the answer to these questions, of course. Were Susan a real person it would be unfair to make guesses in her absence. But since she is a fictional character we can risk a little speculation. Does painting Christ in the wimpish colors Susan throws around allow her to indulge a deep contempt for Geoffrey and relieve her guilt in seeking sexual satisfaction elsewhere? Since Geoffrey and his Christ are so appalling, what can a woman do? In a paradoxical way, the worse Susan makes them, the more liberty she has. Nietzsche did much the same thing on a grand scale. He determined to see Jesus, or at least the followers of Jesus, as weaklings who, unable to compete in the hard world of talented men (*sic*), decide to make a virtue of necessity and stand true human dignity on its head. They call self-sacrifice and suffering noble and godly, and success and power ignoble and of the devil. It is a neat argument. It makes believers look very prissy—and Nietzsche look pretty macho.

There is truth in both positions. Geoffrey may well be despicable. And Christians have at times hidden cowardice and resentful feelings behind lofty doctrines of self-sacrifice. But it is not the whole truth. And it is a truth that may partly serve the interests of its teller. I don't want to push this line any further in exegesis of the story. But it is worth bearing in mind for ourselves. Our functional christologies are partly *our* constructs. At least something in our hearts wants it that way because it suits us. So the clash between our functional views of Christ and the normative Christ is likely to be painful and self-revealing. History shows that not many can take it straight. Not for nothing does Jesus go the way of the cross. Sometimes *we* want the real Christ well out of the way too.

There is no space to attempt a response in detail to each of the points raised in the sketch of Susan's functional Christ. In the chapters that follow I will look at the first *three* only, namely the immaterial Christ, the sombre Christ, and the male-gender Christ.

The other two, the religious Christ and the parochial Christ, are equally interesting and important; indeed, a massive literature has grown up around each. Liberation theology has fought hard to interpret Christ in ways that break his "Babylonian captivity" within the narrow confines of religion. The "political Christ" whose solidarity is with the poor and oppressed of the world, and whose grace stands in judgment on those who wield power unjustly, is a figure of increasing importance worldwide. Likewise the problem of pluralism, or as we call it in Australia, multiculturalism. In the face of a plurality of religions and philosophies, each claiming to provide human access to the grace and truth of spiritual power, and many now reaching something like cultural and historical parity with Christianity, how, if at all, can Christians continue to claim some final and

definitive saving presence of God in Jesus Christ? Efforts to rethink christology in the light of religious pluralism are everywhere evident. But to
do justice to each of these would take another full study in itself. I will
touch upon them only briefly in what follows. For those interested to
pursue such lines of inquiry more fully, the appropriate literature is vast
and readily available.[26]

---

[26] On liberation themes see, for example, Gustavo Gutierrez, *A Theology of Libera-
tion: History, Politics and Salvation*, edited and translated by Sister Caridad Inda and
John Eagleson (Maryknoll, N.Y.: Orbis, 1988 [first published 1973]); Jon Sobrino,
Christology at the Crossroads: A Latin American Approach, translated by John Drury
(London: S.C.M. Press, 1978); Juan Luis Segundo, *Faith and Ideologies*, translated by
John Drury (Maryknoll, N.Y.: Orbis, 1984); Ignacio Ellacuria and Jon Sobrino, eds.,
Mysterium Liberationis: Foundational Concepts in Liberation Theology (Maryknoll, N.Y.:
Orbis, 1992) 77–158; Curt Cadorette et al, eds., *Liberation Theology: An Introductory
Reader* (Maryknoll, N.Y.: Orbis, 1992) 77–158.

On pluralist themes see David Tracy, *Plurality and Ambiguity: Hermeneutics,
Religion, Hope* (London: S.C.M. Press, 1988); John Hick, *An Interpretation of Reli-
gion: Human Responses to the Transcendent* (New Haven: Yale University Press, 1989);
Wilfred Cantwell Smith, *Towards a World Theology* (London: Macmillan, 1981); Hans
Küng et al, *Christianity and the World Religions: paths of dialogue with Islam, Hin-
duism and Buddhism*, translated by Peter Heinegg (London: Collins, 1987).

8

Great Body, Shame about the Artist

In the previous chapter we considered the distinction between functional and normative christology, that is, between Christ as we perceive him and Christ as he actually is in the revelation of God. The argument was that the Christ of revelation—insofar as we are able to determine this revelation—must be the ongoing judge of our various functional Christs, nudging and luring them, in the context of debate within and beyond the Church, toward better congruence with reality. In the second part of the chapter we analyzed a particular functional christology, using Alan Bennett's character, Susan the vicar's wife, as the example. There is no doubt Susan feels acutely the Christ *question*. Her life is deeply fragmented and unfulfilled. She longs for something better. But it is equally true that the Christ who functions in her life is unable to mediate the healing she craves. He is in fact part of the oppression that crushes her.

What I want to do in this and the following two chapters is take the template, so to speak, of an Athanasian-style incarnational christology and place it over Susan's functional christology to see where it fits and where it doesn't. By such a comparison I hope we might be able to move toward a BA—better account—theology, for Susan in the first instance, but also for the wider context of Church and society. We begin with the question of the ethereal or immaterial view of Christ.[1]

Body and Spirit

A strong dualistic tendency runs through Christian history. Perhaps it is a tendency that runs deep in the human psyche *per se*. The tendency is to be suspicious and fearful, if not contemptuous, of things material,

---

[1] See above pp. 130–31. As I have said, I am not going to pursue a detailed exegesis of Athanasius' christology in its historical context. I am interested only to follow the *intention* of Athanasius in maintaining that in Christ God makes divine reality present in a particular historical form.

especially the material of the human body. *Intellectually* this dualism confronts us in the various forms of Neo-Platonism and Gnosticism that draw sharp distinctions between the spiritual and the material, the eternal and the temporal. Plato himself is often regarded as the source of views that interpret the world of time and space as shadowlike, only half real in comparison to the realm of pure Forms. His famous parable of the cave seems to imply that mind or soul is somehow imprisoned in the world of matter and sees only by reflection the light of divine truth. To reach the light proper one must escape the shackles of the cave, that is, the finite world of physical being.[2] In the *Phaedo* Plato moves from implication to direct statement:

> In this present life, we think that we make the nearest approach to knowledge when we have the least possible intercourse or communion with the body, and do not suffer the contagion of the bodily nature, but keep ourselves pure until the hour when God himself is pleased to release us.[3]

These are strong images. To be embodied is like suffering from a disease. It is a "contagion" that corrupts the self. Purity and health mean deliverance from this unhappy state. In yet another passage Plato likens physical existence to a living death. True life is escape from "the pollution of the walking sepulchre which we call a body, to which we are bound like an oyster to its shell."[4] The struggle to escape is brought to completion at death, "when the soul exists by herself and is released from the body."[5] From this perspective salvation, or return to God, is not resurrection *of* the body, but resurrection *from* the body.

It would be unfair to leave the impression that this deep-seated suspicion, even horror, of the body is the only word Plato has to say on the world of space, time, and matter. In reading Plato it is always wise to take note of both sides of the argument. Dialectic, after all, is essential to the Socratic method. In the *Timaeus* Plato adopts a more positive attitude to earthly life. There he speaks of the physical world as "a shrine for the eternal gods," fashioned after the pattern of "an eternal Living Being" and therefore in itself "the moving image of eternity." In this text it is as if space and time become channels—we might even say sacramental mediums—of eternal realities. The divine life seems to permeate the material world. Dialectic connection rather than dualistic separation marks the re-

---

[2] Plato, *The Republic*, Book 7, 514-517, translated by A .D. Lindsey, edited by Terence Irwin (London: Everyman Library, 1992) 203–206.

[3] Plato, *Phaedo* 67, translated by Benjamin Jowett, *The Dialogues of Plato* (Oxford: Clarendon Press, 1953 [first edition 1871]) 1:417.

[4] *Phaedrus* 250, in *Phaedrus and The Seventh and Eighth Letters*, translated by Walter Hamilton (Harmondsworth: Penguin, 1973) 57.

[5] *Phaedo* 64, in Jowett, *The Dialogues of Plato* 1:414.

lationship of body to spirit, time to eternity.[6] From this position it is no great step to interpret matter as a vehicle for the self-expression of the supreme reality, rather than its antithesis.

It remains true, however, that Platonic suspicion of matter did strongly influence the ethos of the late Greco-Roman world. Neo-Platonism and Gnosticism both "drove a wedge between spirit and body and situated the heart of life in the mind."[7] The life of the body is the death of the soul and vice versa. True spirituality then comes to mean a transcending of this world, the participation of the human mind or spirit in an eternal realm of values, of beauty, truth, and goodness. One enters this divine world through progressive apprehension of special knowledge that lifts the soul away from the corrupting and transitory character of the material world of pain and death in which the body is imprisoned. A dualistic anthropology as well as cosmology is a part of this perspective. Soul and body are separable substances awkwardly "nailed and riveted together" in this life, and destined for eternal divorce.[8] Heaven and earth are related as light is to darkness, goodness to evil. To be present in the one is to be absent from the other.[9] The early Christian communities lived in this ethos. Platonic suspicion of the material interacted with more holistic views of body/spirit drawn from the Hebrew Scriptures. The virus of dualism "infected" the consciousness of classic Christianity and, to use a vivid phrase of James Nelson, it has been a "sexually transmitted disease" ever since.[10] It is enough to recall Paul's attitude to marriage as a regrettable concession to human weakness, Augustine's fateful linking of original sin and sexual

---

[6] Plato, *Timaeus 7*, in *Timaeus and Critias*, translated by H.P.D. Lee (Harmondsworth: Penguin, 1965) 50–51. Cf. Keith Ward, *Religion and Revelation: A Theology of Revelation in the World's Religions* (Oxford: Clarendon Press, 1994) 205–206.

[7] Paul Collins, *God's Earth: Religion as if matter really mattered* (Melbourne: Dove, 1995) 103. The whole section on pp. 99–110 gives a brief and lucid account of the historical influence of dualistic anthropologies on early Christian theology. For an extended and brilliant treatment of the question of early Christian attitudes to embodiment see Peter Brown, *The Body and Society: Men, Women and Sexual Renunciation in Early Christianity* (London: Faber and Faber, 1988); also Alvyn Pettersen, *Athanasius and the Human Body* (Bristol: The Bristol Press, 1990) *passim*, but especially ch. 4.

[8] ". . . each pleasure and pain is a sort of nail which nails and rivets the soul to the body, until she becomes like the body." *Phaedo 83*, Jowett, *The Dialogues of Plato* 1:439.

[9] Cf. Paul's words, "We know that while we are at home in the body we are away from the Lord, for we walk by faith, not sight. We are of good courage, and we would rather be away from the body and at home with the Lord" (2 Cor 5:6-7).

[10] Nelson uses the phrase in a different context, but it seems equally appropriate here. See "On Doing Body Theology," *Theology and Sexuality* 2 (March 1995) 42.

"concupiscence," and St. Anthony's blushing in shame at having to eat or satisfy any other bodily function, to make the point.[11]

In *practical* terms such dualism finds expression in various forms of asceticism—a turning away from the world, the rejection of physical pleasure, especially sexual pleasure, but also pleasures of food, theater, art, and music. It should be acknowledged, of course, that in certain historical circumstances asceticism could be life-transforming and liberating for some people, women especially. Important values—humility, gentleness, magnanimity, courtesy, and the like—were strongly nurtured by traditions of ascetic spirituality.[12] Nevertheless it is also true that a deep fear plays on the human mind. It whispers incessantly that sensuality of whatever kind will draw the soul away from God and hence from what is eternal and enduring, and as a consequence all will be lost in death. In extreme forms such hatred of the material can express itself in violent masochistic attacks on the body—scourging, castration, starvation, sexual abstinence, painful penances, and so on.[13] These are extreme positions, of course. But a more diffuse expression of the same sort of dualism is found everywhere in the Church. It manifests itself in a specific hierarchy of values: celibacy is better than marriage, virgins better than wives, inner spirituality better than social involvement, soul better than body, men better than women, Church better than society, the supernatural better than the natural, *logos*—the conscious realm of mind—better than *eros*—the deep, sometimes unconscious drives and longings of the heart, and so on.[14]

The *Guardian* commentator Joan Smith, reflecting on a journey to Italy, "where the clash of two great cultures, Christian and pagan, is in-

---

[11] See James B. Nelson, *Embodiment: An Approach to Sexuality and Christian Theology* (London: S.P.C.K., 1979) ch. 3, for an extended discussion of sexual alienation in Christian tradition; also, again, Peter Brown, *The Body and Society*.

[12] Cf. Ann Loades, *Searching for Lost Coins: explorations in christianity and feminism* (London: S.P.C.K., 1987) 18–38.

[13] Cf. Sara Maitland's vivid depiction of masochistic practices among medieval nuns. "Women flagellate themselves, starve themselves, lacerate themselves, kiss lepers' sores . . . deform their faces with glass, with acid, with their own fingers; they bind their limbs, carve up their bodies, pierce, bruise, cut, torture themselves. . . . What the hell is going on here?" "Passionate Prayer: Masochistic Images in Women's Experience," in Linda Hurcombe, ed., *Sex and God* (London: Routledge & Kegan Paul, 1987) 127; quoted by Julie Hopkins, *Towards a Feminist Christology* 53. Simone Weil represents a modern version of masochistic spirituality. Cf. her prayer that God grant, in the name of Christ "that I may be unable to will any bodily movement, or even any attempt at movement, like a total paralytic. That I may be incapable of receiving any sensation, like someone who is completely blind, deaf, and deprived of all the senses." Quoted in Loades, *Searching for Lost Coins* 48.

[14] Cf. Paul Avis, *Eros and the Sacred* (London: S.P.C.K., 1989) 81–94.

scribed into the very streets and buildings,"[15] reports how struck she was by the continuing struggle between body and soul that is vividly reflected there in art and life. Disgusted with the reactionary nature of many of Pope John Paul II's pronouncements—on the status of women, the issue of contraception, the problems of population, and the like—Smith abandoned an intended trip to the Vatican with its art treasures. The root cause of such papal blindness, she argues, lies in a negative attitude toward the material world in which we live.

> What I really dislike about Catholicism, and indeed most religions, is the way in which their obsession with the idea of an afterlife appears to sanction the most austere, unforgiving and death-dealing regimes in the world we actually inhabit. . . . [and this] has another baleful effect, which is to turn the mind away from—against, even—the pleasures of the present and especially those of the flesh.[16]

By way of contrast, Smith draws attention to the Baths of Diocletian, built around the turn of the fourth century C.E. and containing libraries, exercise rooms, gardens, and galleries catering for up to three thousand people at a time. In 1561 Pope Pius IV converted the ruins of the baths into "a gloomy, cavernous and thoroughly undistinguished church, Santa Maria degli Angeli." "The Romans gave us baths and pleasure parks," she comments; "the Popes turned them into churches."[17]

This is a one-sided analysis, no doubt. It takes no account of the ruthless policies of imperial Rome toward slaves and other marginalized groups on the one hand, nor of the contribution of Catholicism to contemporary liberation movements on the other. Moreover, standing in the Sistine Chapel looking up at all those Michelangelo bodies—from the famous figure of naked Adam being called into life by the finger of God to the terror-struck, writhing bodies of the wicked, tumbling headlong into the abyss of hell—it is hard not to think that if this is a fair artistic presentation of the Christian story, bodies are right at the heart of it.[18] But still, as Smith contends, the art in the Sistine Chapel is largely about human dependency upon the *divine*—creation, fall, redemption, last judgment. God above is the dominating theme. She contrasts this with the pagan wall paintings of Pompeii and Herculaneum. These pictures may not be great art in the sense of the Sistine. But they are certainly life-enhancing. And it is life in *this* world. "From vigorous erotic scenes to detailed depictions of food, the overwhelming impression is

---

[15] Joan Smith, "Great body, shame about the artist," *The Guardian Weekend* (May 13, 1995) 5.

[16] Ibid.

[17] Ibid.

[18] Paul Collins first drew this forcibly to my attention.

of people who cared very much about how they lived and recognised remarkably few taboos."[19] Michelangelo was great at depicting bodies, but mainly for heavenly ends. Of naked Adam, emblazoned across the front of a T-shirt, Smith makes the wry comment from which I have taken the title of this chapter: "Great body, shame about the artist!" Whether this is intended to be a reference to the otherworldly tendencies of Michelangelo only or to God as the ultimate artisan of the human body is left (deliberately?) unclear.

Susan is caught in the theological turbulence of this historic tension. In her affair with Mr. Ramesh she discovers a joy, a sense of self-worth and wonder in the mystery of her own (and his) sexuality, that she cannot deny. Nor can she pretend it does not disclose something profound about the significance of human life. She wonders tentatively if it might even be a point of revelation, an epiphany of God. She asks Ramesh if Hindus "offer their sex to God," and reports to the camera: "He isn't very interested in the point but with them, so far as I can gather, sex is all part of God anyway. I can see why too. It's the first time I really understand what all the fuss is about."[20] But she knows equally well that the congregation, celebrating the Christ at Evensong with Geoffrey at the time all this is going on, would reject her actions and thoughts with outrage.

They may well have good reason. Adultery might sometimes be the lesser of two evils. In Susan's case life with Geoffrey does seem pretty destructive. Even so, it is worth asking whether the path she has chosen is the best way to deal with it. As I suggested at the end of the last chapter, Susan may not be entirely an innocent victim. Geoffrey at least has the right to be heard. But it is pointless to embark on speculation as to what might come out were Susan and Geoffrey to seek marriage guidance. Bennett's text provides no material for such an exercise. And I am concerned with the more fundamental question: the theology of matter. How are we to understand ourselves as physical *bodies*? On this issue Susan struggles with deep theological ambiguity.

Clearly, dualistic spiritualities are powerful and persistent, inside and out of the Christian faith.[21] I agree with Paul Collins that it is "impossible to abandon deep-seated Christian dualism" with "one quick swipe of the pen." [22] Its roots run too far down into the human constitution. Therefore it cannot be dismissed as shallow, unserious, or merely erroneous.

[19] Smith, "Great body, shame about the artist," 5.

[20] Alan Bennett, *Talking Heads* (London: BBC Books, 1988) 38.

[21] It is important to note that Christian cultures are not the only ones to struggle with the problem of matter/spirit dualism. Some critics of Christian asceticism seem to speak as if the whole blame for such distortions were to be laid at the feet of the Christian tradition. See James B. Nelson, *Embodiment* 45.

[22] Paul Collins, *God's Earth* 97.

There *is* a corrupting potential in sensuality. One does not have to read Plato to know that.[23] The collapse of the human person into states that border on mere materiality is appalling. We see it all around. Sex as commodity. Medicine as sophisticated plumbing techniques—engineering in the flesh—with breathtaking indifference to the whole person of the sufferer. Employment as harnessing of physical labor. Economics as pursuit of material profit. Education as accumulation of marketable skills. Drugs and alcohol anesthetizing conscious rationality. And so on. Well we may fear that delicate and immaterial human values—values of truth, beauty, honor, respect, love, and the like—are set to be disparaged or even destroyed by a dominating sensuality, if we are not on our guard.

This fear is symptomatic. It arises from what I called in the discussion of humor the "anthropological paradox."[24] We are embodied beings, physical systems of flesh and blood. Our bodies are subject to implacable laws of nature—physical, chemical, biological, and psychological. We have teeth. We bite, chew, swallow, and digest the substance of other living entities that share this earth with us. Our bodies take what they need of this other life, then discharge the waste in ghastly lumps. To propagate our species we are driven almost irresistibly to sexual intercourse, itself an astonishing, carnal congress, the biological aim of which seems to have precious little to do with our own individuality other than to use it to further the stream of life itself. It is as though life flows through us and, once having achieved its end, ruthlessly pushes us into the past. Death and its consorts, age and sickness, are the great realities and symbols of our embodied state. We decay and die as material bodies. The whole dumb physicality of it seems to stand against our sense of ourselves as individuals—as unique, personal, and irreplaceable. It seems to undercut our awareness of eternal values. Truth and goodness and beauty apparently transcend this dying world and remain while we, who know them in part and seek to know them more, are doomed to destruction. The paradox that this sense of our unique value and the touch of things eternal in our being, which we sum up with words like "personality," "soul," or "spirit," is somehow "nailed and riveted" to a gasping, lusting, eating, defecating, aging, sickening, dying material form is so powerful as to be overwhelming

---

[23] Although Plato is eloquent on the subject. "For the body is the source of countless distractions by reason of the mere requirement of food, and is liable also to diseases which overtake us and impede us in the pursuit of truth; it fills us full of loves, and lusts, and fears, and fancies of all kinds, and endless foolery, and in very truth, as men say, takes away from us the powers of thinking at all. Whence come wars, and fightings, and factions? Whence but from the body and the lusts of the body?" *Phaedo* 66, Jowett, *The Dialogues of Plato*, 1:417.

[24] See above 52–54.

at times. Kierkegaard said the thought of it was enough to drive him to the edge of madness. Swift's famous couplet puts it bluntly:

> Nor wonder how I lost my Wits;
> Oh! Caelia, Caelia, Caelia shits.

Is it surprising that people fight against it? Is it any wonder that adolescents, when they hit that point of physical maturation where sexual drives emerge with all their urgency, just at the very time when they are required to cement a sense of their own personal identity, pursue questions of meaning, and take full responsibility for their actions, swing wildly from utter indulgence in sensuality—sex, drugs, alcohol—to dreamy otherworldliness, awash with ideal values, pure and disinterested love, and bold self-sacrificing altruism? The anthropological paradox haunts them relentlessly, as it does us all. The split and struggle between spirit and body is there. And it can lead to chaos. Thus the spirituality of those who turn inward and upward to escape the anguish of the body is certainly understandable. But likewise we can sympathize with the actions of those who turn outward and downward to escape the torment of the spirit and conscience. Not for nothing do Susan and others retreat into alcohol and sex.[25]

Christ and Matter

The theology of the incarnation seeks unity and reconciliation in the midst of this startling human paradox. It proclaims a spirituality of radical embodiment by affirming the positive relationship of matter and God at the very foundation of being. Athanasius' case for such an embodied spirituality rests on three main affirmations.

(1) Everything that exists is the direct expression of the creative will and sustaining energy of God, and God cannot create anything that is evil or worthless. In deliberate opposition to Plato's claim "that God made the world from pre-existent and uncreated matter," Athanasius argues that God cannot be conceived of as God if any reality other than God exists independently of God. Such independence would undermine the unity and unrivaled ultimacy that are defining characteristics of divinity. God creates *ex nihilo*, from nothing. "For he could in no way be called Creator if he does not create the matter from which created things come into being."[26] The fundamental ontological contrast is not between matter and spirit, but between Creator and creature. Human being as one unified reality in *all* aspects—body, mind, and spirit—is the good creation of God.

---

[25] One of the most brilliant explorations of this paradox that I know is Ernest Becker, *The Denial of Death* (New York: The Free Press, 1973).

[26] *De Incarnatione* 2, edited and translated by Robert W. Thompson (Oxford: Clarendon Press, 1971) 139.

(2) Having been called by God into being from the *nihil*, finite reality reflects its origins. It cannot exist *a se*, of its own constitution. God sustains it in being. In turning away from God (sin), human beings turn from being to non-being. Death becomes their destiny (cf. Ps 104:27-30). To avert this destruction God, in an act of loving kindness, entered the realm of human ungodliness to reconcile it once more with divine being and hence with life. In Jesus Christ, God

> took to himself a body, and that not foreign to our own. . . . And thus taking a body like ours, since all were liable to the corruption of death, and surrendering it to death on behalf of all, he offered it to the Father. . . . [that] the law concerning corruption in men might be abolished—since its power was concluded in the Lord's body and it would never again have influence over men who are like him . . . .[27]

Insistence that God assumed our flesh in order to reconcile us with God (and therefore with life) is the ultimate defense of the essential goodness of created being, including the embodied self that is our existence, in all its strangeness, depth, and vitality.

(3) The creative and redemptive action of God in and through the body is not of passing interest, as if humanity, though presently in an embodied state, were destined for some more exalted, asomatic existence. Athanasius will not allow that Christian hope looks to be liberated finally from the body. Rather he interprets salvation as liberation *in* the body from the corruption of sin and death. This is the meaning of resurrection. "The trophy of his [Christ's] victory over death was the showing of the resurrection to all, and their assurance that he had erased corruption and hence that their bodies would be incorruptible."[28] Athanasius is rather more confident of the fact of the resurrection of Christ—and indeed of what the assertion of such a "fact" might mean in the first place—than we in the post-Enlightenment world find possible. But, when all is said and done, whatever else the symbol of resurrection means, it does affirm the eternal significance of *bodies*, not merely of disembodied "souls."[29]

The devaluation of the flesh, of the material substance of the world, of sexuality; the suspicion of art and games and theater; the indifference to questions of justice and the spiritual importance of food and shelter and bodily care; these attitudes are heretical—literally unchristian—judged from the point of view of Athanasian christology. On the grounds of creation, incarnation, and resurrection we understand that our humanity as a

---

[27] *De Incarnatione* 8, p. 153.

[28] See *De Incarnatione* 22, p. 189. Cf. Alvyn Pettersen, *Athanasius and the Human Body* 189.

[29] Cf. Nelson, "On Doing Body Theology," 57; also Collins, *God's Earth* 104–110.

whole is God's concern, not simply some supposed "spiritual" aspect of it. Christ is the Christ of full human being. It is simply not the case that the more we avoid "intercourse or communion with the body" the closer we move toward God. The reverse is nearer the truth. According to this classic reading of the gospel the most intense, undistorted, limpid encounter with God that is possible within human experience takes place precisely in the flesh. Not in the temple, not in words, not in moral endeavor, not even in mystical ecstasy is found the primary intersection between the human and the divine, but in the body of Christ. God's divinity is manifest most powerfully in God's humanity. We meet God in the body. To deny this is to "persist in a vain attempt to be more spiritual than God."[30]

On this account Susan's functional christology is inadequate. Her Christ is not fully human. She herself recognizes this and fumbles toward a better view. "If Jesus is all man I just wish they'd put a bit more of it into the illustrations," she says.[31] If Christ is supposed to be the definitive manifestation of the "grace and truth" of God (John 1:14), then until the full humanity of Jesus is actually recognized and received Susan can never really feel that God, the God of this truth and grace, is the source of her whole being and is concerned with the full realization of the possibilities of her life. While Christ is an Arian part-human Susan must inevitably sense that those parts of her life that are beyond the picture of Christ she entertains have no secure base and hence no ultimate value, because they have no foundation in God. If Susan's functional Christ is what Christianity means by life, much of her life is judged worthless. It is not real life. She can't buy that judgment, of course. Life is too insistent. But she feels oppressed by it. Unfortunately this is how numbers of people in the churches (and outside) experience Christianity. It manifests itself as a restrictive, life-denying, polite niceness.[32] A false functional christology has much to answer for this sorry situation. True spirituality, built on the real Christ for us today, is embodied—a blood and bone, material spirituality. In the words of Matthew Fox:

> Christian spirituality . . . is a rootedness of being in the world. In history, time, body, matter and society. Spirit is found there (or better, here) and not outside these essential ingredients to human living. This means that economics and art, language and politics, education and sexuality are equally

---

[30] Nelson, *Embodiment* 77.

[31] Alan Bennett, *Talking Heads* 37.

[32] Cf. Dorothy Sayers' remark: "Question: 'What are the seven Christian virtues?' Answer: 'Respectability; childishness; mental timidity; dullness; sentimentality; censoriousness; and depression of spirits.'" *Creed or Chaos and Other Essays in Popular Theology* (London: Methuen, 1949) 24; quoted in Loades, *Searching for Lost Coins* 20.

an integral part of *creation* spirituality. And, not least of all, joy. The joy of ecstasy, and shared ecstasy in celebration.[33]

Fox tends to build his understanding of spirituality on the doctrine of *creation*. Human life is fundamentally good because God made it so. Christology builds an understanding of human wholeness even more securely. It builds on the incarnation and resurrection. Not only did God create our human totality; if Athanasius is correct, in Christ God took this humanity directly into divinity. No more fundamental affirmation of human being can be conceived. Susan needs to hear the truth of this affirmation. Her humanity *is* accorded greatest dignity since it is exactly the humanity adopted by God, whatever the exclusions, degradations and rejections she experiences at the moment. Fundamentally she is God-affirmed in her being as a woman, despite what Geoffrey and the fan club may say and do.

Theology and Experience

It is important to note the dialectic relationship between experience and revelation in this discussion. Good theology has some critical and constructive things to say to Susan's situation. It is critical of the repressive, anti-body culture in which she is immersed and that she has internalized in much of her own self image. "Look at me, the hair, the flat chest, the wan smile, you'd think I was just cut out for God."[34] It is also critical of the image of God that goes with that. This God is a prude. Hardly the One whose creative Word dreamed up sex in the first place! Both the self-image and the God-image need to be reconstructed in the light of a more adequate christology.

But the conversation also runs in the *other* direction. Susan's life experience, especially to do with her embodiment as a woman, is a critique of disembodied views of Christ such as she has encountered in the Church. Her sense of the fundamental realities of life makes her unhappy with the theological theory she has been offered. If such theology makes nonsense of loving and healing sexuality, so much the worse for the theology. Susan feels this in her bones. But she is unable, or too timid, to say it out loud. Alice Walker in the novel *The Color Purple* has her wonderful character Shug say about erotic experience: "God love all them feelings. That's some of the best stuff that God did. And when you know God loves 'em

---

[33] Matthew Fox, ed., *Western Spirituality: historical roots, ecumenical routes*, (Fides/Claretian, 1979) 5 (italics added); quoted in Kenneth Leech, *True God: An exploration in spiritual theology* (London: Sheldon, 1985) 243.

[34] Bennett, *Talking Heads* 31.

you enjoys 'em a lot more. You can just relax, go with everything that's going, and praise God by liking what you like."[35] She could be speaking for Susan. And Geoffrey's theology would benefit from paying heed. But much functional christology in the Church, even when it gives lip service to the orthodoxy of incarnation, finds it extremely difficult to believe and act as if God in Christ were embodied to *that* extent. Can God and sex really be thought together? And if they can, does this not challenge the simple ethics of marriage that Geoffrey espouses?

Of course there is a danger here. We ran into it once before with Karl Barth's critique of theologies of experience. "You cannot speak of God," Barth asserts, "by speaking of man [or woman!] in a loud voice."[36] If strong feelings were always a reliable guide to divine revelation we would have to see lust, anger, jealousy, and vengeance as defining characteristics of the divine. Plato was afraid of exactly this and simply split such passions off from any reference to God, consigning them wholly to the mortal realm, that is, the realm of the body. A theology of incarnation can't do that. These emotions *are* given theological expression in Scripture. God is depicted as angry, jealous, vengeful, and so on. But incarnation theology requires a dynamic balance. The whole self is neither body nor spirit but *embodied-spirit*. All physical vitalities are qualified by conjunction with spiritual values. Bodily hunger can become the "sin" of gluttony. It is also the foundation of sacramental communion, the meal of friendship, and the feast of Eucharist. Anger can be self-righteous rage that seeks revenge at all costs. It can also be "righteous anger" that is the expression of love appalled at cruelty or injustice. Lust can lead to unspeakable evil. But physical desire is also the spring of passionate love. The struggle to work out what reconciliation of body/spirit means in the light of the incarnate God and in the complex circumstances of daily living is the task of Christian discipleship and ethics. Rules like "marriage gives the OK to sex" help.[37] But they cannot encompass the whole mystery of human sexuality. Applied woodenly they may at times destroy rather than promote incarnate love.

The Church today is badly in need of a coherent and plausible sexual ethic. Issues of marriage, divorce, sexism, homosexuality, and lesbianism all demand attention. As James Nelson puts it, we are now in a situation where many Christians are "openly saying that they no longer want to leave their sexuality at the front door before entering the church."[38] This

---

[35] Alice Walker, *The Color Purple* (New York: Washington Square Press, 1982) 178. I owe this reference to an excellent class paper on theology and narrative presented by Zoe Hancock at St. Mark's in 1994. James B. Nelson uses the same quotation in "On Doing Body Theology," 50.

[36] See above p. 82.

[37] Bennett, *Talking Heads* 30.

[38] Nelson, "On Doing Body Theology," 39.

instinct is absolutely right if incarnational christology holds sway. I cannot here try to develop a sex ethic in general, or even to solve Susan's dilemma in particular. Suffice it to say this: An incarnational theology, in my view, would try to take into account the following factors. (1) It would affirm Susan's desire to find sexual love and joy in the midst of a situation that has militated against her. In this sense her experience with Mr. Ramesh is a good thing. (2) It would question whether, as it stands, the affair is an appropriate resolution of the problem. However wonderful and healing the experience may be, it flies in the face of other important values—honesty, promise-keeping, and trust, for example. And it requires a level of duplicity to maintain itself that undercuts the meaning of human community. Were it known, a whole network of relationships to which Susan belongs would change. This may be no bad thing, of course. But it remains a factor to be dealt with, not simply swept under the carpet. For as long as this interpersonal issue is not addressed, genuine reconciliation of embodied life, which is always social life, is unrealized.[39] (3) It would argue that mere capitulation to the *status quo ante* is not a happy outcome. Thus it would be critical of the path that, for a variety of reasons—Mr. Ramesh's move, her own fear of leaving what is known and secure—Susan eventually takes. As we saw, she is brought back into the fold and winds up going to "two churches instead of one." Neither really understands what her spiritual struggle is all about. What is more, Susan goes back into the marriage with Geoffrey. But nothing has changed. Inevitably, therefore, part of her rekindled vitality and love will die. This is hardly life fulfilled.

How these (and other) factors might be weighed in a compassionate and open assessment of the situation, and with what practical outcome, is impossible to say. A theology of incarnation requires that this work be done in the context of the relationships as they are, good and bad. Such a process, were it to take place, would look very different, ethically and pastorally, from the one portrayed in Susan's story. She knows vaguely that this *should* be the case. But her theological context gives her no way of appropriating it. Her choice is stark: capitulate or leave.

---

[39] Kierkegaard argues that sincere openheartedness is the essential characteristic of true marriage. "If the history of your inward development possesses something unutterable, if your life has made you participant in secrets, if in one manner or another you have devoured a secret which cannot be elicited from you except at the cost of your life, do not ever marry." *Samlede Værker,* edited by A. B. Drachman, et al. 20 vols. (Copenhagen: Gyldendal, 1962–64) 2:106, quoted by Reidar Thomte, *Kierkegaard's Philosophy of Religion* (Princeton: Princeton University Press, 1949) 40.

Sin and Grace

There is more in the implication of christology for human life than affirmation of the goodness of being. However important that is, it remains true that Susan *experiences* her life as incomplete—fragmented, distraught, alienated from what she knows she should and might be. A lot of her life is anything but good. And it is not a great deal of help to say "God accords your life fundamental dignity" if nothing matching that affirmation is experienced from day to day. The inevitable brokenness of a good life is the tragic reality of human history. This is the doctrine of sin in both its major forms: *Original* sin is the quality of fatedness in the human experience of alienation. Before ever we choose it, we discover ourselves already in the midst of a broken world. *Intentional* sin is the aspect of self-chosen alienation. We indulge such limited freedom as we command in ways that contribute further to human conflict and estrangement. Sin is fact and also act.[40]

Susan exemplifies the truth of a fallen world. Though she probably wouldn't use the language, she actually experiences the reality to which it refers. It is true that theological concepts of sin, especially the idea of original sin, which seems to imply a necessary corruption of the entire human enterprise, individual and social, have been used to undercut the dignity of human life by portraying it as worthless, depraved, and brutish. Matthew Fox and his sympathizers as well as many feminists have made that point insistently. Against extreme misanthropic interpretations of the doctrine they have a valid case. But what Augustine (and the Reformers) meant in using the term was not that there is nothing of value in human life. That is an obvious absurdity and represents a denial of the significance of creation. What they meant was that any and every aspect of human existence is open to possible corruption and self-alienation. *And* any and every aspect of human existence is likely in *fact* to be tainted by such corruption. Sin is possible and sin is also actual.[41] Thus, as we have had occasion to note, it is possible to twist one's humanity—or have it twisted—by an unbalanced indulgence of sensuality, the material dimension of life. And it is just as possible to have one's life distorted by repression of physicality and a flight into irresponsible otherworldliness. Susan has felt the force of both. She has a loveless marriage with Geoffrey on the one hand and a passionate but ultimately impossible sexual liaison with Mr. Ramesh on the other. She has a desiccated religious life

---

[40] Cf. Reinhold Niebuhr, *The Nature and Destiny of Man* (New York: Charles Scribner's Sons, 1964) 1:255–260.

[41] Cf. Paul Ricoeur's discussion of original sin, *The Conflict of Interpretations: Essays in Hermeneutics* (Evanston: Northwestern University Press, 1974) 269–286.

that reduces her almost to invisibility at one moment, and an addiction to alcohol that destroys her self-control and reduces her to insensibility at another. Her self-esteem is in pieces. She wonders where her life has gone. She is both victim and agent in the situation. Her baleful lot is partly given, partly chosen. The situation, which she has partly helped to cause, has gone beyond her ability to control. This is her distress. "Sin generates entanglements from which human beings cannot free themselves simply with moral appeals and sanctions."[42]

Christianity's claim is that there is healing grace available in Christ to reconcile alienated human life to itself and to its true source: forgiveness of sin, hope in the face of despair, life in the midst of death. But Susan's functional Christ is unable to help her in the areas where she needs it most. She knows Christ is supposed to be redeemer. She knows Geoffrey is in "the redemption business." But where her need is sharpest, Christ is absent, or present only as a stern and judging eye. Is this a miscarriage of meaning? Or is Christianity manifestly unable to deliver what it clearly seems to promise, as Russell, Levinas, Daphne Hampson, and others suspect?[43]

I find myself struggling here. I feel real sympathy with Susan's predicament. My life, too, has jagged edges of incompleteness, frustration, sadness, dashed hopes, unhappy relationships, false religion, and faltering faith. It is easier to hang on to the *idea* of incarnation as a general affirmation of the essential goodness of human life—the feeling, so to speak, that life is meant to be good, if not easy—than to hold on to the *hope* that incarnation is the presence in history of a healing grace that actually reconciles the shattered pieces of a life like Susan's, or addresses the social injustice of a million unemployed, or makes a difference in a world facing the catastrophic epidemic of AIDS and the appalling destruction of the natural environment. The problem of suffering, as always, is the deepest challenge to the claims of christology. At times it certainly appears that "the world was *not* changed by the Christian sacrifice."[44] And yet paradoxically it is also true that the cry of anguish generates christology in the first place. The centerpiece of the gospel is the passion narrative. Athanasius was right. The issue is the possibility and the reality of divine grace. If christology can't deliver here, it can't deliver.

[42] Michael Welker, *God the Spirit*, translated by John H. Hoffmeyer (Minneapolis: Fortress, 1994) 317.

[43] Questioning the claim that in Christ the estrangement of sin is overcome, Daphne Hampson suggests that, given the state of things, "One could argue that brokenness and alienation are fundamental to the world." *Theology and Feminism* (Oxford: Basil Blackwell, 1990) 61.

[44] Emmanuel Levinas, *In The Time of the Nations*, translated by Michael B. Smith (London: The Athlone Press, 1994) 162. See above, p. 136.

A famous phrase of St. Gregory Nazianzen (ca. 329–389) puts the case. Arguing against christologies that refuse to recognize that in Christ God assumes into divinity the whole of human being in all its complexity—body, mind, spirit, will—Gregory says, "That which he [Christ] has not assumed, he has not healed."[45] If any and every aspect of our human existence is open to distortion, as it seems to be, and if healing of our humanity is to come from God, as it seems it must, then all that we are must be touched by the presence of God's grace. God's grace must invade with hope and love every last frontier of our human experience.

Is this true? It seems a wild claim. Some of the places we human beings maneuver ourselves into, or are thrust into by others, or by the force of circumstances, are places of horror and abandonment and violence. Is God in such places? Or are they literally God-forsaken? outside the reach of God's presence and hence beyond the realm of grace and hope? In a classic passage Paul argues the negative case.

> Who will separate us from the love of Christ? Will hardship, or distress, or persecution, or famine, or nakedness, or peril, or sword? As it is written, "For your sake we are being killed all day long; we are accounted as sheep to be slaughtered." No, in all these things we are more than conquerors through him who loved us. For I am convinced that neither death, nor life, nor angels, nor rulers, nor things present, nor things to come, nor powers, nor height, nor depth, nor anything else in all creation, will be able to separate us from the love of God in Christ Jesus our Lord (Rom 8:35-39).

This furnishes a pretty impressive list of places that might appear to be candidates for godforsakenness. And many, like Susan, who have been in such places can bear witness that they seem, as far as one can humanly tell, utterly devoid of God and grace. Is Paul talking nonsense? How can he say *nothing* can separate us from the love of God? How does he know that?

If there is an answer to this, I can only think it rests on christology. Paul's argument depends on the assumption that in the death and resurrection of Jesus Christ, God's love was given "for all of us" (Rom 8:32). But it needs something like a no-holds-barred incarnational christology to sustain it. Arius' Christ cannot give it. That Christ cannot seriously bring God into the realm of creation at all. God touches us at best through a long chain of mediators, of whom Christ is the foremost. But God, as God, remains always at a safe distance. Arius' God cannot look matter in the face. Death is beyond divine comprehension. Death is matter's crisis as sin is spirit's crisis. Both death and sin reveal an abyss that yawns in the heart of human existence, a nothingness that is empty of God. The place

---

[45] Gregory Nazianzen, *Epistle* 101, translated by C. G. Browne and J. E. Swallow, in Edward Hardy, ed., *Christology of the Later Fathers* (Philadelphia: Westminster, 1954) 218; quoted in Keith Ward, *Religion and Revelation* 260.

of godforsakenness. God and sex, God and death, God and sinfulness, simply cannot be *thought*, much less *brought* together. If we find ourselves in such places as these we find ourselves separated from God, if Arius is right. What God in Christ did not assume he did not heal. And Arius' God was reluctant to assume quite a bit.

The same is not true for Athanasius or Paul. According to their view Christ plunges not only into matter, he plunges into sin and death. This is the importance of the cross in the story of Jesus. Not only does Christ take flesh, he goes the way of the cross. The way of death. And not even natural death. He goes the way of sinful, shameful, cruel death.[46] If the incarnation of God is an unexpected thing, the death of the incarnate God, and in this manner, is astonishing. A great reversal seems to be enacted. Jesus, who went to the outcasts, finds himself viciously cast out—cast out of the fellowship of his friends, out of the community of the synagogue, out of the society of the city. Jesus, who presumed to forgive sins, is condemned as the worst of sinners. Jesus, who wept over the city of Jerusalem—God's city—suffered "outside the gate" (Heb 13:12-13). "Outside the gate" is a theological as well as a geographical location. It means outside the boundaries of God's favor, outside the place of God's habitation. In the theological world of the time the cross bears the curse, not only of human beings, but of God (Deut 21:22-23). To be hanged on a tree—judged blasphemous by the religious authorities and lawless by the civil authorities—was to be thrown beyond the horizon of God's mercy. It meant outer darkness, the place of no hope and no return. By his cry from the cross Jesus testifies to his entry into that place: "My God, my God, why have you forsaken me?" (Mark 15:34). Abandoned by all, he dies abandoned too, it seems, by God. Except that this, too, is *God*.

The ultimate implications of this story were only gradually grasped by the early believers. Paul expressed their understanding in the theology of grace that knows no boundaries. The meaning of the destiny of Jesus is that God enters our realm. God takes our place.[47] The truth of the story of Jesus is thus stranger than the truth of the parable Jesus told of the prodigal son (Luke 15:11-32). In that story the father waits at home for his son's return. But in the story of Jesus, interpreted through Athanasian eyes, God makes the journey to the "far country" where the prodigal has

---

[46] Cf. Athanasius' words: ". . . our Lord and Saviour Christ, did not himself contrive death for his body lest he should appear frightened of a different death, but accepted and endured on the cross that inflicted by others, especially by enemies, which they thought to be fearful, ignominious, and horrible, in order that when it had been destroyed he might be believed to be life, and that the power of death be completely annihilated." *De Incarnatione* 24, p. 193.

[47] Cf. Karl Barth, *Church Dogmatics* IV, 1, translated by G. W. Bromiley (Edinburgh: T & T Clark, 1956) 157–357.

wasted his substance and descended to eating with the pigs. God *becomes* the prodigal—hungry, outcast, brutalized, and condemned to death. All that belongs to our fate in the "far country," God in Christ assumes. God takes godforsakenness into God's own heart and overcomes it in resurrection life. God takes our death into divine life in order that we might discover divine life in our death. That, I think, is how Paul arrives at the theological assertion that *nothing* can separate us from the love of God.

This view of Christ is not Susan's. A good deal of her experience is not assumed by the functional Christ she knows and therefore is certainly not healed by him. Her Christ scarcely penetrates the quiet desperation of the very proper vicarage in which she lives, much less the strange fascination of Mr. Ramesh's shop. Her Christ is absent from her place of meaningless work and seems only to reinforce her gender oppression. Her Christ stands aloof from humor and is suspicious of festivity. By Melanchthon's test—that to know Christ is to know his benefits—this Christ is a failure. He is neither really God nor really human. He is an Arian Christ, a contradiction of the process of salvation he is supposed to represent.

Will Athanasian-type christology help? This is difficult to answer. In theory, yes. The Christ of the manger and the cross is precisely the Christ who reaches to the extremities of human despair. But the realization of salvation remains an eschatological hope. Tragedy and great suffering persist in our lives and in the life of the world. Athanasian BA christology says that we are not alone in this. Hell will not have the last word. But there are times when it is devilishly hard to hang on to this affirmation. The theory seems overwhelmed by brute experience. Then I find all there is is faith in the story. I *hope* that hell will not conquer because in telling the story of the crucified and risen Christ I see God entering the worst darkness I can confront and overcoming it from within. Paul's great affirmation—*nothing* can separate us from the love of God—makes sense on these grounds alone.

9

The Black Scarecrow

Thus spake Zarathustra: "I bade them laugh at their gloomy sages, and whoever had sat as a black scarecrow, cautioning, on the tree of life."[1] He speaks for Susan. Her functional Christ is a black scarecrow. He sits gloomily on the tree of her life and frightens off a whole range of fluttering joys that might otherwise have alighted there. "You never see pictures of Jesus smiling, do you?" Susan asks, to be told by Geoffrey that she should "think of Our Lord as having an inward smile." She hits back. "Do you think he ever smirked?" But Geoffrey sees neither a joke nor a serious theological point in the question. He suddenly remembers he "was burying someone in five minutes and took himself off."[2] That sums it up. There is a touch of death about this religion. It smells of the mausoleum, musty and decaying. Life has gone from it.[3] Susan observes others. "Sunday afternoon. Families having a run out. Wheeling the pram. Walking the dog. *Living.*" But for her, life always seems elsewhere. She is left wondering "what happened to *our* life."[4]

Instinctively following Zarathustra's advice, Susan sees her best defense against the scarecrow Christ in humor. She pokes fun at the fan club with its petty rivalries, at the bishop and his pompous ways, at the Church's attitude to sex. Those emissaries who "believe that they promote the interests of God," says Nietzsche, "want to make sure that we do not laugh at existence, or at ourselves—or at [them]." But "*in the long run* every one of these great teachers of a purpose was vanquished by laughter . . . and returned into the eternal comedy of existence."[5]

[1] Friedrich Nietzsche, *Thus Spake Zarathustra*, translated by R. J. Hollingdale (Harmondsworth: Penguin, 1969) Part III, "Of Old and New Law-Tablets," 214.

[2] Alan Bennett, *Talking Heads* (London: BBC Books, 1988) 37.

[3] "Do we smell nothing as yet of the divine decomposition? Gods, too, decompose." Nietzsche, *The Gay Science*, translated by Walter Kaufmann (New York: Vintage Books, 1974) Book III, 125, 181.

[4] Bennett, *Talking Heads* 31 (italics added).

[5] Nietzsche, *The Gay Science*, I, 1, pp. 74–75.

Unfortunately Susan cannot sustain the joke. In the final sequence of the monologue we see her having lost her lover, being "on the wagon" (i.e., off the booze), and dutifully attending Evensong *and* the weekly AA meetings. The heaviness in her spirit is painful. She is repressed, self-pitying, and glum. "I never liked going to one church so I end up going to two. Geoffrey would call it the wonderful mystery of God. I call it bad taste. And I wouldn't do it to a dog. But that's the thing nobody ever says about God . . . he has no taste at all."[6] This, too, is Nietzsche's conclusion. In the final analysis it is not an intellectual issue. Can you believe in God? It is a question of life. Does it have zest? "What is now decisive against Christianity is our taste, no longer our reasons."[7] If it *tastes* like death, why call it life?

I have deliberately paired Susan's intuitions with Nietzsche's commentary. Christian existence is often experienced as sombre or even sour. People watching from outside get the feeling that the faithful are straight-laced, oppressively earnest and unable to laugh at themselves. Somewhere in their extensive corpus of nonsense Peter Cook and Dudley Moore have a sketch. In it the New Testament church at Ephesus is getting ready to have a picnic. Boats on the lake. Fluffy clouds in the sky. Children playing. They are organizing the sandwiches and wine when suddenly: Knock, Knock, Knock at the door. It's a letter. "Who's it from?" they shout as they gather around. "It's from Paul." "Well, open it, open it! What's he say?" There is a pause while the envelope is ripped open. "Hey you Ephiscans, stop having fun!" Signed "Paul." This is Nietzsche's point. As son of the manse Nietzsche knew religious life from the inside. In angry disillusionment he wrote of Christians: "They would have to sing better songs to make me believe in their Redeemer: his disciples would have to look more redeemed!"[8]

Nietzsche's assessment is that believers are killjoys. To the extent that this is right we need to ask: "Is our lack of joy due to the fact that we are Christians, or to the fact that we are not sufficiently Christian?"[9] Is it true that the pagans always throw the best parties? Are we suppressing something that really belongs to our life? We know the theory. According to the psalm, "When the Lord restored the fortunes of Zion, we were like those who dream. Then our mouth was filled with laughter and our tongue with shouts of joy" (Ps 126:1-2). Or in the words of the Christ, "I have said these things to you so that my joy may be in you, and that your joy may be complete" (John 15:11). But our knowledge is not matched by our courage. We dare not affirm the world and ourselves. We seem too timid to let joy take hold of us. If we do let go for a moment

---

[6] Bennett, *Talking Heads* 41.

[7] Nietzsche, *The Gay Science*, III, 132, p. 186.

[8] *Thus Spake Zarathustra*, "Of the Priests," Part I, p. 116.

[9] Paul Tillich, *The New Being* (London: S.C.M. Press, 1964) 142.

we feel silly or guilty. And we often bring down on ourselves the malicious criticism of others who themselves are frightened of joy.

Nietzsche's attack on the scarecrow Christ is many-sided. But three main elements stand out.

(1) Physicians of the soul (as he calls them)—moralists and theologians—are all too eager to point out the dark danger of life. Evil lurks at every turn. Human beings are inevitably snared by it. Once caught, they are unable to free themselves. So things are bad.

> . . . all of them [i.e., preachers] try to con men into believing that they are in a very bad way and in need of some ultimate, hard, radical cure. Because humanity has listened to these teachers much too eagerly for whole centuries, something of this superstition that they are in a very bad way has finally stuck. Now they are only too ready to sigh, to find nothing good in life and to sulk together, as if life were really hard to *endure*.[10]

The doctrine of sin is a *sulky* doctrine. It teaches that we are guilty *and* helpless. Guilt encourages a sense of caution. The less you do the less you can do wrong. Helplessness engenders a sense of dependence. Only someone else can save us. Both dispositions cut the nerve of joy, which is to live our lives as our *own*, freely and with zest, wherever it takes us.

(2) The "hard cure" is always associated with an implacable distinction between good and evil. The good is defined by certain moral demands. And the call is to *obey* these "thou shalts" and "thou shalt nots." Nietzsche dubs this the "Spirit of Gravity"—compulsion, dogma, moralism, and the rest. The trouble is, it masks weakness, not strength. It betrays the need for a prop, "a support, backbone, something to fall back on." Not being willing to risk taking command of themselves, life-shy people urgently need someone who will take command for them. Once "a human being reaches the fundamental conviction that he *must* be commanded, he becomes 'a believer.'"[11]

(3) Both these perspectives coalesce for Nietzsche in the life-denying image of Christ on "the worst of all trees, the Cross."[12] There the scarecrow hangs. Suffering, pain, degradation, weakness, failure—these things are held up as admirable and fundamental: in fact, divine. The Christian lifestyle therefore cannot be anything but slavish and sombre. All that is little, poor, sick, and weak is celebrated in its vision. In a direct attack on Paul's interpretation of Christian life in 1 Corinthians 1, Nietzsche writes:

---

[10] Nietzsche, *The Gay Science*, Book IV, 326, p. 256.

[11] *The Gay Science*, Book V, 347, p. 289. On Nietzsche's attitude toward morality see Lev Shestov, *Speculation and Revelation*, translated by Bernard Martin (Athens, Ohio: Ohio University Press, 1982) 184–192.

[12] Nietzsche, *Thus Spake Zarathustra*, "Of Old and New Law-Tablets," Part III, p. 221.

God has chosen what is weak and foolish and ignoble and despised in the eyes of the world. . . . God on the cross—do we still not understand the terrible background significance of this symbol?—Everything that suffers, everything that hangs on the cross, is divine. We all hang on a cross and therefore we are all divine. . . . We alone [i.e., the Christians] are divine. . . .

Given this perspective on the divine, Nietzsche concludes that "Christianity is the greatest misfortune of the human race thus far."[13] It kills the taste of life. It gives freedom away. It makes a virtue of dependence. It glorifies passive pain. This is not the religion of joy. The "man of sorrows" is its defining type. Real joy is the opposite. Joy lives in self-determination, in freedom of the will, in defiance of slavish convention, in living to the full. Such a "spirit would take leave of all faith and every wish for certainty, being practiced in maintaining [itself] on insubstantial ropes and possibilities and dancing even near abysses. Such a spirit would be the *free spirit* par excellence."[14]

Note the thrust of this critique. Nietzsche is not attacking incarnational christology as if some other type were *better*. He assumes incarnation is at the heart of Christian faith. His aim is to highlight its consequences. Incarnation means the cross is not simply the unfortunate end to the life of one dedicated to God. Religious martyrdom is common enough in history. But its meaning is ambiguous. It may or may not be a genuine revelation of the purposes of God. The martyr could have been plain unlucky, in the wrong place at the wrong time. He or she may even have been mistaken and their sorry end be a repudiation by God. But the case of Christ is different. God is uncompromisingly implicated in the destiny of *this* life. That is what incarnation is—"God on the cross." The cross is the true destiny of God in the world, not of some more or less fallible servant of God. This is the divine way. The cross of Christ cannot be interpreted as accident or misfortune. That is what is unacceptable to Nietzsche. Servitude, weakness, suffering, and death are deified.

Susan's problem is not that she has misunderstood the Athanasian Christ. She has understood him too well. Christianity is in essence—not by distortion—a life-pinching stance. The choice is stark—"Dionysius against the Crucified."[15] Life against death. If she wants to live well, Susan must have done with Christ and the God he incarnates.

---

[13] Nietzsche, "Antichrist," #51, *Twilight of the Idols and The Anti-Christ*, translated by R. J. Hollingdale (Hamondsworth: Penguin Books, 1972) 168–169. Cf. Karl Barth, *Church Dogmatics* III, 2, translated by Harold Knight, et al (Edinburgh: T & T Clark, 1960) 231–242.

[14] Nietzsche, *The Gay Science*, Book V, 347, p. 290.

[15] Nietzsche, *Ecce homo* 433. "They called God that which contradicted and harmed them." *Thus Spake Zarathustra*, "Of the Priests," Part II, p. 115.

Jesus and John

This critique of religion goes a long way back. It is there in the New Testament. We catch a glimpse of it in the strange Lukan text on the comparison between John the Baptist and Jesus and their respective attitudes to life and faith. In the text it is Jesus speaking.

> To what then will I compare the people of this generation, and what are they like? They are like children sitting in the marketplace and calling to one another, "We played the flute for you, and you did not dance; we wailed, and you did not weep." For John the Baptist has come eating no bread and drinking no wine, and you say, "He has a demon;" The Son of Man has come eating and drinking, and you say, "Look, a glutton and a drunkard, a friend of tax collectors and sinners!" (Luke 7:31-34)

A sharp distinction is drawn here between the religious approach of John the Baptist and that of Jesus. Ironically, despite the marked difference between them, neither, apparently, was acceptable. Be the music dance or dirge, "this generation" remained unmoved. "There were Jews who found John too unsociable to be sane and Jesus too sociable to be moral."[16] But it is not the indifference of reception that both John and Jesus suffered that I want to examine. Rather, I am interested in the distinction between their religious styles. John's religion—let us call it religion "Type A"—is depicted in the text as the religion of the fast. Self-denial is its hallmark, the wail its hymnody. In contrast, the religion of Jesus—"Type B" for sake of argument—is portrayed as the religion of the feast. Eating and drinking (to excess!) is its symbol, the dancing flute its music.[17]

It is important to emphasize that I am dealing here with *types* of religious disposition. I am not attempting a historical comparison between the personalities and teachings of Jesus and John, an enterprise unlikely to

---

[16] G. B. Caird, *The Gospel of Luke* (London: Adam & Charles Black, 1963) 112.

[17] The distinction I am making here is not the same as the one famously drawn by Kierkegaard. In the *Postscript* Kierkegaard distinguishes between what he calls Religion A, which is the religion of immanence—it rests on the assumption that the truth of God is immanent in human subjectivity—and Religion B, which is synonymous with Christianity properly interpreted, and affirms that fellowship with God is achieved only through the revelation of God in history (i.e., in Christ). My distinction is nearer to the one Kierkegaard makes between the "ethical" and the "religious" stages of human existence. See his *Concluding Unscientific Postscript* 493–98. For a lucid discussion of Kierkegaard's various "stages" of existence (aesthetic, ethical, and religious) see Reidar Thomte, *Kierkegaard's Philosophy of Religion* (Princeton: Princeton University Press, 1949) chs. 2–6, *passim*. The film "Babette's Feast," based on a Karen Blixen story, is a wonderful study of the comparison and contrast between the two styles of religious disposition—the fast and the feast.

succeed in any case for want of data.[18] Even less am I intending to draw a distinction between Judaism and Christianity using these names as the catalyst. The temptation is there, of course. The uneasy relationship between the Synagogue and the Church is already evident in the text. When Luke has Jesus say, "I tell you, among those born of women no one is greater than John; yet the least in the kingdom of God is greater than he" (Luke 7:28), it is hard not to detect a confusing mixture of respect and rivalry between the two groups. And there is little doubt which comes out on top. It is too easy for Christians to make straw figures and then boost their own morale by knocking them over. "John" (read: Synagogue) is the stern religion of legalism and command. "Jesus" (read: Church) is the joyful faith of grace and forgiveness. To our shame this sort of thing has too often been preached. But the time is past when it can be treated seriously. Jesus was a Jew from birth to death. His first followers, whose reception of him as the Christ shaped the life and thought of the earliest Christian communities, were also Jews.[19] The line between law and grace, command and gift, judgment and forgiveness, does not run between Judaism and Christianity. It runs straight down the center of both traditions. Of the life-denying demands of religious moralism in Christianity enough has already been said by Nietzsche to make the point clear.

I had occasion to witness a remarkable expression of this. The Chapel at King's College Cambridge ran a series of Jewish/Christian dialogues during the Lent term of 1995. I happened to be there on a Sunday when Rabbi David Goldberg from the Liberal Synagogue in London preached the sermon at the morning Eucharist. A few weeks earlier the much publicized ceremonies held to mark the fiftieth anniversary of the liberation of the concentration camp at Auschwitz had taken place. Goldberg chose to preach on forgiveness. He referred to the speech given at the Auschwitz ceremony by the Nobel Peace Laureate and Auschwitz survivor, Elie Wiesel. The words of Wiesel's speech had been quoted and re-quoted in the world media for days afterwards.

> Although we know that God is merciful, please God do not have mercy on those who have created this place. God of forgiveness, do not forgive those murderers of Jewish children. Do not forgive the murderers and their accomplices. Those who have been here: remember the nocturnal procession

---

[18] G. B. Caird, for example, speaks rather too knowingly of "the deep gulf that separates his [i.e., Jesus'] radiant friendliness from John's forbidding austerity." *The Gospel of Luke* 111.

[19] Elizabeth Schüssler Fiorenza writes, "It is . . . misleading to speak about 'Jesus and his Jewish background' as though Jesus' Judaism was not integral to his life and ministry, or to describe the behavior of Jesus' disciples over and against Jewish practice as though the first followers of Jesus were not Jews themselves." *In Memory of Her: A Feminist Reconstruction of Christian Origins* (New York: Crossroad, 1983) 105.

of children and more children, frightened, quiet and so beautiful. If we could simply look at one, our heart would break. Did it not break the heart of the murderers? God, merciful God, do not have mercy on those who had no mercy on Jewish children.[20]

The weight of those words reiterated by a Jew in the context of a Christian service of worship was palpable. Goldberg went on:

Such feelings at such a time and in such a place are utterly human—humanly understandable and probably *humanly* unavoidable. But they remain [here he spoke with great deliberation] they remain *theologically* unacceptable. It is better to take the hard road and believe that after Auschwitz there is no God than to pretend to address God and then tell him how he should make up his mind. Wiesel's prayer at Auschwitz makes God in our own image. It acknowledges God, but then dictates what is and is not for God to do. Forgiveness is hard and maybe impossible for human beings in such circumstances. It certainly calls for repentance and the admission of responsibility for crimes unspeakable. Without that there can be no acceptance of the "guilty other" as far as humans beings are concerned. But God? That is a different story. "For my thoughts are not your thoughts, nor are your ways my ways, says the Lord. For as the heavens are higher than the earth, so are my ways higher than your ways and my thoughts than your thoughts" (Isa 55:8-9). If we would believe in God and not be religious sentimentalists we must let God be God in his judgment *and his mercy*.[21]

Only a Jew could speak in such terms. Listening, I felt it made many Christian treatments of the theme of divine forgiveness pale by comparison.

The Fast

Type A religion is the religion of "fasting." It is serious, upright, and utterly committed. It is acutely aware that the world is a battleground in which good and evil, justice and injustice are locked in mortal combat. Denial of self, separation from wickedness, the call for resistance of evil, are close to its center. The gospels (especially Matthew) paint John in strong ascetic colors. He bursts on the scene in the desert, complete with hair shirt and leather belt. Locusts and wild honey are his food. He preaches the judgment of God on a "brood of vipers," meaning the members of the religio-political establishment. The center of his message

[20] *The Independent*, Friday, 27 January 1995.
[21] The sermon was preached on 12 March, 1995. I have set the words as a quotation although I have no actual text from which to quote. They are a reconstruction made from notes I took at the time. It seemed better to try to retain the immediacy of direct speech in the report. Although the full text was much longer than this condensation I hope that I have managed to remain faithful to the substance of the sermon.

is a call for strict repentance since, even now, "the axe is lying at the root of the trees" (see Matt 3:4-12).

After the Holocaust it has become manifest again that the extraordinary history of the Jewish people, a history of suffering and dispersal, is a testimony to "an apparently unsaved world" and the irreducible demand—the divine demand—for justice in the midst of it. In the words of Emmanuel Levinas, it is "as if Jewish destiny were a crack in the shell of imperturbable being and the awakening to an insomnia in which *the inhuman is no longer covered up and hidden* by the political necessities which it shapes, and no longer excused by their universality."[22] A profound experience of the inhumanity of human actions, especially the injustice and cruelty that lurk in the corridors of power, shapes the Jewish understanding of God, from the experience of "bondage in the land of Egypt" to the present day. There is a terrible honesty about this faith. It is a religion in which the "fast" is of fundamental importance. But the fast is understood in a particular way. In Isaiah 58, which has a central place in the liturgy of Yom Kippur, the point is made. The "pious" ones, practiced in the rituals of faith, challenge God for inaction. "Why do we fast, but you do not see? Why humble ourselves, but you do not notice?" To which the Lord replies:

> Look, you serve your own interest on your fast day, and oppress all your workers. Look, you fast only to quarrel and to fight and to strike with a wicked fist. Such fasting as you do today will not make your voice heard on high. Is such the fast that I choose, a day to humble oneself? Is it to bow down the head like a bulrush, and to lie in sackcloth and ashes? Will you call this a fast, a day acceptable to the Lord? Is not this the fast that I choose: to loose the bonds of injustice, to undo the thongs of the yoke, to let the oppressed go free, and to break every yoke? Is it not to share your bread with the hungry, and bring the homeless poor into your house; when you see the naked, to cover them, and not to hide yourself from your own kin? *Then your light shall break forth like the dawn, and your healing shall spring up quickly. . . . Then you will call and the Lord will answer* (Isa 58:3-9; italics added).

Levinas draws three fundamental conclusions from this text. (1) The distinction between what is "specifically religious," that is, actions of devotion or worship directed exclusively toward God, and the sphere of ethical obligation, or duty toward the human neighbor, is called in question. Kierkegaard's view that religion represents a "higher stage" of existence beyond the ethical is rejected.[23] (2) Religion is in essence nothing other than

---

[22] Emmanuel Levinas, *Beyond the Verse: Talmudic Readings and Lectures*, translated by Gary D. Mole (London: The Athlone Press, 1994) 4 (italics added). I am heavily indebted to the essay "Demanding Judaism," 1–10, for the section that follows.

[23] See n. 17 above.

the fulfillment of moral obligation toward the neighbor. What matters is not "faith" but "doing." The accomplishment of the ethical *is* the accomplishment of the religious. Levinas is explicit on this point. "[T]he religious is at its zenith in the ethical movement towards the other man . . . the very proximity of God is inseparable from the ethical transformation of the social . . . it *coincides* with the disappearance of servitude and domination." Doing good *is* the act of religious belief itself. (3) In absolute agreement with Nietzsche, but with diametrically opposite evaluation, Levinas argues that Jewish faith "expresses above all the obstinate negation of a political and social order which remains without regard for the weak, and without pity for the vanquished." For Nietzsche this is the disposition of slavery. For Levinas it is the hope of divine liberation.[24]

The "fast"—that is, the ethical element of relationship with God—is an inescapable aspect of all genuine religion, Christianity included. Jesus himself acknowledged it. He was baptised by John (Mark 1:9). He knew that faith in God creates a kind of anti-society in the midst of an unjust world. The kingdom of God and God's righteousness, by its very existence, is a critical disturbance of the *status quo*. There are broods of vipers about. They do need smoking out. Jesus, like John, began his ministry with a call to repentance (Mark 1:15). He was severe on economic enterprise understood as an end in itself. "You cannot serve God and wealth," was his assessment (Matt 6:24). For would-be followers there is, to use Kierkegaard's phrase, an "either/or" quality to discipleship. And there is no disguising the cost. "If any want to become my followers, let them deny themselves and take up their cross and follow me" (Mark 8:34). Jesus' commitment to the will of God plunges him into resistance of all forms of evil—injustice, illness, suffering, and death. The powers that be in this world, spiritual and civil, recognize the threat of his actions and words. They take him with utmost seriousness. The struggle goes down to the wire, bringing Jesus eventually to condemnation, punishment, and death, just as it did to John. Faith in God in this world implies a taking

---

[24] All quotations are from Levinas, *Beyond the Verse* 4–6; italics on the word "coincides" added. Cf. also the vivid story Levinas tells in another place. It concerns Hannah Arendt. "When she was a child in her native Königsberg, one day she said to the rabbi who was teaching her religion: 'You know, I have lost my faith.' And the rabbi responded: 'Who's asking you for it?' The response was typical. What matters is not 'faith,' but 'doing.' Doing, which means moral behavior, of course, but also the performance of ritual. Moreover, are believing and doing different things? What does believing mean? What is faith made of? Words, ideas? Convictions? What do we believe with? With the whole body! With all my bones (Psalm 35:10)! What the rabbi meant was : 'Doing good is the act of belief itself.' That is my conclusion." Emmanuel Levinas, *In the Time of the Nations*, translated by Michael B. Smith (London: The Athlone Press, 1994) 164.

of sides that is as serious as it can be. There is a cross right in its heart. The effort, the self-denial, the struggle involved in religion Type A are always required. Where they are not found religion is rightly criticized as self-indulgent, untruthful, and unjust. Liberation theologies of all stripes have learned this, basically from the Jewish example and the Hebrew Scriptures. The story of the Exodus and its reinterpretation in the political theology of the prophets have been central.

Nietzsche is right. There *is* a negative element in Christianity and Judaism. It cannot be ignored or passed over lightly. Sometimes the so-called "creation spirituality" of Matthew Fox and his followers, for all its value, tends in this direction. With its concern for "a dancing God" and the understandable desire to move beyond a faith of negativities and repressions, it risks becoming unrealistically optimistic about humanity.[25] But the argument that the negative assessment of the world is the result of gloomy preaching is a mistake. Nietzsche's view that "*because* humanity has listened to these preachers much too eagerly . . . something of this superstition that they are in a very bad way has finally stuck" is mischievous. No doubt there are doomsayers who exaggerate the darkness of life. But the doctrine of sin is powerful because it names, rather than invents, the experience of suffering, evil, and death. These days there are revisionist historians who claim that the Holocaust is a fabrication.[26] It never happened. Talk about it is gloomy and inaccurate, a false picture of the world. Nietzsche cannot be held responsible for such travesties, of course. But his theory that any interpretation of the world that sees that things are "in a very bad way" is fundamentally the result of some sort of a theological conspiracy invites such revisionism. It can only be rejected in disgust by people of goodwill. The inhuman must not be covered up and hidden. Both the prophets and the Christ negate the world and the self *to the degree that the world and the self are set against justice and against God.* The cross does reveal that history is fallen, that sin abounds, and not just in obviously evil people, but also in the lives and actions of history's best. It is good people, the religiously sophisticated and politically dedicated, not the overtly wicked, who crucify Jesus. The real Christ confronts us with two negative elements: "the requirement of self-giving and the denial of the self, on the one hand, and the death on the cross,

---

[25] Cf. the words of Kierkegaard: "The bustling parsons and their advisors from the laity, who wish to deliver man from fear of the terrible, are opposed to me. It is true that anyone who wants to attain anything in this life would be better off forgetting about the terrible. But anyone who sets himself problems of a religious nature must open his soul to the terrible." *Stages on Life's Way* IV, 341, quoted by Lev Shestov, *Kierkegaard and the Existential Philosophy*, translated by Elinor Hewitt (Athens, Ohio: Ohio University Press, 1969) 186.

[26] David Irving is perhaps the most notorious of revisionists.

on the other," and both "coincide to express the negation of the world and of our human being in the world, which out of self-concern eliminates him who comes not only to save us but represents as well our own authentic selfhood."[27]

What about joy? We said earlier that joy is the state that attests the fulfillment of our lives. Joy is the state we enter when we are united with what answers our deepest needs and puts us in touch with the purpose for which we were made.[28] Conversely, sorrow is the sense of being deprived of that fulfillment. A real clash of values occurs here. For Nietzsche fulfillment of being means realization of one's own freedom. Joy craves admiration, not sympathy; strength, not weakness. Joy is Dionysian. "Not good taste, not bad taste, but *my* taste" is what counts.[29] Slavish obedience to the rules and conventions of others, hand-wringing about the sorry state of things, timid capitulation to the constraints of society, and all dressed up in divine livery—these are the killjoys of religion. Joy is to be free of them and to soar like the eagle.

Christianity and Judaism stand foursquare against it. The issue is solidarity with those who suffer. Human fulfillment understood from this religious tradition is impossible without community. True humanity is essentially *co-humanity*, a being-with the other. While the other is unfulfilled, I am likewise unfulfilled. *My* taste cannot be finally realized without *your* taste. Barth is in full agreement with Levinas on this point. Faith in God forces us to face the suffering of the world. It will not let us be human without struggling to alleviate it. "In the person of Jesus [crucified] a whole host of others who are wholly and utterly ignoble and despised in the eyes of the world (of the world of Zarathustra, the true world of men), the hungry and thirsty and naked and sick and captive, a whole ocean of human meanness and painfulness" must be recognized as our neighbors and *ourselves*.[30] (Cf. Matt 25:31-46). If joy cannot be had while also acknowledging the right of these, too, to be joyful, that is, fulfilled in *their* humanity, then there is no joy in Christian and Jewish existence.

It would be a long and difficult exercise to debate this conflict adequately. In its extreme forms Nietzsche's "superman," the one who creates his own world of values, seems isolated, locked up in himself, even deluded. In the realm of politics it is worse. An appalling use of power, with utter indifference to the suffering it creates, lurks in the wings. Nietzsche cannot be blamed for the atrocities of Nazism toward the Jews, but neither is it an accident that his name was associated with the rise of

[27] Langdon Gilkey, *Through the Tempest: Theological Voyages in a Pluralistic Culture*, edited by Jeff B. Pool (Minneapolis: Fortress, 1991) 108.

[28] See above pp. 160–61.

[29] Nietzsche, *Thus Spake Zarathustra*, Part III, "Of the Spirit of Gravity," p. 213.

[30] Barth, *Church Dogmatics* III, 2, p. 241.

National Socialism. His critique of the scarecrow Christ stands. It must be heeded. Timid, self-pitying, stern Christianity is a disaster for many. But, on the other hand, genuine humanity as *co-humanity* is a truth that must never be forgotten. This is the message of the Holocaust and the cross. Without it the "good conscience" of the established order remains unchallenged and terrible injustice continues unabated. If this means tears mixed with joy, so be it.

Susan stands in need of Nietzschean-type counsel. As we have seen, she is in some ways instinctively Nietzschean already. She laments a lack of joy in her experience and feels in her heart that this is critique enough of Geoffrey's Christ. Oppressive religious structures, passionless relationships, trivial permissions, and massive exclusions, these things make for a boring, which is to say, unreal life. A good dose of *The Gay Science* to shake up such sombre theology would be no bad thing for Susan.[31] More importantly, her life would be much enhanced were she able to assert her own freedom, *her* taste against the fan club's. To watch the final scene and see Susan knuckle down to it all again is to look despair in the eye. Why doesn't she choose Dionysius, for Christ's sake! That's the point. Sometimes "Nietzsche's blasphemies and curses sound sweeter to God's ear than the most solemn halleluiahs."[32] Susan needs to be redeemed from the redeemer she has internalized. It would be for Christ's sake if *that* Christ were exposed and dismissed. The real Christ suffers in the suffering of the weak. But his call, too, is to *do* something to change the orders of oppression, not least religious oppression that operates in his name. But can she . . . ?

The Feast

Religion Type B is the religion of "feasting." According to the text Jesus came eating and drinking and consorting with "sinners." This is in sharp contrast to John. Jesus does not withdraw from the world. He is not found in a hair shirt out in the wilderness. He stays in the cities and towns where the people are. He involves himself in their personal and political struggles. Dinner parties, weddings, and wine in abundance are on the agenda (John 2:1-11). Careless of the eyebrows it raises, Jesus hap-

---

[31] The first English translation of *Die fröhliche Wissenschaft* as *The Joyful Wisdom* misses Nietzsche's meaning. *Wissenschaft* means science, not wisdom. The word "gay" in English has now acquired a new meaning associated with homosexuality. Walter Kaufmann argues that despite this new connotation the best translation remains "gay" rather than "joyful" or "cheerful." "'Gay science,' unlike 'cheerful science,' has overtones of a light-hearted defiance of convention; it suggests Nietzsche's 'immoralism' and his 'revaluation of values.'" "Translator's Introduction," *The Gay Science* 5.

[32] Shestov, *Speculation and Revelation* 186.

pily mixes and often sides with women, outcasts, tax-collectors, lepers, and sex workers (Luke 7:36-50). He stays in touch with Synagogue and Temple, debating the religious leaders on their own ground (Luke 6:6-11). Above all he seems compassionate and nonjudgmental. The sick need a physician, not a sermon (Mark 2:17). Where he is uncompromising, it usually has to do with matters of religious formalism. The word that sums up his attitude hits straight at the heart of oppressive religious regimes. "The sabbath was made for humankind, and not humankind for the sabbath" (Mark 2:27). In other words, religious life that constricts human flourishing is a contradiction in terms. The call to repentance remains. The commitment to action on behalf of the righteousness of God is undiminished. The religion of the feast is not callous. It is not a joy that parades itself while turning its back on the suffering of others. Any such interpretation is stopped in its tracks by the cross. Yet there *is* a joy hinted at here that seems to demand conditions that cannot be contained within the strictly ethical framework of relationship to God and to other human beings that marks Type A religious dispositions. What is it?

"No religion excludes the ethical," according to Levinas.[33] And he is right. But it is also true that, in the final analysis, the Church or Synagogue is not justified, or their place under God secured, *only* because they serve the cause of justice. Many groups do that. It is deeply true that you cannot love God and treat human beings like dirt (1 John 4:20-21). But love of God is not valued and valuable because it achieves certain moral ends. The worship of God is not a means to some other end, social, moral, or even spiritual. It is an end in itself. Schleiermacher, in his famous *Speeches on Religion to Its Cultured Despisers*, refused to recommend faith in God to his educated and skeptical audience by demonstrating its helpfulness for socially desirable goals. Faith that is used as a means, not an end, he argued, is faith already in some way falsified. "You need not fear," he says to his listeners,

> that I shall betake myself in the end to that common device of representing how necessary religion is for maintaining justice and order in the world. Nor shall I remind you of an all-seeing eye, nor of the unspeakable short-sightedness of human management, nor of the narrow bounds of human power to render help. Nor shall I say how religion is a faithful friend and useful stay of morality, how, by its sacred feelings and glorious prospects, it makes the struggle with self and the perfecting of goodness much easier for weak man.[34]

---

[33] Levinas, *Beyond the Verse* 5.

[34] Friedrich Schleiermacher, *Speeches on Religion to Its Cultured Despisers*, translated by John Oman (New York: Harper & Row, 1958) 18. Cf. Jürgen Moltmann, *Theology and Joy*, translated by Reinhard Ulrich (London: S.C.M. Press, 1973) 79.

Faith in God has its own integrity, according to this reading. If we try to defend faith for its utilitarian value it threatens to dissolve into something else. If our dealings with God are determined wholly by ethical relationships with other human beings God becomes superfluous, a disappearing point, a word without independent reference.

This argument is open to radical critique, of course. Marx, Levinas, Gutiérrez and Ruether could all "deconstruct" it easily enough. This view of religion clearly belongs in a context of basic security and comfort. It makes sense for "the cultured," as Schleiermacher's own title indicates. Only those who are sure they know where the next meal is coming from can speak about "the sacred feelings and glorious prospects" of religion as if these were somehow separable from the struggle to survive. Schleiermacher's conviction that the essence of religion is neither a "knowing" nor a "doing," but a qualification of "feeling,"[35] is music to a tyrant's ears. Hitler could live with it.

This is not the place to debate the subtleties of Schleiermacher's view of the relationship between religion and ethics. But, allowing for this critique, the basic point is still worth pondering. Is religion exhausted in the ethical? Kierkegaard, Luther and, in an odd way, Nietzsche (not to mention St. Paul!), agree with Schleiermacher in saying no. At stake is freedom, both human and divine. The ethical is the unconditional demand—"thou shalt." Nietzsche felt in his bones that God cannot be thought of independently of command. If God exists, a universal and necessary and inescapable "thou shalt" lowers over human life. Command means submission to another's will. And "once a human being reaches the fundamental conviction that he *must* be commanded, he becomes a believer." Creativity, self-realization, freedom to determine the future, are lost. Life cannot be lived on its own terms in such a straightjacket, at least not with zest and daring. Hence Nietzsche's break with God. Much better, he felt, to believe "nothing is true [i.e., universally, divinely given]; everything is permitted."[36]

Kierkegaard likewise struggles with the problem of freedom and fulfillment in connection with the "thou shalts" of religion. But, unlike Nietzsche, Kierkegaard refuses to identify God and the ethical. If God is the ethical, then God is subject to the ethical. Then the ethical is God. Then the "thou shalt" strikes at *God's* freedom. If the ethical is the highest, then Abraham is lost. He is a monster, not the "father of faith." His will-

---

[35] Schleiermacher, *The Christian Faith*, translated and edited by H. R. Mackintosh and J. S. Stewart (Edinburgh: T & T Clark, 1968) 5. "The piety which forms the basis of all ecclesiastical communions is, considered purely in itself, neither a Knowing nor a Doing, but a modification of Feeling, or of immediate self-consciousness."

[36] Shestov, *Speculation and Revelation* 192.

ingness to "give up" his son Isaac cannot be understood in terms of the religious category "sacrifice," it can only be judged by the ethical canon "murder."[37] If the ethical is the highest, then Job is lost. He protests his innocence before God, but the whole world contradicts him. In ethical terms his counselors are right. God has judged him wrong. By denying this Job makes himself guilty of both ignorance and arrogance, in addition to whatever moral shortcomings must be assumed to account for his present affliction.[38] Kierkegaard pushes his distinction right into the question of the incarnation. If God is bound by ethical necessity he is powerless to do anything for his Christ. "The menacing 'you must' strikes at His [i.e., God's] freedom; He can weep, suffer, despair, and yet, not only can He not respond to the call of His crucified Son, but He must pretend that powerless love and powerless charity are 'the one thing that is needful,' reserved for both mortals and immortals."[39] The resurrection gives the lie to this interpretation. God is not so bound by necessity. God raises the dead Christ. In other words, "God means nothing is impossible."[40] There is something "higher" than universal ethical maxims: divine grace, the freedom of God to love *unconditionally*.

If the ethical is the highest, Susan is also lost. On the one hand, she is judged a moral failure at central points of her existence. She has committed adultery. She has lied. She has lost her self-control in drug abuse. She despises those who belong to her inner circle. On the other hand, she seems powerless to follow Nietzsche's advice and take charge of her own existence. The effort involved in choosing freedom is beyond her. Courage and strength fail her. The constricting conventions of the scarecrow Christ are an order of magnitude greater than her power to resist them. She capitulates. Great injustice surrounds her. But she cannot challenge it, much less change it. She is victim of her circumstances. The call to *do* something about it is simply beyond her. If religion is exhausted in the ethical, Susan seems bound to be destroyed by it. If human value is measured according to Nietzsche's scale, Susan is trash.

Religious consciousness, at least in its Christian form, is aware that beyond the "thou shalt" in relationship with God lies a deeper word—"thou art." Life is gift before it is demand. The value of *being* underlies the value of *doing*. There is a fundamental *passivity* of human life in relation to God, although it is realized only in dialectical tension with the

---

[37] Kierkegaard, *Fear and Trembling*, and *The Sickness Unto Death*, translated by Walter Lowrie (Princeton: Princeton University Press, 1968) 38–64.

[38] Kierkegaard, *Repetition*, translated by Walter Lowrie (Princeton: Princeton University Press, 1941) 128–31.

[39] Shestov, *Kierkegaard and the Existential Philosophy* 242. Cf. Søren Kierkegaard, *Journals* II, 364, quoted by Shestov, *Kierkegaard* 188–189.

[40] Shestov, *Speculation and Revelation* 192.

demand for action. Schleiermacher called it our "absolute dependence" on God.[41] The capacity to act, even to act in defiance of God, is not self-grounded. Ultimately it is rooted beyond itself in the creating and sustaining grace of God. Levinas is prepared to acknowledge this. "God holds you without letting you go, but without enslaving you: a relation in which, despite the subordination it formally outlines, the difficult freedom of man arises."[42] Already I have tried to argue this case in terms of the doctrine of creation.[43] In this context it emerges again in terms of the doctrine of justification.[44]

Probably more than any other single thinker in history, Luther struggled with this problem. He sets out his basic insight into the dynamics of religious life in the sentence: "Man is justified by faith."[45] He is summarizing Paul. "For we hold that a person is justified by faith apart from works prescribed by the law" (Rom 3:28). Luther intends this as an open definition. It describes *human* existence as such, not simply Christian existence.[46] The human being is not fundamentally constituted by what he or she does, but by the free affirmation of God, that is, by grace. The righteous person is the one judged "all right" by God, not one acquitted before some ethical tribunal, however lofty. "We do not become righteous by doing righteous deeds but, having been made righteous [by God], we do righteous deeds."[47] There is always the danger, as Levinas points out, that such a doctrine will cut the nerve of ethical responsibility and weaken the demand to act for justice in a sinful world. Paul faced the same accusation at the dawn of the Christian era (cf. Romans 6). Yet whatever the truth in Nietzsche's bold claim that we must "make ourselves," or in Levinas' view that ultimately the ethical is the religious, it remains doubtful that we can constitute our own *beings*. Whatever we can do to make our lives our own is something other, and presupposes the fundamental mystery of what makes a person into a person. The value of being human is more than, though it also includes, the ethical value of

[41] Schleiermacher, *The Christian Faith* 12.

[42] Levinas, *Beyond the Verse* 9. For a somewhat different assessment see the discussion of Levinas' views of the relationship to God and the relationship to the human other in Eberhard Jüngel, *Theological Essays II*, translated by Arnold Neufeldt-Fast and J. B. Webster (Edinburgh: T & T Clark, 1995) 91–99.

[43] See above, pp. 148–51.

[44] For what follows see especially Jüngel, *Theological Essays II*, chs. 10 and 11, *passim*.

[45] Martin Luther, *The Disputation Concerning Man*, in *Luther's Works*, edited by Jaroslav Pelikan and H. T. Lehmann (Philadelphia and St. Louis: Fortress and Concordia, 1955–1986) 34:139.

[46] Jüngel, *Theological Essays II*, 216.

[47] Luther, *Disputation Against Scholastic Theology*, in *Luther's Works* 39/1, 283; quoted by Jüngel, *Theological Essays II*, 229.

freely chosen actions and intentions. Deeper than all human efforts at self-realization, or at setting to rights the inhumanities of history, is the promise that human persons are already accepted and approved in the prior judgment of God. And this is true in spite of the judgment a strict ethical view can and must make.

The final mystery of religion is that God overcomes, or better, re-creates, the ethical in the flow of divine life. Faith receives life from God before it is asked to give life for others. This view of grace has remarkable consequences. While ethical judgments cannot be avoided, in the final analysis

> The justification of sinners forbids one to identify the *best* or even the *most atrocious deed* with the "I" of the agent. It demythologizes the myth of superhumans who surpass themselves with their successes, and allows us to discover behind the facade of the self-righteous individual who confuses him- or herself with life's achievements a human being worthy of mercy. And similarly it also demythologizes the myth of inhuman beings who have become non-persons through the atrocities they have committed, and even in the worst case allows us to discover behind a wretched life story the person to whom God himself has been merciful.[48]

The terrible test case of this theology is the Holocaust. Is the ethical judgment, the inevitable and utter condemnation of such inhumanity, the absolute and final word of God? Just this is the matter at dispute between Elie Wiesel and David Goldberg. This Jewish debate makes it abundantly plain that the issue of divine forgiveness that lies at the heart of religion Type B is not confined to Christian sensibility. Yet in the Christian view it is central. The cross of Christ reveals *both* God's resistance to evil and its destructive consequences in life *and* the grace that bears for us the self-destruction that our own participation in evil wreaks in our existence.

A person has value even when he or she can do nothing, or has done so much that the knot of the past seems too tangled to untie. Susan laments what might have been. "Once upon a time I had my life planned out . . . or half of it at any rate. I wasn't clear about the first part, but at the stroke of fifty I was all set to turn into a wonderful woman." She then lists all the things she should have achieved, in the Church and beyond. "But I can *do* none of these things. I'm even a fool at the flower arrangement."[49] This is where Susan's functional Christ fails once more. He will not let her get beyond a sense of condemnation. On ethical grounds— good ethical grounds, not mere pious convention—she finds herself judged guilty. She doesn't even have the courage to tell the truth about it all. No matter which way she turns or how hard she tries, she always seems to be

[48] Ibid. 256.
[49] Bennett, *Talking Heads* 34 (italics added).

in the wrong. The Christ who can "suspend the ethical"[50] for the sake of the creation of new possibility is the Christ who can bring life to a situation that, from an ethical perspective, appears to be hopeless. God's unconditional love, an unearned valuing of a life outside of its achievements, is the meaning of grace, the truth of the incarnation. Tillich's words about grace, if Susan could hear them, might be the beginning of a genuine transformation.

> *You are accepted*, accepted by that which is greater than you, and the name of which you do not know. Do not ask for the name now; perhaps you will find it later. Do not try to do anything now; perhaps later you will do much. Do not seek for anything; do not perform anything; do not intend anything. *Simply accept that you are accepted!*[51]

To suspend the ethical in the moment of grace does not mean to *abrogate* it. The passionate commitment—which implies both repentance and action—of religion Type A remains. But its demand is mediated through compassion. Its "thou shalt" is uttered within the context of a deeper "thou art." The name of *this* Christ Susan does not know. If Tillich is right, she can only discover it in the experience of liberation it brings.

For religion Type B there is an intrinsic religious delight. The old catechism is right. Our human purpose is to glorify God and to enjoy God forever. In that sense worship is as much like play as it is like social critique. It celebrates an intrinsic value. If the resurrection is true, if the creation of new possibilities of life in the face of death and of all the "might have beens" is really open in our history, if the alienation of the human heart and the corruption of human society have in fact been overcome in God's grace in Christ even though we must await its final manifestation, then the community of faith, as bearers of that possibility and witnesses to that new reality should, of all people, live with a sense of joy and wonder in the world. This is the religion of the feast, the religion of the Eucharist. Its ethos is gratitude because its foundation is gift. It is disposed to laugh as well as to weep. Although the old order remains in history, death, its final sting, has been overcome. Faith Type B lives from a victory already won.

A Concluding (very) Unscientific Postscript

I want to conclude with some reflections on alcohol. The Lukan text speaks of Jesus as a drunkard. Susan is a regular drunk. Why? To put the question in a broader framework: Why do so many people drink, and with

---

[50] Cf. Kierkegaard's discussion of the "teleological suspension of the ethical" in the case of Abraham and Isaac, *Fear and Trembling* 89–90.

[51] Paul Tillich, *The Shaking of the Foundations* (Hamondsworth: Penguin, 1969) 163.

such dedication? Alcohol is a massive social issue, of course. But is it also spiritual? The adages we use about it point to a deep ambivalence in the fascination of alcohol. *"In vino veritas"*—in wine is truth. The psalmist speaks of "wine that gladdens the human heart" (Ps 104:15). But wine is also seen as a "mocker and brawler" (Prov 20:1). And the old Freudian quip has it that "the super-ego is soluble in alcohol." This ambivalence about alcohol confronts us again in the wine of the Eucharist. Communion wine is symbol both of the death of Christ and of the joy of the coming kingdom. Wine, it seems, represents both the degradation and the ecstasy of human experience. It can mean destruction. It can mean joy.

The tension between religion Type A and religion Type B sometimes crystallizes around the issue of drink. I was raised in a religious atmosphere that took a thoroughly negative attitude toward alcohol. "Drink" was of the devil. It was banned from the house. The mark of a good Christian was abstinence, with one exception—"the Lord's Supper." None of this nonsense about "grape juice" in the Brethren Meeting! Jesus used *wine* at the Last Supper. My childhood memory of the great glass cup of strong-smelling, blood-red liquid ("port" I heard it whispered) that passed my nose as it went the rounds of the solemn Brethren communion service, is full of all sorts of sinister and delicious secrets. If this stuff was so dangerous, what strange power and delight must it hold? Though hardly seven years old, I had imbibed the feeling that for religion mysterious pleasures, especially liquid ones, were dark and forbidden. Given this background, perhaps it is no wonder I have an interest in the way the theologians deal with the question of alcohol!

Paul Tillich, though certainly no wowser, is deeply suspicious of intoxication. Joy and ecstasy belong to human life. They are in fact the marks of life fulfilled, the consequences of the spiritual movement in which the self is united with its ground in God. On that point Tillich is adamant. Life in Christ is life raised to a new height of fulfillment. Intoxication is a pseudo-high. It gives the semblance of joy, but in the end produces spiritual self-destruction.

> Intoxication is an attempt to escape from the dimension of the spirit with its burden of personal centredness and responsibility and cultural rationality. Although ultimately it can never succeed, for the reason that man bears the dimension of spirit, it does give temporary release from the burden of personal and communal existence. In the long run, however, it is destructive, heightening the tensions it wants to avoid. Its main distinguishing feature is that it lacks both spiritual productivity and Spiritual creativity. It returns to an empty subjectivity . . . . It makes the self a vacuum.[52]

[52] Paul Tillich, *Systematic Theology* (Welwyn, Herts: James Nisbet & Co., 1964) 3:126–127.

This could be the Brethren elders speaking. And Susan can easily be interpreted in its light. She drinks to avoid pain, to dull the sense of loss and meaninglessness. She wants relief from the burden of her existence. To that extent alcohol is a substitute salvation. She turns to the bottle partly because her functional Christ is impotent. He is bad Type A, judgmental, unrelenting, and nay-saying.

But there is another side to her drinking. *In vino veritas.* Wine does help Susan see and say some of the truth of her existence. It may be dutch courage, but it is courage nonetheless. It enables her to stand up to Mrs. Shrubsole and the flower arranging competition and to name it for what it is, not love of God, but love of self and of Geoffrey. And the wine certainly dissolves Susan's superego. Under its influence the repressive morality that cripples her vitality is lifted. A lot of what follows may be inappropriate, as Mr. Ramesh notes, inquiring of her with "troubled face . . . if intoxication was a prerequisite for sexual intercourse, or whether it was only when I was going to bed with him . . . I had to be inebriated."[53] But, for all that, the wine does allow her to express her physical being as never before and to experience real if limited joy in doing so.

William James has a more positive attitude toward alcohol and its spiritual significance. James does not see it in terms of an escape from the burdens of existence, at least not a purely negative escape. He interprets it rather as an expression of the deep longing of the human spirit for that which is greater and more complete than the self by itself. In fact, for James drinking alcohol is a form of the mystical striving for transcendence.

> The sway of alcohol over mankind is unquestionably due to its power to stimulate the mystical faculties of human nature, usually crushed to the earth by cold facts and dry criticisms of the sober hour. Sobriety diminishes, discriminates, and says no; drunkenness expands, unites, and says yes. It is in fact the great exciter of the *Yes* function in man. It brings its votary from the chill periphery of things to the radiant core. It makes him for the moment one with truth. Not through mere perversity do men run after it. . . . it is part of the deeper mystery and tragedy of life that whiffs and gleams of something that we immediately recognize as excellent should be vouchsafed to so many of us only in the fleeting earlier phases of what in its totality is so degrading a poison. The drunken consciousness is one bit of the mystic consciousness, and our total opinion of it must find its place in our opinion of that larger whole.[54]

Susan is a "very drunken lady," as she says. But Geoffrey and the fan club can see nothing of what it is about, apart from moral failure. Their

[53] Bennett, *Talking Heads* 39.
[54] William James, *The Varieties of Religious Experience: A Study in Human Nature* (London: Fontana Library, 1961) 373.

energies are directed toward bringing her back to the fold. But Susan's drinking, if read in terms of James' hermeneutic rather than Tillich's, is a deep struggle for the *Yes* function of the human spirit, a longing to move from the "chill periphery of things to the radiant core." Susan's functional Christ is the scarecrow of sobriety that "diminishes, discriminates, and says no." Her intoxication is, in part anyway, her sigh for joy: misplaced and temporary, of course, and, as Tillich maintains, escapist and destructive. But it is *also* the cry for grace. From the data we are given in the story it could be argued that it is a more authentic cry than the prayers of many of the church people, for all their religiosity.

Is it something like this that the accusation of drunkenness and gluttony against Jesus is about? His disposition is an ecstatic embrace of the *Yes* function of life as the gift of God. Unless the Christ can be understood as the source and meaning of such "yes-ness" to life he will be always the Christ of religion Type A, never of religion Type B.

As Tillich argues and James hints, the problem with alcohol as a salvation substitute is that in the end it lacks spiritual productivity and creativity. It does *not* reconcile the splits and alienations that distort human life, inwardly or outwardly. Its "highs" empty rather than fill the spirit. Susan with her scarecrow Christ is caught between a rock and a hard place. On the one hand there is a kind of unhappy religion Type A. It knows that human life is displaced from its home. It knows there is corruption that warps even the most generous of human relationships. It knows there is injustice that oppresses and exploits in even the most enlightened of politics. But it is unable to do much about these threats except by hard moral resistance, struggle, and self-denial. Yet this in turn seems to breed a kind of horrible "holier-than-thou" attitude. And it fails to conquer the darkness anyway. On the other hand there is cynicism about the human condition, which despairs that anything in this sorry world can ever really be mended. Susan can find no exit between the two. She tries to assuage her longing for joy in the consolations of the bottle.

Is real joy in spite of the ruination we see all about us possible? Incarnational christology believes so. Hope, salvation, new possibility enter history as God's gift, not merely as our effort. They can and must be furthered by determined self-denial and hard moral endeavor. But they are founded on the redeeming self-involvement of God in our human story, as manifest in the suffering and risen Christ. God creates. And God makes creation new. Change does come through human attitude and action. Religion Type A is right. But it is not *created* by us. Its source is deeper. It grounds in God's unconditional love. Religion Type B is also right. Fast and feast belong together. But feast is the deeper reality. In vino *religio* veritas?

10

A Different Kind of Play

Dorothy Sayers wasn't married to a clergyman. But she was the daughter of a clerical family of Anglo-Catholic persuasion. Whether she ever wondered, like Susan, what being married to Jesus would have been like is unknown, to me anyway. But in 1946 she put down her considered judgment on Jesus of Nazareth and his attitude to women. He was, she argued,

> A prophet and teacher who never nagged at them, never flattered or coaxed or patronised; who never made arch jokes about them, never treated them either as "The women, God help us!" or "The ladies, God bless them!"; who rebuked without querulousness and praised without condescension; who took their questions and arguments seriously; who never mapped out their sphere for them, never urged them to be feminine or jeered at them for being female; who had no axe to grind and no uneasy male dignity to defend; who took them as he found them and was completely unselfconscious.[1]

This is about as far as could be from Susan's experience. Her sphere is well and truly mapped out for her. The Jesus she knows and his official male representatives simply take it for granted that her being is derivative and her function subservient—to them, naturally. This holds as firmly in the home as it does in the Church. As vicar's wife she is expected "to be on parade" at her husband's every performance. When she chooses not to go to Evensong, Geoffrey feels compromised. "Then I'd better pretend you have a headache," he says grudgingly. Some of the congregation have their worries that she isn't quite doing her job. At the church door Mrs. Shrubsole takes her aside. "We must cherish him," she whispers, nodding toward the vicar. To the bishop, Christ's vice-regent on earth, she is "Mrs. Vicar." His interest in her boils down to one thing—

---

[1] Dorothy L. Sayers, *Unpopular Opinions* (London: Gollancz, 1946) 122; quoted in Ann Loades, *Searching for Lost Coins: explorations in christian feminism* (London: S.P.C.K., 1987) 20–21.

and that addressed to Geoffrey: "How outgoing is Mrs. Vicar?" He means: Will she play the ecclesiastical game as required? When the Carnation milk is knocked over at lunch and Susan gets a dishcloth to "sponge his gaiters," the bishop gives her a funny look. "It's Mary Magdalen and the Nivea cream all over again," she says deadpan into the camera. The women on their knees at the feet of the "lords." "The ladies," says the bishop. "Where would we be without them?"

Susan's questions, far from being answered, are not even noticed. On theological matters like belief in God, ordination of women, work in the Church, her opinions are irrelevant. "So long as you can run a tight jumble sale," she concludes, "you can believe what you like." The nearest she gets to holding a position of genuine significance in the Church is when Geoffrey uses her as an illustration in his preaching on redemption—the story of "the drunken flower-arranger" who was "my wife." "We met it [i.e., 'the problem'] with love," he cries, seizing her hand. And so, "from being a fly in the ointment" Susan finds herself "transformed into a feather in his cap." The look on her face and the tone in her voice as she says it indicate the depth of exclusion she feels.[2]

The cries—public and private—of women in society and in the Church who find themselves put down, pushed to the margins of things, or treated violently, are inescapable. In its diverse forms the feminist movement has emerged as a passionate protest against this unhappy reality. It vigorously opposes gender injustice, promotes equality between men and women, and defies customs, attitudes, and structures that violate the dignity of women. Feminist thinking gives voice to the fact that in much of its theology, liturgy, and practice, the Christian tradition has failed to mediate to women a sense of liberation and joy. In fact, often the reverse. It has restricted, disempowered, and belittled them. Susan's experience is a case in point. Even if we allow that her perspective may be biased, and that Geoffrey and the fan club are not quite as she perceives them, the point remains. And were it all true down to the last detail hers would by no means be the worst of situations. That in the space of little more than two decades feminist theology has made its influence felt worldwide is a measure of its power and persuasiveness. Any attempt to talk about God that hopes to be taken seriously today must confront the challenge of this theology.

I confess to approaching this aspect of the question in fear and trembling. It is a major problem in the Church. There is a lot of pain and anger around. Some of it threatens to split the Church. Certainly it has led to a depletion in the ranks. Can a male presume to say anything on

---

[2] Quotations from Alan Bennett, *Talking Heads* (London: BBC Books, 1988) 31, 32, 40; see also the discussion above, pp. 126–28.

the question? Will not such speaking be just another example of the very issue women have identified: males spouting and probably spouting male theo-ideology? Sometimes I feel there is a gap, an antagonism, between women and men in the Church so deep as to make words trivial or offensive. Is it better to be silent? Is this a topic on which only those are qualified to speak who have lived the problem personally, women themselves? On the other hand—and this is the ragged rationalization I give for pressing on with the task—if we cannot talk across the gender gulf within the Church, then our claim to bear witness to a "new creation" that can reconcile the most profound of human alienations is a mockery. It is a sectarian story we are telling, not the gospel of universal creation and redemption.

I am encouraged in this task by the bravery and determination of many women friends in the Church. They have chosen to stay and certainly not, as is perhaps the case with Susan, for want of somewhere else to go. They stay because they still detect in Christianity a grace and spirit of liberation that is real. Despite it all these women see something worth fighting for in the strange mystery of God that emerges from the story of Jesus. They are not yet ready to abandon it to unchallenged patriarchal control. The spiritual toughness of such women is crucial for the future of the Church. It is conversations with them that are reflected in what follows.

I am going to take a number of things for granted. Perhaps they are still regarded as matters for debate in some circles. Feminism is by no means monochromatic either in or outside of the Church, and of responses made to it, almost no generalizations whatever are safe from challenge. Nevertheless in my judgment, and for the sake of this conversation, I will assume that feminism and its theological expression have substantially demonstrated the following points: (1) That patriarchy as an ideology exists. By ideology I mean a more or less comprehensive understanding of human existence that operates, consciously or unconsciously, to justify the interests of a particular group (in this case males) by representing these interests as the demands of disinterested justice and/or the expression of the will of God.[3] Patriarchy enshrines the view that male dominance is the way the world is structured by nature or God, that it has been

---

[3] Cf. Schubert M. Ogden, *The Point of Christology* (London: S.C.M. Press, 1982) 94–95. An influential definition of patriarchy comes from Adrienne Rich. "Patriarchy is the power of the fathers: a familial-social, ideological, political system in which men—by force, direct pressure, or through ritual, tradition, law and language, customs, etiquette, education and division of labor, determine what part women shall or shall not play, and in which the female is everywhere subsumed under the male." *Of Woman Born* (New York: W. W. Norton, 1976) 57; quoted in Susan Brooks Thistlethwaite, *Sex, Race, and God: Christian Feminism in Black and White* (London: Geoffrey Chapman, 1990) 138.

this way since the beginning, and that to interfere with this order is to defy values that are sacred and thus to risk confusion and destruction. Such a view, bolstered by whatever claimed authority from science, history, philosophy, or Scripture, is nevertheless a rationalization whose purpose is to sanctify a power relationship that advantages the man at the expense of the woman. (2) That patriarchal ideology is entrenched in the Christian tradition. Its influence can be detected everywhere, from language, liturgy, art, and theology to ordination, marriage, and employment opportunities. It is even present in the biblical texts themselves. As a consequence a "feminist hermeneutics of suspicion" is needed to detect and then counteract the impact of such bias in thought and action. The time is past when "androcentric codifications of patriarchal power and ideology [can] claim to be the revelatory Word of God."[4] (3) That patriarchy has been extremely damaging to many women in their self-understanding, their status in the world, and their (perceived) standing before God. Any adequate response therefore calls for genuine repentance and amendment of life. (4) That God is not a patriarch.

The Word Became *Male* Flesh

The issue between women and the Church is nowhere more sharply focused than in the question of christology. It may be possible to think of God as essentially beyond gender specification. It may be possible to conceive of a theological anthropology that genuinely affirms women as made "in the image of God." It may even be possible to imagine a community of religious faith in which women share equally in leadership, authority, and sacramental power with men. But everything seems to come to grief on the affirmation that defines Christianity itself, namely, that Jesus of Nazareth is the Christ of God. Though all else about him may be in dispute, this is agreed by everyone. Jesus was a male. Naomi Goldenberg puts it bluntly.

> Jesus Christ cannot symbolize the liberation of women. A culture that maintains a masculine image for its highest divinity cannot allow its women to experience themselves as the equals of its men. In order to develop a theology of women's liberation, feminists have to leave Christ and the Bible behind them. Women have to stop denying the sexism that lies at the root of the Jewish and Christian religions.[5]

Daphne Hampson arrives at the same conclusion. It hardly matters whether the view of Christ is one that follows classic theology by affirm-

---

[4] Elizabeth Schüssler Fiorenza, *In Memory of Her: A Feminist Theological Reconstruction of Christian Origins* (New York: Crossroad, 1983) 32.

[5] Naomi Goldenberg, *Changing of the Gods: Feminism and the end of traditional religions* (Boston: Beacon, 1979) 22.

ing his being as of "one substance with the Father" or one that is more inclined to stress the historical aspect of his life, neither sort of christology is compatible with the values and aspirations of any feminism worth the name. "Christian feminism," according to Hampson, is a contradiction in terms.

> However "high" a Christology one may have, the divine nature of Christ is still bonded to the human nature of a human who was male. However "low" a Christology, this human person, who is a man, is not simply human but his human nature is bonded to a divine nature.[6]

This is a far-reaching critique in anyone's terms. Liberation theologians sometimes complain that "christology has obscured history," meaning that the real Jesus, Jesus as he actually lived and acted, has been obscured and distorted in the history of christological interpretation of him. This "real" Jesus does not support and is not reflected by oppressive christologies of one kind or another. Goldenberg and Hampson go farther. They argue that it is not merely the *interpreted* Christ that is the problem, but the male identity of Jesus, both in history and in theology, which prevents women from finding liberty and fulfillment in him. It is God incarnate in *male* flesh that is the difficulty. Christology inevitably obscures rather than reveals God for women. This is a critique not of the form but of the substance of theology. It is not as if we can get off the hook by claiming a misleading "functional" view of Christ to be corrected by reference to some "normative" Christ. Whether the approach is via history or dogma, as long as the male figure is given unique theological weight, the problem remains. As a consequence Hampson regards herself as "post-christian." "Christian feminists want to change the actors in the play, what I want is a different kind of play."[7]

There is a certain irony in the fact that this radical feminist stance shares fundamental presuppositions with the most conservative of (masculine) Christian perspectives. For these latter views, also, the maleness of Christ is neither incidental nor accidental. What it means for them, however, is not a social construct—patriarchal ideology, which must be changed—but the order of creation, which cannot be changed. The Fatherhood of God, headship in marriage, authority of the clergy and so on are essentially and fundamentally associated with maleness as a given of *revelation*. Hampson quotes the words of the American Protestant, Thomas Howard.

---

[6] Daphne Hampson, *Theology and Feminism* (Oxford: Basil Blackwell, 1990) 59. Cf. also Rosemary Radford Ruether: "Christology has been the doctrine of the Christian tradition that has been most frequently used against women." *To Change the World: Christology and Cultural Criticism* (London: S.C.M. Press, 1981) 45.

[7] Hampson, *Theology and Feminism* 162.

> Jews and Christians worship the God who has gone to vast and prolonged pains to disclose himself to us as he not she, as King not Queen, and for Christians as Father not Mother, and who sent his Son not his daughter in his final unveiling of himself for our eyes. These are terrible mysteries and we have no warrant to tinker with them.[8]

These "terrible mysteries" are in no way supposed to denigrate women. Women have their God-given place in the created scheme of things. But it is the place of "sacrificial giving," of reception, of following, of nurturing. Howard makes his case by appeal to "revelation." The Bible mediates this understanding of God. And the Bible is to be received as God's own self-manifestation. It is not to be tinkered with.

Again it is somewhat ironic that Protestants of this persuasion find themselves, on the women's issue as almost no other, at one with conservative Roman Catholic perspectives. For the same framework of thought also makes a convenient case for sacramentalists. Official Catholic doctrine has consistently used the christological argument against the ordination of women. The sign of the sacrament must be congruent with that which it signifies, the argument runs. A woman in the sacramental role, because of her biological constitution, obscures the requisite congruence. Therefore in representing Christ, and through him God, the priest must of necessity be male. The priest "acts . . . *in persona Christi*, taking the role of Christ to the point of being his very image."[9] Thus the maleness of Christ appears to be a crucial link, if not the anchor pin, in a chain that sustains a male-dominated interpretation of the world, the Church, the ministry, the sacraments, and ultimately God *himself*.

It is important to emphasize again the main thrust of this argument. It is christology at its best—at least in terms of the argument I have been presenting in these chapters—not christology as its worst that is the problem. An Arian-leaning interpretation of Christ is easier to deal with than an Athanasian one. If Jesus as the Christ is not in some sense *uniquely* related to God the christological offense to women does not arise with the same force. If Jesus is *only* human, a person who, say, knew and loved God in an intense and infectious way, then the fact of his being male *is* incidental. Then it is his message, not his being that is significant. At least his message is separable from his being. It can be adopted and applied as well by women as by men. But the cost of this is the rejection of any substan-

---

[8] Ibid. 66. The original is taken from a speech given by the Anglican bishop Graham Leonard to the General Synod of the Church of England in 1978. There is no further indication of the original source of Howard's comments.

[9] *Inter Insigniores: Declaration on the Question of the Admission of Women to the Ministerial Priesthood*, 15 October, 1976, in Leonard Swidler and Arlene Swidler, eds., *Women Priests: A Catholic Commentary on the Vatican Declaration* (New York: Paulist, 1977) 43–44; quoted in Hampson, *Theology and Feminism* 68.

tial christology at all. Jesus becomes a prophet, a teacher, a rabbi, a guru. There are plenty of those, and of both genders. The trouble is, if Jesus is simply the historical founder of the Christian movement why does he occupy such a central and unrivaled place in the theology, liturgy, and prayer of the Church? Isn't that idolatry? It is the *togetherness* of Jesus with God, however this is understood in detail, that allows for Christian worship to take the shape it does. Jesus as the Christ is the manifestation of the divine. But exactly that connection—the "hypostatic union" as classic christology called it—permits both sacramentalists and revelationists to defend the conclusion that male is, if not identical with, then at least more symbolically or sacramentally appropriate to divinity than female.

This conclusion can be challenged. Any argument that leads to the conclusion that God is more male than female is an argument that has lost touch with the "infinite qualitative distinction" (Kierkegaard) between heaven and earth. It has confused finitude with the conditions that make finitude possible. God is certainly the condition of gender ("male and female God created them" [Gen 1:27]). But it is Feuerbachian projectionism with a vengeance simply to reverse the proposition and say gender is the condition of God; worse still to make the reversal asymmetric—*male* gender is the condition of God, but not female.

But Hampson (and others), rightly in my view, make the case basically on *ethical* grounds. It is not so much the abstract theological problem of the analogical relationship between finitude and infinitude, nor even the specific problem of the special relationship between Jesus of Nazareth and God, that is at stake. It is *soteriology*—the matter of salvation in Christ as developed by the classic christology of people like Athanasius, Gregory Nazianzen, and Melanchthon, that is in question. Athanasius said, "God became man so that men might become divine;" Gregory, "That which he [Christ] has not assumed he has not healed;" Melanchthon, "To know Christ is to know his benefits."[10] But if the Word of God has assumed male humanity *only*, doesn't this exclude the being and experience of half the human race? Where then the benefit for women?

Hampson is not impressed by the argument that Athanasius and his followers, in speaking about the assumption of human nature by the Logos, did not mean "male humanity" to the exclusion of female. They meant simply "humanity," as an essence or universal, has been taken on by God. And humanity as a universal is gender inclusive. If ever such language made sense (which Hampson is not prepared to concede), it only made sense from within a Platonic worldview where universals, rather than particular instances of universals, can be said most truly to exist. Such a worldview has long gone. We live in an age where the reverse is felt nearer the

---

[10] See above, pp. 148–51; 156; 158.

truth. The real is the particular. The universal is the abstract. Inevitably, therefore, in our context the christological question becomes not how universal humanity, but how this particular human being, is incarnate God. But then gender specificity is inescapable, and we are back to the old problem. "Is it not the case," Hampson concludes, "that such a religion is by its very nature harmful to the cause of human equality?"[11]

This is a powerful argument. In the previous chapter we saw how Levinas defended the view that religion at its zenith is precisely "the ethical movement toward the other [person]." The presence of God "*coincides* with the disappearance of servitude and domination."[12] All liberation theologies are agreed on this judgment. If religion is more than this it certainly cannot be a "more" that is really less than this. Theology that leads to injustice is *ipso facto* bad theology. You cannot love God and treat women as dirt. Feminism thus uncovers a particular variation on a general uneasiness with doctrines of grace that move for a "suspension of the ethical." As Kaufmann argued against Kierkegaard, any so-called "revelation" of the will of God that leads you to plan the murder of your only child is abhorrent, whatever fancy theological theories of "obedience" and "sacrifice" you spin out. Murder is murder, and that's what Abraham is plotting against Isaac.[13] Likewise it is "cheap grace" (though very expensive for women) that allows men to suspend the principle of justice in the call for gender equity on the grounds that "revelation" or "sacramental congruence" require them to take a position of superiority over women. It is a threadbare defense to argue that "headship," "priesthood," and access to the lion's share of power are not "inequality" but really true dignity appropriately "nuanced" to account for God-given differences. "The sacrificial animal does not share the spectators' ideas about sacrifice," says Nietzsche, "but one has never let it have its say."[14] Just so. Justice says: "Ask Isaac about sacrifice before you jump to his father's theological conclusions." Ask women about the benefits to them of male redeemers.

Were Daphne Hampson to advise Susan on her options for a better life, it is pretty clear what action she would recommend.

> Many a woman . . . has had to turn her back upon the religion within which she grew up. It simply became impossible. For any woman apprised of what

[11] Hampson, *Theology and Feminism* 53. For the discussion of universals and particulars see pp. 53–58.

[12] See above, p. 167.

[13] "What Kierkegaard sanctions in effect is fanaticism: the attitude of those who willingly suffer everything for their unquestioned faith, and who commit atrocities for it, too." Walter Kaufmann, *The Faith of a Heretic* (New York: Doubleday Anchor, 1963) 73; cf. also pp. 70–76, *passim*.

[14] Friedrich Nietzsche, *The Gay Science*, translated by Walter Kaufmann (New York: Vintage Books, 1974) III, 220, p. 210.

the history of women has been, the question of theodicy raised by the [Christian] conception of God has made that conception of God unthinkable. That God, moreover, was clearly not made in her image, and became superfluous as she came to herself and acquired a feminist consciousness.[15]

It is something of a theological surprise to see it put quite so nakedly that God, to be God, should be "made in her image"—or any finite image, for that matter. But that aside, the judgment is clear. To the extent that Susan's life is deeply shaped by a Christian view of God she, unlike the prodigal son, cannot "come to herself" (Luke 15:17). To be herself in a way that fully liberates her potential as a woman, she must break with the Christian tradition. Even were she to discover a reconstructed christology and be part of a therapeutic process to renegotiate the power structure of her marriage to Geoffrey, and even were she to spearhead a revolution in the Church community and move it toward more democratic structures, she would still lack true fulfillment. Patriarchy by any other name is still fundamentally against her. And this God is a patriarch through and through. Jesus tells her so. The Church is consequently unable to articulate in thought or express in life a theology that affirms her as equally created in the image of God, equally indwelt by the Holy Spirit, equally recipient of liberating grace, equally responsible for her decisions, both sinful and virtuous, as Geoffrey and the bishop.

Jesus the Feminist

Some of the best attempts to answer this kind of critique start with a re-examination of the person of Jesus. Like the tactics of the liberation theologians—understandably so since their causes are not dissimilar—some feminists turn to the historical Jesus as the touchstone of their christology. They try to demonstrate that for all the patriarchal interpretation of Christ in the tradition of the Church, Jesus of Nazareth, in his concrete historical existence, was remarkably free from patriarchal attitudes. And this is true despite the fact that he lived in a rigidly patriarchal society.

Others are wary of this approach. Julie Hopkins, for example, regards the efforts to show that Jesus of Nazareth was no sexist as "rather worn out," though she is prepared to allow that "once the focus is shifted to the life-style and praxis of the Jesus Movement a new vision of power between the sexes in the inbreaking of the Kingdom of God is revealed."[16] Judith Plaskow and Susan Thistlethwaite caution that such endeavors risk falling into unfortunate anti-Jewish sentiments. In an effort to demonstrate how inclusive Jesus was in dealing with women the whole Jewish

---

[15] Hampson, *Theology and Feminism* 173.
[16] Julie Hopkins, *Towards a Feminist Christology* (London: S.P.C.K., 1995) 34–35.

context in which he lived is often depicted, on the basis of comparatively few statements, as misogynist. "In short, the price of Jesus the feminist was yet another slam at the Jews, hardly a dissent from traditional patriarchal theology."[17]

It may be that statements like that of Dorothy Sayers with which we began this chapter are somewhat idealistic, reflecting a pre-critical attitude to reading the gospels. It may also be true that some investigations of the life of Jesus portray his "uniqueness" at the cost of neglecting his essential Jewishness. We have already had occasion to reject such maneuvers.[18] But careful research into the life of Jesus need not be anti-Jewish. As Elizabeth Schüssler Fiorenza argues,

> [To] reconstruct the Jesus movement as a Jewish movement within its dominant patriarchal cultural and religious structures is to delineate the feminist impulse *within Judaism.* The issue is not whether or not Jesus overturned patriarchy but whether Judaism had elements of a critical feminist impulse that came to the fore in the vision and ministry of Jesus.[19]

As with the doctrine of divine forgiveness, the line between patriarchy and feminism does not run between Judaism and the Jesus movement but through the heart of each faith. Even if we insist that much of the Jesus material in the gospel story is evidence of the "Jesus movement," that is, of the communities who received Jesus as the inaugurator of the eschatological kingdom of God rather than of the immediate words or actions of Jesus himself, we can still get a sense of the attitude he took in relation to women and, equally important, the attitude women took to Jesus. Despite the critics this seems an exercise worth doing. The literature on the issue is immense. I can only take the space for a brief indication of its contours.[20]

First, Jesus' attitude to God. Jesus' language about God is diverse and colorful. In his parables he depicts God in relation to human beings as a woman searching for a lost coin, a shepherd looking for lost sheep, a father longing for reunion with lost sons, a baker woman kneading dough, a birth experience that precipitates people into new life, an employer who offends the workers by being too generous, and so on.[21] The inbreaking of "the kingdom of God," as Jesus calls it, unveils a compassionate, lib-

---

[17] Judith Plaskow, "Christian Feminism and Anti-Judaism," *Cross Currents* (Fall 1978); quoted by Susan Thistlethwaite, *Sex, Race, and God* 94.

[18] See above, pp. 163–64.

[19] Schüssler Fiorenza, *In Memory of Her* 107 (italics added).

[20] For what follows see particularly Schüssler Fiorenza, *In Memory of Her* ch. 4; also A. Roy Eckardt, *Reclaiming the Jesus of History: Christology Today* (Minneapolis: Fortress, 1992) 105–134.

[21] Luke 15:3-32; John 3:4-8; Matt 20:1-16. Cf. Elizabeth A. Johnson, *She Who Is: The Mystery of God in Feminist Theological Discourse* (New York: Crossroad, 1994) 79–82.

erating God, radically opposed to structures of domination and exclusion. Even Jesus' controversial use of the term "Father" for God seems to undermine rather than bolster unjust male power. Bernard Cooke, for example, analyzes with great care Jesus' experience of God as *"Abba,"* which means "dear father," or even "daddy."[22] This view of God is profoundly anti-patriarchal, Cooke maintains. It discloses a divine love that is the very reverse of hierarchical power and control. The abba relationship points to a love that is infinitely concerned for the well-being of the beloved. It is prepared to suffer and serve for the liberation of others, male or female, slave or free, Jew or Greek. The fact that such a love was present and revealed in the *man* Jesus is crucial, Cooke believes. In a woman such a revelation might well have been no fundamental challenge to patriarchy, but only what was to be expected. The fact that it appeared in a male, however, means male injustice is radically challenged in the male.[23] If this is not enough to make the point, structures of patriarchal domination are explicitly rejected in the Jesus movement.

> But you are not to be called rabbis, for you have one teacher and you are all students. And call no one your father on earth, for you have one Father—the one in heaven. Nor are you to be called instructors, for you have one instructor, the Messiah. The greatest among you will be your servant. All who exalt themselves will be humbled, and all who humble themselves will be exalted. (Matt 23:8-12).

On this text Schüssler Fiorenza comments: "Thus liberation from patriarchal structures is not only explicitly articulated by Jesus but is in fact at the heart of the proclamation of the *basileia* of God."[24]

Second, Jesus' attitude to women. One of the glories of feminist biblical hermeneutics has been the recovery of women's stories within the biblical tradition. Again, only a hint of the richness of this reconstruction can be given here. The Samaritan woman at the well (John 4) is not judged by Jesus for her moral shortcomings, though they belong to the classic type that patriarchy loves to stress and condemn. Instead, quite remarkably, he entrusts to her the preaching of the messiah's presence, a secret he had thus far kept from his own male disciples. The Syro-Phoenician woman of Matthew 15 begs for Jesus to heal her demon-possessed daughter. At first she is ignored by him and pushed aside by his disciples. She persists, falling on her knees with a heart-wrenching plea: "Lord, help

---

[22] See above, ch. 4, *passim*.

[23] Bernard Cooke, "Non-Patriarchal Salvation" in Joann Wolski Conn, ed., *Women's Spirituality: Resources for Christian Development* (Mahwah, N.J.: Paulist, 1986) 274–286. See also Edward Schillebeeckx, *Jesus: An Experiment in Christology*, translated by Hubert Hoskins (New York: Seabury, 1979) 256–271.

[24] Schüssler Fiorenza, *In Memory of Her* 151.

me." Even then she receives the not very politically correct response, "It is not fair to take the children's [i.e., Israel's] food and throw it to the dogs." Still not to be put off, she continues to press the justice of her cause. In the end she forces Jesus to concede that redemption also extends to non-Jews, an amplification of the grace of God that escaped completely the insight of the males, and perhaps even Jesus himself up to that point. More unexpected still is Jesus' attitude to sex workers, the very lowest of women. Of them he said—and this must go back to Jesus himself, so startling and unacceptable is its implication—that they go into the kingdom of heaven before the righteous male religious leaders (Matt 21:31). Summing up, Schüssler Fiorenza writes:

> Only when we place the Jesus stories about women into the overall story of Jesus and his movement in Palestine are we able to recognize their subversive character. In the discipleship of equals [i.e., the Jesus movement] the "role" of women is not peripheral or trivial, but at the center, and thus of utmost importance to the praxis of "solidarity from below."[25]

It is remarkable stuff. If indeed Jesus combined an anti-patriarchal attitude with an anti-wealth and anti-privilege stance he could hardly have picked a more provocative and unacceptable combination of ideas to espouse, given the political realities of his time. No wonder he was perceived as a threat to the social structures.

Finally, the attitude of women to Jesus. Once the question is raised it is again astonishing how much material comes to light. In the gospel of Mark, for example, the writer introduces four leading male disciples at the start: Simon, Andrew, James, and John. At the end he presents four leading women disciples: Mary of Magdala, Mary the daughter or wife of James, the mother of Joses, and Salome. Schüssler Fiorenza comments that whereas in the story the males (to a man) deny, betray, and abandon Jesus "the women disciples, by contrast, are found under the cross, risking their own lives and safety. . . . [T]hey are well aware of the danger of being arrested and executed as followers of a political insurrectionist crucified by the Romans."[26] An unknown woman anoints Jesus' head with oil, an act he interprets as a prophetic recognition of his death (Mark 14:3-9). Martha of Bethany gives primary confession to full christological faith, at least for the Johannine community (John 11:27). Moreover, the gospel story is uniformly insistent that the first witnesses to the resurrection of Jesus were women. This, the most crucial of all events that determine the meaning of Jesus' life and ministry, stands on the testimony of women. In the Gospel of John, Mary of Magdala stands at the cross of Jesus, discovers the empty tomb, and is the first to experience and

---

[25] *In Memory of Her* 152.
[26] *In Memory of Her* 320.

bear witness to the presence of the resurrected Jesus. Peter and the beloved disciple come on the scene later, but return home without really understanding (John 20:9-10) . Thus in a double sense Mary "becomes the *apostola apostolorum*, the apostle of the apostles," the "primary apostolic witness to the resurrection."[27] Schüssler Fiorenza concludes: "Therefore, wherever the gospel is preached and heard . . . what the women have done is not totally forgotten because the Gospel story remembers that the discipleship and apostolic leadership of women are integral parts of Jesus' 'alternative' praxis of *agape* and service."[28]

Three important results of this approach to christology through the history of Jesus of Nazareth are worth noting in this context.

(1) It blunts the edge of that form of radical feminism that sees patriarchy as a monolithic structure that thoroughly permeates and (therefore) vitiates the entire Jewish and Christian traditions. Here is a patient, historically critical, and systematically detailed study of the origins of Christian faith and its Jewish context that gives the lie to such broadbrush generalizations. It uncovers anti-patriarchal forces in the stories of both women and men, and especially those who came into the orbit of Jesus of Nazareth.

(2) It seeks to transform the religious tradition away from sexist injustice by critical confrontation with elements that are already in the heart of the tradition itself. This is a dialectical reading of the dynamics of revelation in history. The biblical texts, including the gospels, reflect the androcentric culture and history in which they emerged. How could they do otherwise? But they also enshrine, as great prophetic traditions do, a powerful and mysterious "Word of God" that, though in the idiom of the situation to which it comes, is not completely subservient to it. This Word critically confronts the context with a judgment and invitation that relativizes its claims and opens a way for transformation and renewal. Feminist readings of the Bible are "geared toward the liberation of women but also toward the emancipation of the Christian community from patriarchal structures . . . so that the gospel can become again a 'power for salvation' of women as well as men."[29] Prophetic traditions are in this sense always open to correction and self-correction. They live in the tension created by the Spirit between what is given and concrete and what is new and yet to be.

(3) Finally, this kind of approach makes it clear, should anyone be in doubt, that christology has to do with a way of life more than with a conflict of ideas. Feminist and liberation theologians agree that Jesus and the

[27] *In Memory of Her* 332.
[28] *In Memory of Her* 334.
[29] *In Memory of Her* 31.

movement that sprang up around him focused on the coming reign of God as "good news" for the poor, the sick, and the outcasts of the day. Jesus pledged himself to liberate his people. His ministry, suffering, final victory, and new community signified love, grace, and peace for all, but especially for the needy. Women, who in many instances were found among the poorest and most endangered of groups in society, responded warmly to his mission. On these grounds Jesus can be understood as a liberator of women, even today. He stands for solidarity with all who long for freedom from oppression. The liberation he came to bring was addressed to the situation in his own time. It can and must live again in our time. And its actualization may well lead us to as radical a critique of contemporary religion and society as it did in the first century of our era. The cross is no accident.

Susan could benefit from reinterpreting her situation in the light of these observations. Not only would they raise her self-esteem by putting her in touch with others who understand exactly the kind of struggle she is engaged in, but they would also provide her with a powerful leverage for change. She can challenge the ecclesiastical setup in which she is immersed on the grounds of the very tradition it claims to represent. In the final analysis it would be a critique of a destructive functional christology in the name of a BA (better account) christology. I am not suggesting that this is a panacea. Despite the splendid work of much feminist thinking, the struggle of women in the Church goes on. It is a slow business. In particular cases, such as Susan's, many factors other than theological ones are in play. Psychological, economic, social, and emotional forces all shape the pastoral situation. If anything constructive were to be done these factors would have to be taken into account. But for all that, the christological matter is vital. The feminist Jesus is a powerful ally.

All this is gain. But questions remain. As with any approach to the religious significance of Jesus via historical research into his life and context, the results of these investigations remain tentative and debatable. Was Jesus quite so feminist as he is portrayed? Can we honestly conclude from what can be known of his sayings and parables that he was concerned to address the socio-economic and politico-religious dimensions of patriarchy? Nicolas Slee, for example, has shown that "of the main characters in the synoptic parables of Jesus, 211 are male and only 21 female (of whom 10 are bridesmaids!)."[30] Not an outstanding strike rate, one would have thought. Perhaps it is more plausible to take a neutral stance. "Jesus was neither a feminist nor a misogynist. His central mes-

---

[30] See Nicolas Slee, "Parables and Women's Experience," *The Modern Churchman*, 26/2 (1984) 25–31. The sentence quoted is from Hopkins, *Towards a Feminist Christology* 35.

sage simply lay elsewhere."[31] Can such uncertainties really be the basis for an affirmation of the fundamental theological significance of women in the divine scheme of things? Will any message from the past, especially a past now so far removed in time and tradition from our own, speak with the healing power required to deconstruct patriarchal religion and reconstruct new and just communities in its stead?

The question of Daphne Hampson will not be silenced. The advantage of a "low" christology, that is, one that approaches Jesus as essentially just another human being, is that his maleness "then would seem to be of no more import than his or her sexuality in the case of any other human being."[32] We can examine Jesus' words and actions and take from them what seems to be of help, as we would, say, with Socrates, or Moses, or Hampson herself. The problem then is, why bother with Jesus? If Jesus is a human like any other there is no christology, but only a Jesus message. There may well be others whose actions and words on the matter of gender justice are more accessible and more to the point that those of Jesus. "A Christian position must necessarily hold of this human being Jesus that he existed (or exists) in relation to God as no other."[33] This is what makes him important. This is what places his name in the center of Christian liturgy and worship. And this is what makes him crucial in Christian understandings of *God*. It is not that God *tells* us what God is like, or even shows us the divine nature as in a mirror. It is rather that God makes divine reality present in a particular historical form.[34] We are back with Hampson's original complaint. This christological theory appears to make the maleness of Jesus integral to an understanding of God. And that shuts out half the human race. It is to the question of christologies of incarnation and the feminist critique of them that I want now to turn.

A Thought Experiment

One way of looking at christological debate is to see it as a kind of "thought experiment" in progress. It asks the imaginative question: What happens if we assume "X"? The Athanasius/Arius controversy can be set in this light. What happens to Christian life, faith, worship, prayer, etc., if we imagine that Jesus is not "of one substance with the Father" but is of the highest order of created being? As we have seen in previous chapters,

[31] Judith Ochshorn, *The Female Experience and the Nature of the Divine* (Bloomington, Ind.: Indiana University Press, 1981) 173; quoted by Hopkins, *Towards a Feminist Christology* 23.

[32] Hampson, *Theology and Feminism* 62.

[33] Ibid.

[34] Cf. Keith Ward, *Religion and Revelation: A Theology of Revelation in the World's Religions* (Oxford: Clarendon Press, 1994) 193.

if this is assumed some gains can well be claimed. For a start it is much easier to think about both God *and* Jesus if you are not caught in the vice of trying in some way to speak of God *in* Jesus. God is creator. Christ is creature. These may be complex ideas. But they are far easier to deal with separately than trying to "weld" the two somehow. On the other hand, given the lived experience of the Christian community, especially the experience of salvation mediated by Christ, the "easier" position (at least according to the judgments made at Nicea and Chalcedon) failed in important ways to capture the living spirit or "logic" of the faith. If all creatures stand in need of divine grace for their being, and Christ is "merely" a creature, does he not also stand in need as we do? Whence then his help? Thus a kind of "rule" for speaking theologically about Jesus was hammered out. Put negatively (and somewhat frivolously) it says: "to call Jesus a very, very, very, god-like man is not enough." Put positively (and more formally) in Athanasius' words, "*God* became man so that men might become divine." That raises all sorts of other questions. How did it happen? What kind of "becoming" is this? Was he then a "real" man? And so on. The rule doesn't tell you what to say so much as what not to say. If this rule is not respected, speaking about Christ, as far as *Christian identity* is concerned, will be inappropriate. A similar sort of thing can be said about Gregory's dictum, "That which he [Christ] has not assumed he has not healed." This gives expression to the outcomes of another thought experiment: What happens if Christ is thought of as divine? Again the classic judgment was that this does not express what faith really needs to say. The rule this time is, "to speak of Christ as a very, very, very human-like god is not enough." It must be real humanity. Christian talk about Christ that transgresses either of these rules ends up not saying what needs to be said and saying what does not need to be said concerning the Christian relationship to God in Jesus Christ.

We can think of more recent christological thought experiments. Lessing and Reimarus in the eighteenth century asked: What happens if we reject all dogmatic interpretations of Jesus and assume only what can be known of him from critical historical reconstruction? Kierkegaard in the nineteenth century went in the opposite direction. He explored the consequences of assuming that nothing concrete is known of the historical figure of Jesus. What happens if we have only a "footnote" to history to the effect that at such and such a time God took human form?[35] Chris-

---

[35] Hermann Samuel Reimarus, *Fragments*, translated by R. Fraser, edited by Charles H. Talbert (London: S.C.M. Press, 1971). Søren Kierkegaard, *Philosophical Fragments or A Fragment of Philosophy*, translated by David F. Swenson and Howard V. Hong (Princeton: Princeton University Press, 1962) 130–131. "If the contemporary generation had left nothing behind them but these words: 'We have believed that in such and such a year the God appeared among us in the humble figure of a servant,

tology in the twentieth century has been battling with both these experiments and the "rules of doctrine" they might imply ever since.

Suppose that, as our century draws to its close, a shepherdess, wandering the shores of the Dead Sea, were to stumble upon a cave and there discover hidden in a sealed stone jar a manuscript as old as, in fact older than any yet known to the scholars. And suppose, after exhaustive research of the most rigorous kind, it were found to have originated in the very earliest of the "Jesus communities" of Palestine. Every indication is that its author or authors were eyewitnesses to the words and events they report. And suppose that on deciphering the text we learn that the true secret, the dark "messianic secret" of the Jesus movement, was not that Jesus had been conceived out of wedlock, nor that he had merely swooned on the cross and the "resurrection" was nothing more than a lucky recovery, not even that he was secretly married to Mary of Magdala. The real messianic secret was that Jesus was in fact Jesua. The Christ was a woman. Judas' act of betrayal was not to tell the authorities where Jesus was that fateful night. They knew well enough already. It was to tell them that "he" was in fact "she." In fury at the deception they organized for her disposal. For all the reasons now divined by modern theologians this truth had to be suppressed at the time for fear that her message and meaning would not be heeded. But, after much debate, the community decided the story should be written down and securely hidden that the truth might not be finally lost but, one day, in the providence of God, might be found and take effect.

The scenario is fanciful. But the question of implication is not. Feminist theology is in the process of exploring the ramifications of just such a thought experiment. What would be the consequences for Christian faith and life were such a "discovery" to come to light? Would it spell the complete dismantling of Christian spirituality and relationship to God? It is not hard to see how startling changes could be argued for. Patriarchy would be ruled out immediately. All the implications presently drawn from male christology would have the gender signs reversed. God would be she not he, queen not king, mother not father, who sent her daughter not her son as her final unveiling. There would be no question of the authority of women in the Church. The only issue would be whether men could share sacramental dignity with them. Headship in the family would, of course, be with women. It would be hoped that men might fare rather better under such a regime than has been the case for women in the present gender hierarchy. So we could go on.

---

that he lived and taught in our community, and finally died,' it would be more than enough. . . . this *nota bene* on a page of universal history would be sufficient . . . and the most voluminous account can in all eternity do nothing more."

Conservatives reject it outright. They are convinced it is the destruction of Christian spirituality. The incarnation in male form is no accident. It models the meaning of divinity. God cannot and has not become incarnate in female flesh. We must simply accept this "terrible mystery." Radical feminists agree and rest their case. The experiment proves it. Christianity can never be anything but fundamentally sexist. Abandon it. Some, who wish to remain both Christian and feminist, insist on facing the implications. If we cannot "speak of the Divine incarnated in a female body, 'truly God and truly female,'" Julie Hopkins argues, then "Mary Daly was correct when she observed, 'If God is male then the male is God.'"[36]

Others think the issue is a red herring. Jesus' sex is of no more importance than his height or ethnic origins when it comes to what about him is significant *theologically*. For Anne E. Carr, feminist "women in the church insist that sexuality has nothing to do with saviorhood."[37] Moderates make the point that while God *could* have chosen to take human form in female flesh, given the circumstances of history at the time it was expedient not to. Elizabeth Johnson joins Bernard Cooke in maintaining that there is "a certain appropriateness . . . to the historical fact that he [Jesus] was a male human being. If in a patriarchal culture a woman had preached compassionate love and enacted a style of authority that serves, she would most certainly have been greeted with a colossal shrug."[38] Roy Eckardt is less sanguine. "It appears to me that in the light of the dreadful tale of male oppression of women, it would have made more sense in the long run for God to have sent a woman." "Was this possible?" he muses. But does not answer. "That is a problem for God rather than for us."[39] Maybe. But God does seem to have put the ball in our court for the moment.

Rule 4?

I want to push this experiment a bit farther. But to do so I need to make a theoretical digression into what George Lindbeck has called "the nature of doctrine."[40] If this seems tedious, skip the following paragraphs and pick up the story at the next section when it is all over!

By doctrine Lindbeck means "communally authoritative teachings regarding beliefs and practices that are considered essential to the iden-

---

[36] Hopkins, *Towards a Feminist Christology* 85.

[37] Anne E. Carr, *Transforming Grace* (San Francisco: Harper & Row, 1984) 187; quoted in Eckardt, *Reclaiming the Jesus of History* 133.

[38] Johnson, *She Who Is* 160.

[39] Eckardt, *Reclaiming the Jesus of History* 254, n. 17.

[40] George A. Lindbeck, *The Nature of Doctrine: Religion and Theology in a Postliberal Age* (Philadelphia: Westminster, 1984).

tity or welfare of the group in question."[41] In a now famous argument he compares three different interpretations of the nature of doctrinal statements and the way they function in the theological tradition.

(1) The first he calls the "cognitive/propositional" theory. In this view doctrines function as "informative propositions." They are truth claims about objective realities. To speak of God incarnate in Christ means to conceive in mythical or metaphysical terms of the conjunction of divine and human essences in the one being, Jesus of Nazareth. Conservative theology often takes this position.

(2) The second option Lindbeck calls the "experiential/expressive" theory. In this perspective doctrines are understood not as objective truth statements so much as symbols giving expression and form to religious experiences, attitudes, and orientations. To speak of incarnation in this framework means to speak of the human experience of God carried to its highest pitch. If to experience God is to feel oneself absolutely dependent upon God (Schleiermacher), then, in Jesus Christ this experience reaches its most intense and perfect manifestation. A good deal of liberal theology follows this line.

(3) While not dismissing the value of these perspectives on doctrine, Lindbeck himself favors a third option that he calls the "cultural/linguistic" theory. This model understands religion as a "comprehensive interpretive medium," that is, a symbolic or categorical framework through which human beings interpret their experience, understand their world, and order their lives. Religions provide communities with idioms—rituals, languages, stories, forms, ideas—to enable them to deal with whatever is regarded as most important in human existence, the "ultimate questions of life and death, right and wrong, chaos and order, meaning and meaninglessness."[42] Doctrines are the *rules* that govern the way the interpretive system works. To change the image, doctrines are to religious life what the rules of grammar are to the operation of language. They do not tell you what to say so much as describe the conditions under which anything that is said can make sense. "The novelty of rule theory . . . is that it does not locate the abiding and doctrinally significant aspect of religion in propositionally formulated truths, much less in inner experiences, but in the story it tells and in the grammar that *informs the way the story is told and used.*"[43]

A bald summary like this does no justice to the fascinating discussion Lindbeck undertakes to illustrate and defend his thesis. But for my purposes it is sufficient. I want to explore how a rule theory of doctrine might assist in the feminist "thought experiment" on which I am embarked. How

---

[41] *Nature of Doctrine* 74.
[42] *Nature of Doctrine* 40.
[43] *Nature of Doctrine* 80 (italics added); see also pp. 16; 30–39.

does Lindbeck's cultural/linguistic theory help deal with a theological interpretation of incarnation? The most significant gain over the other theories is that rule theory allows a clear distinction between doctrine and the terminology or conceptuality in which it is formulated. Thus the doctrines of Chalcedon, for example, can be said to remain in force in different linguistic and conceptual worlds provided the new expressions generate equivalent consequences in the revised context. The words and concepts may be different, but the rules governing their use remain the same.

It is more difficult to sustain this distinction in the frameworks of the propositional and expressive models. If incarnational doctrine intends to refer primarily to the being of the Christ as such it is difficult to see how, if there is a change in gender as proposed, the *whole* edifice is not changed as a consequence. We simply get a mirror image system with all the problems of gender justice reversed. Likewise if incarnational doctrine is referred to experience. Feminists complain that their experience, women's experience, cannot be summed up in the experience of a male, however perfect. Their side of the experiential equation is left out. The Christa experiment overcomes this nicely. Women's experience is now central. But what of men? In both cases we seem to be caught on a switchback of either/or. And, in any case, the whole thing is hypothetical since the incarnation "in fact" was in a male. Can rule theory help?

It is important to note that the "rules" that govern or describe the operation of religious idioms are not necessarily *consciously* in mind for those who live within the idiom, not even when they are in the process of debating theological doctrines. Like rules of grammar they are "second order" propositions, sentences describing how sensible sentences work. Competent speakers of a language may never refer to, or even know, the rules of their grammar. They know from long practice how to speak meaningfully, what makes sense and what doesn't. The rules are implicit, nonetheless, and there are times, in novel circumstances, say, or on occasions of disagreement, or when learning a new language, when reference to the rules is helpful. Most theological controversies are about matters of immediate concern in a particular context. How shall we speak responsibly of God in an age of science? How is discipleship of Jesus Christ to be understood in circumstances of social injustice? And so on. Those who argue such questions from a Christian perspective do so using all the materials that make the faith what it is—the biblical story, liturgies, prayers, art, humor, theological ideas and ethical maxims of the tradition. But as the debate clarifies the issues and some points of view win acceptance and others are put aside, the implicit "logic" of the discussion can be analyzed and the "rules" governing it made explicit.[44]

---

[44] *Nature of Doctrine* 82–83.

Lindbeck detects three basic "regulative principles" at work in the shaping of the classic doctrines of incarnation and the trinity. *Rule 1:* The monotheistic principle: there is only one God, the God of the Hebrew Scriptures. *Rule 2:* The principle of historical specificity: the stories of Jesus refer to a real human being who was born, lived, and died in a particular time and place. *Rule 3:* The principle of christological maximalism: "every possible importance is to be ascribed to Jesus that is not inconsistent with the first rules." These principles reflect the implicit sense of religious self-understanding in the Christian community from earliest times, Lindbeck argues. Their joint application to the various controversies that emerged in the course of time constrained the early believers "to use available conceptual and symbolic materials to relate Jesus Christ to God in certain ways and not in others."[45] It is not hard to see how the application of these rules might work to the exclusion of the classic "heresies" of christology—docetism, Gnosticism, adoptionism, Arianism, Nestorianism, and so on. By the same token, "what ultimately became Catholic orthodoxy was a cognitively less dissonant adjustment to the joint pressure of these three rules than any of the rejected heresies."[46]

Here, then, is Lindbeck's main contention: "if the same rules that guided the formation of the original paradigms are operative in the construction of the new formulations, they express one and the same doctrine."[47] This means that terms and concepts used in discussing christology can change radically according to circumstance and need, while yet remaining faithful to the fundamental intention of the original impulse of faith. That intention is to live life according to the conviction that Jesus is of central importance for the right ordering of the complex relationship that human beings have with God the final mystery that grounds and encompasses their lives, and with each other and the world.

I want to emphasize two points before applying this theory to feminist christology. (1) The so-called "regulative principles" of doctrine are working principles that are only discovered in the process of theological debate. They are not known *a priori*. Rules of grammatical structure emerge from studying the way a living language works, not the other way around. Similarly, learning how to apply the story of Jesus to the ultimate questions of life is a process of trial and error, learned in the doing of it. (2) The rules are therefore, in principle at least, open to amendment, clarification, modification, or addition. Further debate, deeper reflection, and new circumstances may lead to the uncovering of other regulative principles, consistent with the fundamental sense of faith that belongs to the community but previously unsuspected or inadequately formulated.

[45] *Nature of Doctrine* 94–95.
[46] *Nature of Doctrine* 95.
[47] *Nature of Doctrine* 95.

As I said earlier, feminist theology has, in the matter of a decade or two, become influential on a world scale. No serious Christian thinking can ignore it. This means that increasing numbers of thoughtful Christians—genuinely "competent speakers in the Christian idiom" to use a Lindbeck-like phrase—are more and more convinced that the way we have been using christological language is inappropriate. It is "ungrammatical" in terms of the "feel" of the idiom. It seems to lead us to say and do things we don't want to say and do as Christians, and not to say and do things we do want to say and do (cf. Rom 7:15!). And that, we feel, is not the way "the grammar" ought to operate. The original intention of christological doctrine—"that *everyone* who believes in him may not perish but have eternal life" (John 3:16)—is badly obscured by the use to which christological language has been put in patriarchal contexts. In order to recover the original meaning of the Christ, attention must be given to the rules that governed the formulation of classic christological doctrine to see whether they are being appropriately applied in our new context of concern with gender justice, and also whether the new context has led to the uncovering of modifications or additions that need to be made to those rules in order that the original intention might be made clear once again.

I want to argue that feminist theology, in the course of its controversy with established theology, has in fact brought to light at least one implication of and one addition to these regulative principles of christological doctrine. I will mention the implication briefly and then concentrate on the additional rule.

The implication. Lindbeck's second rule affirms historical specificity. Jesus was born, lived, and died in real time and space. As a summary statement this is fair enough. It reflects Gregory's rule. I am not chiding Lindbeck for not developing it further. The important point is this. Classical christology affirmed this rule but applied it rather abstractly. The creed jumps from birth to death in the Jesus story—"Born of the virgin Mary, suffered under Pontius Pilate." It says yes to time and place of birth and death, but completely neglects to say what *kind* of life Jesus lived in the time between. It is hard to avoid the feeling that in applying this rule the classic creed assumes that the life of Jesus is not of theological significance, at least not of the same order of significance as his birth and death. Kierkegaard was exploring a variation on this classic view in his "footnote" experiment. But this means that a crucial issue is neglected: What were the historical actions, words, and alliances that resulted in Jesus being brought to the sorry condemnation of the cross? Why did he choose this path? Whom did he offend? Whom did he support? And why? Along with a number of movements in modern theology, including nineteenth-century liberalism and twentieth-century liberation theology, feminist theology insists that an implication of Rule 2 is that the concrete historical details of the life of Jesus of Nazareth must be taken into *theological* account. It is not enough to say he was "true man." We must also say "and he was this *kind* of man." The sort of impact that this application of the rule has on shaping Christian understandings of God and of the "cost of discipleship" are glimpsed in the discussion of the feminist Jesus above.

More significant is the claim that a fourth rule should be considered in any contemporary christological debate. As a tentative formulation I put it thus. *Rule 4:* Rule 3 may not be so interpreted as to yield non-equivalent theological consequences in relation to matters of gender difference. Another, though less helpful way of stating this rule would be to say that only those things may be claimed as *theologically* essential for Christ as could equally well be claimed for the "hypothetical Christa."

Is this an advance? Does it not in fact introduce a false image—a hypothetical counter-factual, as the logicians might say—into christological debate? The "scandal of particularity" in historical Christian faith seems to be that there *is* the male Christ and *is not* the female Christa. To try to balance the two things—one fact, the other "thought experiment"—is in effect to turn the incarnation into a myth or mere idea. We could work out the meaning of christology simply by imagining an incarnation first in male, then in female form. Do we need either to be real? If we were stuck with the idea that doctrine is essentially propositionally formulated truth—was it this or was it that?—this criticism would be serious. But rule theory is not making ontological statements. It is advising how to draw appropriate theological conclusions within a Christian idiom from ontological statements. It is still possible, indeed necessary, to maintain that God was in Jesus Christ. Rule 2 of the schema requires that. Real, historical, fleshly presence is demanded by good christological grammar. But the question then is: What further theological conclusions can legitimately be drawn from this in the light of Rule 3? And this is where the Christa experiment helps to clarify things. Universalizing maleness is a theological scandal. Whatever the "scandal of particularity" means, it cannot mean this.

This is not the first time issues of this kind have been faced by the Church. Take the question of suffering and death. Jesus Christ suffered and died, and in an appalling manner. Does this mean that, because he is God incarnate, we must say God also suffered and died? Does a simple "as on earth so in heaven" rule apply here? The so-called "patripassianists," those who believed that such a rule does apply, argued that christology implies that since Jesus suffered the Father also suffered. Their opponents, sensitive to the fact that at the very least it seems odd to say "God dies," felt the reverse to be the better case. God does not suffer.

The question is not: Did Jesus suffer or not? The answer to that is not in doubt. The question is: What rules apply in drawing legitimate theological conclusions from this "fact"? In the course of history opinion has been divided on the matter. Those who held that suffering cannot be attributed to God tended to carry the day in earlier times. But the weight now seems to have shifted. "Competent speakers" of the Christian language now argue strongly for the "rightness" of speaking of a suffering God, or at least of suffering in God. The issue of slavery is similar. Where once slavery appeared to be an acceptable social organization within a Christian framework, this is no longer the case. It is now universally agreed that the rule against slavery has the weight of dogma. Christian faith and theology cannot be so interpreted that slavery remains an option within its horizon. In short, rules for the proper interpretation of the Christian idiom can change, develop, and be refined in the course of debate aroused by new situations.

Feminists are not arguing that Jesus is an imaginary figure, easily "balanced" by a hypothetical Christa. Still less are they debating his gender. The Christa experiment simply forces the problem of gender equity to be faced squarely. The question in a cultural/linguistic framework of understanding doctrine is as always: What kind of rule(s) guide the theological use to which the basic story is put? Until recently much theology has simply assumed that, on the gender issue, the male image is dominant. And it has used this assumption in a "grammatically careless" fashion in theological construction.[48] Now this unthinking application is under powerful challenge. Its operation leads to all the baleful consequences feminist theology has so carefully documented. It seems hard to resist the conclusion that the current way of doing and saying things is flawed. The rules need to be re-examined. Lindbeck's theory of doctrine provides a way of doing that without destroying the fundamental intention of the original story of incarnation. Rule 4 as I have defined it suggests a way of making the appropriate adjustment. The first formulation is to be preferred to the second. While it is not as vivid or confronting, it also does not give the impression that it is reducing the christological question to one of myth or idea. Its character as a regulative principle is obvious.

Continuity and Discontinuity

What difference would the application of Rule 4 make to christology? I believe it to be far-reaching, and (obviously) in line with the best

---

[48] There are, of course, counterimages in the tradition that have a feminine interpretation of christological ideas, e.g., Julian of Norwich, Bernard of Clairvaux, Anselm, etc. These counterexamples are now being vigorously explored.

of feminist theology. A few pointers only can be given here. First in relation to God and language about God: If incarnational christology—God was in Christ—allows us to speak responsibly of the "humanity of God" (Barth), and if this means it is appropriate to use anthropomorphic images to describe God and God's dealings with the world, and if we find it is fitting to use male models and call God "father" or "he" or refer to divine power as the "seed" of the world then, by the operation of Rule 4, we must also be able to speak with equal legitimacy of God as "mother" or as "she" and to refer to her power as the "womb" of the world. Furthermore, to the extent that such images are limited and need to be qualified by the reminder that God is "beyond" gender—as indeed God is beyond all finite imagery—neither group of gender images holds analogical priority over the other. In other words it is not more *nearly* right to speak of God as father than God as mother, or to use the masculine rather than the feminine pronoun. If a Logos (masculine) view of the incarnation is legitimate, so is a Sophia (feminine) interpretation. We can speak as meaningfully of Sophia-Christ, or wisdom incarnate in Jesus of Nazareth, as of Logos-Christ or the word incarnate.[49] It is worth noting that this approach does not imply—as some feminist perspectives do—that gender is unimportant in theological language. On the contrary. It takes the sexuality of the incarnation with full and joyful seriousness. Sex and God are to be thought together in theologically significant ways.[50] Rule 4 indicates the way in which this can be done appropriately and with the ethical integrity that Daphne Hampson calls for. Theological equivalence is the regulative principle.

Similar kinds of change are implied if we turn the christological lens the other way and use it to examine the human condition. If it is said that divine grace in Christ is available to men, then it is equally available to women. This must include the grace of ordination as much as that of the forgiveness of sins. If Christ's call is to a servant ministry it is a call for men as much as it is for women. And so on. What it boils down to is that all patriarchal interpretations of Christian discipleship are ruled out. I think this is exactly in line with the original intention of the doctrine of the incarnation of God in Jesus Christ. It "fits" the grammar of belief.

One further point. Rule 4 as I have stated it does not imply slavish equality of the sexes in all things. It states that the centrality of Christ cannot be so understood as to yield "non-equivalent theological consequences" across the gender divide. But equivalence is contextual. Perhaps I am on shaky ground here. Conservative interpretations make a similar

---

[49] Elizabeth Schüssler Fiorenza, *In Memory of Her*, and Elizabeth Johnson, *She Who Is*, have explored this kind of christology in detail.

[50] Cf. ch. 8 above.

point in support of patriarchal readings. Men and women are equal before God, but—the inevitable sexist "but"—equal in appropriately different ways. He has the power, she doesn't! I hope that application of Rule 4 would make this kind of reading invalid, while allowing for such truth as there is in the affirmation of genuine difference.

Let me illustrate. Take the question of sin. Feminists have often noted that male interpretations of sin focus on matters like pride, self-centeredness and the abuse of power. Christ's presence comes as a judgment against such dispositions and the call to repent of them. But for many women, Susan included, such an interpretation of "sin" is pretty meaningless. Susan's problem is not the overreaching power of self assertion but the exact reverse. She suffers from the loss of a sense of self-worth. In christological terms a doctrine of sin is still applicable, but "theological equivalence" means a markedly different emphasis. The call to "repent" in Susan's case may well be the call to stop accepting the negative evaluation of self under which she currently labors. The equivalence is the call to change. The *meaning* of the change, however, relates to the context in which it is to occur.[51]

Application of Rule 4 would lead to massive changes in Christian existence. It would change the theology, art, liturgy, politics, ethics, language, ritual, and prayer of the Church, and exactly in the way in which women (and many men) increasingly feel is essential if we are to be true to the inclusive salvation of God said to be offered to humanity in Christ.

Does it dismantle Christianity altogether as conservatives fear and radical feminists assert? Is the time of doing theology in a christological way over? I have tried to argue in this chapter against such pessimistic conclusions. Feminist christology, I am convinced, can lead to the unleashing of a whole new vitality in the religion of the incarnation. Without pretending to anything like completeness let me conclude by noting what of the basic structure of incarnational theology remains after the application of Rule 4. I will mention only those issues we have already touched on in the course of these conversations.

(1) The goodness of creation. The idea that the world is created by God *ex nihilo*, from nothing, and is declared by God to be "very good" carries with it the strong implication that everything that has being is valued. This includes our human lives. But the affirmation of incarnation is even stronger. It affirms God's thoroughgoing commitment to the creation in all its dimensions. And it reveals God's uncompromising resistance to all

---

[51] The classic statement of this view of sin from a feminist perspective is by Valerie Saiving, "The Human Situation: A Feminine View" in Carol P. Christ and Judith Plaskow, eds., *Womanspirit Rising: A Feminist Reader in Religion* (San Francisco: Harper & Row, 1970) 25–42.

forces that work for the deflection of creation from its intended destiny in "the peaceable kingdom of God." The value of human life could not be maintained more strikingly than this. None of this is changed by Rule 4.

(2) Matter and spirit. The covenant between God and creation is sealed by the presence of God in the physicality of Jesus. Once this is established there can be no defense of spiritualities that drive a wedge between matter and spirit and favor the latter as "more God-like" than the former. Incarnational christology makes fun of us when we try to be more spiritual than God. None of this is changed by Rule 4.

(3) Ethical seriousness. The ethical and political demands of religious life are inescapable. To know God and to do justice are one and the same. Both Hebrew and Christian Scriptures make plain that there is no "fast," at least none that interests God, without mercy for the suffering, liberation for the oppressed, recompense for the wronged, repentance for the wrongdoer. This emphasis, especially in relation to the suffering of women, is further strengthened by the action of God in Jesus Christ. None of this is changed by Rule 4.

(4) Unconditional love. If there is a "more" in religion, a dimension that does go "beyond" the ethical without abrogating it, in the tradition of the incarnation it is the "more" of God's unconditional love. What is made clear in the life and death of Jesus Christ is that God's fundamental acceptance of the creation is grounded in the gift of love before it is measured by the calculus of deeds. Even when there is nothing we can do to help, or there is so much we have done that it can no longer be helped, the divine "thou shalt" is mediated through the divine "thou art." None of this is changed by Rule 4.

(5) Inclusive salvation. The clear intention of christological doctrine is to affirm that the healing grace of God made present in history in the life and destiny of Jesus excludes none, at least none who do not intend to exclude themselves. God's actions are necessarily inclusive. As in creation, so in new creation, being itself is determined by the intentions of God. "Who can separate us from the love of God in Christ Jesus?" None of this is changed by Rule 4.

(6) Resurrection. Death is always a religious matter. At least all religions have serious things to say about it in terms of their overall "idiom." The religion of the incarnation of God in Jesus Christ asserts a togetherness of God with Jesus that is not broken by death. The cross of Jesus' involvement in the death of the world is taken up by Christ's resurrection into the life of God. This is a manifestation of the fundamental intention of God's purpose in creation. It is part of incarnational hope. None of this is changed by Rule 4.

Feminist christology can and will bring big changes to the Church. They are changes that need to be made not because some "secular movement" demands them, but because they are called for by the truth intrinsic to the religion of the incarnation itself. Without them we are not telling the story of the gospel according to the "rules" that story demands.

Will all this complex and wearisome theology help Susan? Probably not. At least not as it is set out here—although I wouldn't want to pre-empt the possibility that Susan might well be interested in theoretical matters of religion. She does show a certain "taste" for them, despite the indifference of others. She definitely has a "feel" for the implication of certain christological assertions. To that extent she is a "competent speaker" in the Christian idiom. She knows it clashes with a good deal of the religion she has to put up with. But for all that, it is not the theory that will help. It needs the community of faith to start putting the theory into practice in all dimensions of its life. And yet this is really to put the cart before the horse. It is not the grammar that generates the talk. It is the talk that generates the grammar. The community would need to "look more redeemed," especially in its attitudes toward women, if it is to persuade Susan to think again about its redeemer.

Index